Praise for *The Circumference of Home*

"For several generations, we humans have observed that the world is growing steadily smaller. Yet as we slow ourselves back down to the pace at which our legs can stroll or pedal a decent bicycle, the experienced Earth begins to grow larger once again, each locale swelling with unexpected nooks and crannies. Each bioregion finally discloses itself as utterly unique and practically inexhaustible in its complexity and wonder. Here, by virtue of the lucidity of his prose and the quality of his practice, Kurt Hoelting expands the world."

—David Abram, author of *The Spell of the Sensuous* and *Becoming Animal: An Earthly Cosmology*

"A masterpiece in the traditions of Thoreau, Muir, and Abbey....While a poetic and compelling tale, this is also an uncompromising mirror for all of us to face our impact and see what choices we might make that— added together—could literally turn the tide."

—Vicki Robin, author of *Your Money or Your Life*

"Kurt Hoelting first took me on a voyage around southeast Alaska to connect more deeply with the natural world. Now he has modeled for all of us a still more profound connection—this book gives us firm footing to cross the treacherous and challenging ice pack that lies ahead."

—Carl Pope, Executive Director, The Sierra Club

"Even as we strive to transform the way we use energy, we must also re-examine the fundamental principles on which we base our life choices. Kurt Hoelting has taken this challenge to heart, embarking on a voyage of discovery in his native Puget Sound that has transformed his own relationship with the place he calls home. He offers this book as an invitation to the rest of us to embark on similar voyages of discovery, wherever we may find ourselves."

—Alan Durning, Director, Sightline Institute and author of *This Place on Earth*

"We are all struggling with how to take meaningful personal action in response to the climate challenge. Hoelting's thoughtful and self-aware chronicle shows the upside of a smaller carbon footprint. *The Circumference of Home* is an engaging and meaningful account of the constraints and freedoms that emerge when we stop to think about where we are going and how we get there."

—Will Rogers, President, Trust for Public Land

"As Kurt Hoelting reclaims his life from the thrall of the automobile, he finds that he regains the great gifts of time, silence, exuberant good health, deep connection to his northwest home, and ultimately the personal integrity that comes from living a life he believes in. *The Circumference of Home* is a wild bike/kayak/ferry ride among islands and towns. But it is also a journey of the moral imagination, asking the essential question—in a time of dangerous ecological disruption, how ought I to live?"

—Kathleen Dean Moore, author, *Wild Comfort*

The
Circumference
of Home

The Circumference of Home

o o o

One Man's Yearlong Quest
for a Radically Local Life

Kurt Hoelting

Da Capo Press
A Member of the Perseus Books Group

The map on page x was created by Aaron Racicot, using the following Open
Source GIS tools: QGIS (http://qgis.org/); GDAL/OGR (http://www.gdal.org/);
PostGIS (http://www.postgis.org/)

Set in 11 point Kepler by The Perseus Books Group

Library of Congress Cataloging-in-Publication Data
Hoelting, Kurt.
    The circumference of home : one man's yearlong quest for a radically local life /
Kurt Hoelting.
       p. cm.
    Includes bibliographical references.
    ISBN 978-0-306-81774-8 (alk. paper)
    1. Hoelting, Kurt—Travel—United States. 2. Human ecology—United States.
3. Place (Philosophy) 4. Outdoor recreation—Environmental aspects—United States.
I. Title.

GF503.H64 2010
304.20973—dc22

                                                                    2010000832
Published by Da Capo Press
A Member of the Perseus Books Group
www.dacapopress.com

Da Capo Press books are available at special discounts for bulk purchases in the U.S.
by corporations, institutions, and other organizations. For more information, please
contact the Special Markets Department at the Perseus Books Group, 2300 Chestnut
Street, Suite 200, Philadelphia, PA 19103, or call (800) 810-4145, ext. 5000, or e-mail
special.markets@perseusbooks.com.

10 9 8 7 6 5 4 3 2 1

For Sally,
who was with me the whole way.

CONTENTS

Step out onto the Planet
Draw a circle a hundred feet round.

Inside the circle are
300 things nobody understands, and, maybe
nobody's ever really seen.

How many can you find?

—LEW WELCH, *RING OF BONE*

o   o   o

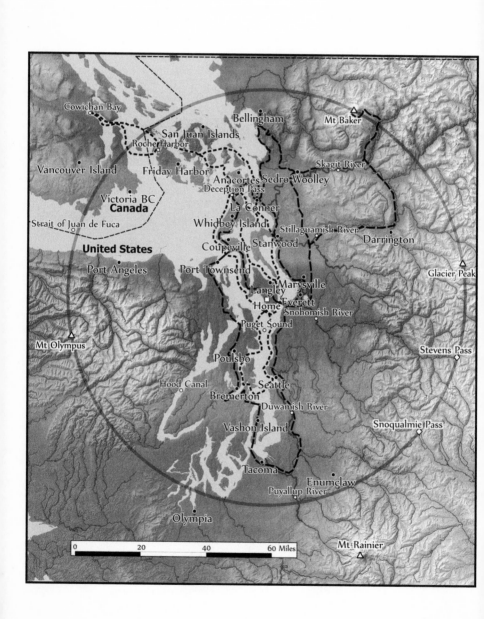

INTRODUCTION

The Ground Zero of Global Warming Is Everywhere

The melting Arctic is the call from the repo man. . . . No matter how many votes, no matter how much lobbying, no matter how much pressure you apply, you can't amend the laws of physics and chemistry.

—BILL MCKIBBEN,
"President Obama's Big Climate Challenge"

A sea of clouds far below in the murky December light is my only clue that I am flying over the center of the Greenland ice cap. My wife Sally and I are on a crowded commercial flight crossing the polar route from Oslo to Seattle, ten days before the winter solstice. From thirty-nine thousand feet, the last sliver of Arctic winter sun is hanging low on the western horizon as we chase its descent through a perpetual sunset, slowly losing ground to the turning of the earth. Soon the darkness will win this westerly race, and the sun will be gone from this far northern latitude altogether, offering nothing but a hint of sunrise to leaven the perpetual darkness of a long winter's night.

A jet-shaped icon blinks on the large GPS monitor at the front of the passenger cabin, updating our position on a virtual map every few seconds, jerking my attention continually back to the inside of the cabin and away from our actual progress across the planet itself. I scan the heads of fellow passengers and the dozens of blinking video monitors in front of each seat and cannot find a single person who is looking out the window as we pass over one of the most remote and storied places on earth.

This trip to Norway has been thick with ironies as I strain for a glimpse of the Greenland ice cap below. Once our jet touches down in Seattle, I will be embarking on a different kind of journey. Beginning on the winter solstice, ten days hence, I have vowed to go car-free and jet-free for a year and to spend that time within walking distance of home, living inside a sixty-mile radius of my home on Whidbey Island in Puget Sound.

The impulse behind this year of local living has been growing in me for a long time. At a personal level, my choice is rooted in a growing sense of homelessness that has accompanied a lifestyle filled with travel. As my frequency of travel has increased for both work and pleasure, I've lost a basic sense of continuity and belonging within the place I've always called home, losing handles on what *home* even means. For a year, I am pushing "Pause" on travel to far-off places in order to renew my relationship with the place I actually live and to rediscover the art of homecoming in an increasingly homeless culture.

But underlying this pull back toward place-based living is a growing concern for the fate of all places in an era of climate change. With global warming now undeniably upon us, and lifestyles like mine the primary engine driving it, changing how I live for the sake of my children's future has become a personal passion, even as the means and motivation for embarking on such a major shift have proven stubbornly elusive.* As our jet wings its way west toward my home ground in Puget Sound, I can feel my excitement building for this new adventure that lies ahead. The burden of living out of step with my own deepest convictions is already starting to lift. I am no longer willing to live at such a bizarre distance from what I know to be true. This much is clear to me. If I can't change my own life in response to the greatest challenge now facing our human family, who can? And if I won't make the effort to try, why should anyone else? So I've decided to start at home, and begin with myself. The question is no longer whether I must respond. The question is whether I can turn my response into an adventure.

As fate would have it, I am making my final approach into this yearlong climate-induced travel fast by flying directly over the ground zero of global warming.

o   o   o

THE BEGINNING OF THE END of my strategy of avoidance came when I took my own online carbon footprint survey.[1] To my amazement, I discovered that my footprint was more than twice the national average, in spite of the fact that I drive a hybrid vehicle and work hard to limit my personal use of energy. Since the average North American carbon footprint is ten times the world average, this was an alarming discovery. For someone who prides himself on living low on the energy food chain, this was not something I could take sitting down.

---

*In this book, I will use the terms *climate change* and *global warming* interchangeably in referring to our present climate emergency. But neither term captures the scale or urgency of the crisis, and the term *global warming* in particular can have a vaguely comforting connotation. It would be more to the point to use the terms *climate destabilization* or *atmospheric deterioration*. But to avoid confusion, I will stick with the terms in common usage.

When I looked more closely at the details of my energy consumption, I discovered that three-quarters of my carbon footprint is a result of frequent jet travel, more than swamping all my other efforts at energy conservation combined. I'd been turning a blind eye on my biggest source of personal carbon emissions, while obsessing on small efforts to rein in energy use in other parts of my life. Yet with family and friends spread to the four winds and a livelihood dependent on frequent travel, I could see no way out of my personal enmeshment in this global crisis. It was a moment of truth that offered no easy solutions.

I'd almost given up finding any answers at all, when the genesis of a creative response ambushed me one morning while I was having breakfast with a friend. I'd watched the dramatic changes happening in my own local climate—the rapidly receding Cascade glaciers and diminishing summer snowpack, the increased rainfall and flooding in the rivers, the obviously warming temperatures. It was written in plain sight, yet still I felt stuck. Tired of feeling powerless, and weary of this treadmill of travel, I overheard myself musing to my friend, "What would it be like if I didn't get into a car for a year? What would it be like to spend an entire year within walking distance of home?"

Just the thought alone brought a wave of relief. The very audacity of this prospect echoed all the way down to my bones. Rarely has a passing notion taken such complete hold of my imagination. In the days and weeks that followed, I could not let it go. I spent hours poring over local maps with a growing excitement about the places I've always wanted to explore close to home. The prospect of doing so under my own power added an aura of adventure that fired my spirit. Using my home as a center point, I drew circles of varying sizes on the map, to see what each contained. The image of "circling home" inscribed itself on my mind as a scope for the adventure. I chose the duration of one year for the project to include a full cycle of seasons, and one full circle around the sun. And I chose the winter solstice as a time to begin because of its symbolism of darkness turning back toward the light.

What really closed the deal, though, was the discovery I made when I drew a circle one hundred kilometers (or sixty-two miles) in radius from my home. The arc of this circle passed directly over the summit of Mount Olympus to the west, the highest point in the Olympic Mountains. It swung north to just include the San Juan Islands, before passing directly over the summit of Mount Baker, the highest point in the North Cascades. From there it passed directly over the summit of Glacier Peak in the east, the highest point in the Central Cascades, crossed Stevens Pass and Snoqualmie Pass on the Cascade crest, then swung around to just touch the southern tip of Puget Sound. To my astonishment, I discovered that my home on Whidbey Island lies at a perfect symbolic epicenter of the Puget Sound basin. With a home circle like this, there was no turning back.

It is this circle that awaits me with open arms when my jet touches down. For the coming year, I will travel exclusively by foot, bicycle, kayak, and public transportation inside this circle, with a portion of each month devoted to explorations under my own power. I still have no idea what I've gotten myself into or how I'm going to make this work. What I know for sure is that I've already set off on one of the grandest adventures of my life.

My goal is straightforward. I want to turn the necessity for change into an opportunity for adventure. I want to inhabit this year as if it were the last I had to live and as if the very future depended upon it. Which in fact it does.

o   o   o

As OUR JET MOVES steadily across Greenland's frozen center, I give up on making visual contact through the mantle of clouds below and try for a nap. But sleep is out of the question. I'm pestered by guilty feelings, caught in the conflicting emotions that this trip has aroused. On the one hand, I went to Norway out of love for my daughter Kristin, who is living there for a year as a Fulbright scholar. On the other hand, I've placed myself at odds with my growing conviction that such trips are a luxury I can no longer afford. I'm keenly aware that my personal share of carbon emissions from this one flight to Europe is equal to driving an SUV for months, or a hybrid car for an entire year.[2] A jet flight that has kept me connected with my daughter is also contributing directly to the destruction of her future. I am making my final approach into a yearlong travel fast caught in a perfect storm of contradictions.

Still more irony came with disturbing headlines on the European news channels in Oslo yesterday featuring reports of devastating floods in my home state of Washington, the result of record rainfall. Unlike such reports in the United States, the European news coverage speculated openly about links to climate change in these events occurring back home, reinforcing my sense that there is no longer anyplace to hide. The ground zero of global warming is everywhere.

With sleep evading me, I glance out my window again. Expecting the usual monotony of clouds, I am so startled by what I see that I gasp out loud. We are crossing directly over the deep-cut fjords and jagged peaks of the West Greenland coastline, which is crystal clear now and bathed in dazzling sunlight. Beyond the stunning wall of coastal mountains, Greenland's famous ocean of ice pushes east into the clouds as far as I can see. To the west, the sea is locked in winter ice as well. I experience a wave of unexpected emotion, and my eyes well up with tears. The landscape is starkly articulated by the long, low rays of winter sun. My face pressed to the window, I strain to watch the last glimpses of the coast as it fades off behind the aircraft.

Despite the appearance of eternal winter below, the actual drama unfolding here is almost too painful to contemplate. I file through the statistics that are so much on my mind these days. Temperatures in the Arctic are rising much faster than in the lower latitudes. The average winter temperature on the Greenland ice cap alone has risen by eight degrees Fahrenheit since 1990. This accelerating rate of warming has speeded the flow of glaciers to the sea and jacked the rate of surface melting far beyond the original estimates of climate scientists. An ice cap 1.6 miles thick and thought to be a firewall against the worst effects of warming is now hanging on the brink of collapse. According to environmental journalist Mark Binelli, writing in *Rolling Stone* magazine, "once the melt reaches a certain level, an irreversible feedback loop will kick in, after which the total disintegration of the ice sheet will be impossible to stop. A total melt would raise the sea level by 23 feet.... [Greenland] is a country where, short of people actually bursting into flames, the physical manifestations of warming could not be more overt."[3]

o o o

THIS BOOK IS NOT INTENDED as another scientific treatise on climate change, and I will not be hammering readers with statistics. Compelling summaries of the evidence are readily available in the scores of books, articles, documentaries, and public testimony that have already been offered by people far better qualified than I am to speak on the subject. I have mentioned a few among these many excellent sources in the endnotes.[4] Instead, this book is for those who, like me, already accept the reality of climate change and of our human role in causing it, yet remain perplexed about how to respond. While the urgency of the crisis is now beyond reasonable dispute, finding the will to respond at a level commensurate in scale has proven far more elusive. We are caught in a widening gap between what we know and how we are living. Elizabeth Kolbert has nailed the scope of this dilemma in the conclusion to her book *Field Notes from a Catastrophe*. "It may seem impossible to imagine that a technologically advanced society could choose, in essence, to destroy itself, but that is what we are now in the process of doing."[5]

o o o

AS A SOURCE OF MOTIVATION for serious personal change, global warming has a lot going for it. Its scale and urgency are also its opportunity. Climate change challenges us to anchor personal choices in a more enduring shift in cultural values about what constitutes the "good life." The benefits of such cultural fads as "slow food," "slow travel," and "staycations" are compelling on a personal level. But climate change ups the ante exponentially, giving us enormous new incentive to bear with the costs and burdens that come with such changes. Knowing that everything worthy of our love really *is* on the line, we are much more likely to face the difficult aspects of these shifts with the courage and fortitude we need to stand our ground. We are more likely to stick it out.

That's why climate change—arguably the greatest challenge ever to face the human family—will never be far from my thoughts and meditations throughout this coming year in circumference, even when the contexts of my adventures are deeply personal and local. If there is a hidden gift embedded in this crisis, it is this potent new motivation to reexamine our lives, to make changes in the direction of more balanced and sustainable living—changes that we have resisted for too long. That our overall quality of life may actually benefit from this effort is a prospect often lost in the public rhetoric about anticipated hardship and self-sacrifice that we've long associated with such changes.

The hope now driving me forward is that the opposite may prove to be true. The climate crisis may be our last, best chance for a broad-based realignment of values that can finally extend our ethical regard into the deepest heart of the living world.

That is also why our climate emergency is not ultimately a crisis of technology or public policy, as it is so often portrayed in the media. Since we ourselves have created this crisis out of an ethic of unrestrained growth, climate change is at root a crisis of meaning, a crisis of moral vision and values. We cannot expect to "jump the chasm" of climate destabilization with a merely technological fix, leaving unchallenged our destructive habits of unbridled consumption. Climate change upends our most cherished assumptions about what it means to be human in a world of exquisitely fragile balances that now threaten to expel us from the biosphere itself. Our pursuit of global climate initiatives and sustainable energy technologies, essential as they are, cannot carry us across this chasm without a commensurate change of heart, one that expresses itself in the nuts and bolts of how we live. Among the three prongs of any realistic climate solution—better energy technologies, more responsible public policy, and the power of personal choice—only this final one lies within our direct individual control. And only this final one can yield immediate progress—starting now—in the quest for a carbon-neutral life. Personal choice is the low-lying fruit that can be harvested without delay, buying precious time until the critical components of greener technology and more comprehensive climate initiatives can catch up with the reality of our runaway climate.

This book, then, is the story of one man's attempt to confront his own complicity in the climate crisis and to do so out of freedom rather than fear. It is an attempt to turn the greatest crisis humanity now faces into an opportunity for self-discovery. My story is not a recipe or prescription for others to follow, but an invitation to launch similar acts of homecoming, wherever we may find ourselves. No two lives are the same, and every place on the planet has its own unsinkable magic. This book is an invitation to turn homeward with an urgency appropriate to our times and with a renewed gratitude for the treasures already at hand. It doesn't matter where we choose to start this adventure. It matters that we begin, and the sooner the better. We already have everything we need. Please join me on this journey to the heart of home.

SECTION I ○ THE BOOT

Walking is the great adventure, the first meditation, a practice of heartiness and soul primary to humankind. Walking is the exact balance of spirit and humility. Out walking, one notices ecology on the level where it counts.

—GARY SNYDER, *The Practice of the Wild*[1]

CHAPTER 1

Footloose in the Geography of Nowhere

o o o

As long as I've got broadband, I'm perfectly at ease with the fact that my position on the planet's surface is arbitrary.

—Bruce Sterling, *The Last Viridian Note*

It is a drab and rainy morning in early January, two weeks after the winter solstice that launched my year in circumference, as I strap on my boots, hoist my backpack, and head out my door for a hike unlike any I have ever taken before. It does not feel like an auspicious beginning. Sally has had her doubts all along, but gives me a cheerful hug, anyway, as I head out in the direction of the ferry. It's raining hard, the kind of Northwest winter rain that is just a hair shy of snow, with enough sleet mixed in to give it the worst qualities of both. In all the years I've lived on the island, this is the first time I've ever walked the four hilly miles from my house to the ferry landing, or thought to, for that matter. And this is just the first part of a much longer journey ahead of me on foot.

I've traveled this route hundreds of times by car, of course. On the face of it, my trip to the ferry could not be more familiar. But any resemblance to previous trips ends at the outskirts of my immediate neighborhood, when I move outside the scope of my normal daily walks. Like most of my fellow islanders, I settled here for the open space and rural character of the island's landscape, only to find my life more tightly bound to my car than ever as I piece together the different fragments of a widely scattered lifestyle with the only piece of indispensable gear that all Americans seem to share in common. This time, though, there will be no car to bail me out. I've just taken a public vow to go car-free for this entire year, and I'm only two weeks into it. That leaves fifty weeks to go. As the sleet bites into my face, I'm inclined to think that Sally is right. I really have lost my mind.

The first mile takes me along familiar trails and side roads. But as I head out toward the highway, with the added weight of a full backpack, I begin to feel like an alien in my own home. I climb the long, steep hill from Maxwelton Valley to the ridge above Cultus Bay, and soon my sweat has joined with the drenching rain that is already seeping down inside my raingear. By the time I turn the corner onto the highway itself, my boots are soaked through to the socks. I consider aborting the mission and trying again tomorrow as I plod along the newly hostile domain of the highway during morning rush hour. With no shield against the traffic and rain, I feel as if I've entered a new kind of wilderness area, but this is no walk in the park. A steady stream of cars pummels past my shoulder on the long hill down to the ferry, drenching me with noise and fumes that linger like a sour, wet fog. Only my refusal to give up before I've even begun keeps me from turning back as I trudge on into the gray light of morning, a solitary salmon in the wrong river, bucking a steady current of cars—a current that seems to have no beginning and no end.

o o o

THIS IS THE FIRST of several expeditions under my own power that I have planned for the year, trips that will eventually take me throughout the Puget Sound basin. In the long hours I've spent poring over maps in preparation for the year, this hike through the Skagit basin seemed like the perfect place to begin, and going on foot seemed like the right mode of transport to kick it all off. But now I'm not so sure. This is a far cry from hiking on a scenic mountain trail.

My plan is to cover 130 miles in ten days, hiking north through the deltas of three major rivers that flow from the west slope of the Cascade Mountains into Puget Sound. From there I'll circle back onto the north end of Whidbey Island to walk its fifty-mile length, making the first of several circles around my home. Each of these rivers—the Snohomish, Stillaguamish, and Skagit—meets tidewater in the sheltering embrace of my home island, creating a continuous estuary of enormous ecological richness. The nearshore heart of this basin lies off the beaten track of I-5's busy commerce and is mostly unfamiliar terrain to me. Much of it is inaccessible tide flats and salt marsh. The plateau that rises from the shore to the Puget lowlands beneath the Central Cascades contains thriving cities melding with the spreading suburbs of Seattle, several Indian reservations, rich farmland across the lower deltas, and the largest remaining salmon runs in Puget Sound.

I start out with only vague notions of what route I will take, where I will sleep, or what I'll find along the way. I know few people on this out-of-the-way passage, so I bring camping gear in case no lodging presents itself. Walking is recreation, not transportation, here in the land that cars built, and my presence on foot with a backpack by the side of a busy highway feels just slightly blasphemous. It is one small gesture of defiance against a cultural orthodoxy that takes cars absolutely for granted.

o o o

LIVING ON AN ISLAND in the sound has its advantages. One of them is that you don't have to wonder where the boundaries of your home terrain lie. Walk in any direction, and you hit a clear line of demarcation where land meets water. Head either way down the beach, and you eventually wind up right where you started. It's a comforting feeling. This morning, though, I arrive at that line of demarcation already soaking wet and feeling the strain on my out-of-shape muscles.

Trips off-island constitute a ritual that we islanders call "going to America." As the ferry heads for the mainland, I gratefully dump my pack on the bench and warm my hands with a cup of hot tea from the ship's galley. I run into a few friends who comment on my wet clothes and backpack. I'm still working on an elevator speech that cuts to the chase about what I'm up to this year, and I botch my attempt at a short answer. They nod their heads politely and back slowly away as I try to explain what I'm doing on this walk. There isn't a big tradition of going on long hikes to Everett from Whidbey Island, especially early on a wet January morning.

Leaving the island is a psychological as well as geographical leap outside that comfortable sense of place that is already fading off in our wake. "Going to America" trades a semblance of rural cohesiveness for an empire of sprawl—shopping malls, commercial strips, instant subdivisions springing up like mushrooms, and ever-more-congested highways. To a greater degree than usual this morning, I'm crossing more than just water. I'm crossing into another state of mind, and I'm doing so without the one tool I normally rely on to make this passage manageable—the private automobile. I'm entering a world where boundaries are much less certain, and the sense of place is less rooted in the natural features of the land. I'm walking into a regional hinterland of seething contrasts that lead away from wholeness and toward fragmentation the farther from the island I get. Low-density housing, light industry, strip malls, and big-box stores that could be mistaken for any city in America offer the prime measure of progress along the way.

The ferry crosses Possession Sound to a landing at Point Elliot in the wealthy suburban enclave of Mukilteo, a series of affluent subdivisions and malls tucked into the hills that rise from the shores of the sound. It was in precisely this spot in 1855 that the Treaty of Point Elliott was signed. In that mock ceremony, the collected tribes of Puget Sound gathered to relinquish all claims to their lands in exchange for reservations, a pittance of cash, and fishing rights to their traditional grounds that were soon roundly ignored. It was a familiar story of promises made and broken in the westward expansion of Euro-American settlers across North America in the nineteenth century. Since that time, most of the forest has relinquished its claim to the land as well. A trip from the island into the corridors of the city these days feels like a signature tour through what James Howard Kunstler has called "the geography of nowhere."[2] Maybe it's the somber weather this morning, or my own feeling of exile from the familiar, but I can almost see the ghosts of these tribes rising out of the morning mist as I trudge off the ferry just ahead of the cars that pour up the ramp after me.

Heading north from the ferry, I feel good to be moving again. It's still rainy and cold, but it will be easier to keep going, now that I've made the crossing, and this alone gives me a boost of confidence. I walk toward Everett through loose-knit subdivisions, picking my way along side streets to avoid the traffic until each street peters out, one by one, into dead-end gullies that funnel me back onto the main drag that is the only continuous road leading north. The steady rhythm of feet on pavement brings comfort and warmth to my body and compensates for the relentless drumbeat of traffic.

As the miles stretch out behind me, I stride on through a tangle of emotions; the satisfaction of being finally under way, buoyed up by the simple pleasure of walking, countered by my growing sense that I am a stranger in a strange land—out of place, out of step, and quickly running out of steam. The harsh pavement underfoot has none of the compliant softness of a hiking trail through the forest, and within hours, my feet are killing me, my senses are battered, and my spirit is sagging.

I begin to notice something else too. Through one neighborhood after another, I pass tidy rows of houses, and driveways adorned with cars, but I see almost no evidence of human inhabitants. Twice I pass joggers, locked in their private iPod reveries to seal them off from the noise of traffic. Once, on a side street, I encounter an older couple walking their dog. We exchange greetings, the only words that will pass between me and another human being all day. In typical suburban fashion, dead-end cul-de-sacs keep steering me back to the main drag, shopping malls stand in for public spaces, and two-car garages take the place of front porches, while fenced backyards are all that remains of open-space commons. The social components of work, family, and community that were once bound together in a village format are compartmentalized here into widely scattered fragments that make little sense on foot. What was originally created around the convenience of cars now remakes the people who drive them into extensions of their own tools. Neighborhoods are consigned to social isolation and add their stream of solo drivers to the congested river of cars on the freeway. It is a familiar story being played out all across America.

o   o   o

I TAKE A LONG DETOUR around a peninsula park to get away from traffic for a time. The rain comes in fits and starts, and the leafless alder thickets fill the gullies with a winter sparseness. I stop for lunch on a bench overlooking the sound with a vista back across to the island. I am already a bit homesick gazing across to my island as I dive back into the river of cars.

So familiar has this pattern become that it's easy to forget how new this way of living still is. Not only do Americans own more cars per capita every year, but the number of miles each of us drives daily has also been steadily on the rise, and the Northwest exceeds the national average in the magnitude of our dependence on cars. Ninety percent of all excursions now take place behind the wheel of a car.[3] Caught between the American ideal of hyperindividualism that drives us to flee the cities in the first place and the spreading web of sprawl that chases us out into the hinterland, we spend an ever-increasing quantity of time in our cars, trying to stitch the scattered components of our lives back together.

The irony is that the very implement of this dismemberment is what we now turn to for solace. In fact, our commutes have become the last refuge of solitary time for many Americans, never mind that the quest for solitude and psychic space is what sent us sprawling into the hinterland by car in the first place. Laura Esther Wolfson captures the strange magnetism of this uniquely American pastime: "The commute is a golden border at the beginning and end of each workday, shedding some of its shimmer onto the leaden expanse in between. . . . There is the unencumbered time, a commodity beyond price for those who sell their waking hours in order to afford a place to sleep. There is the heady state of in-between-ness, a brief release from all worldly entanglement."[4]

Add this all together, and it is no wonder that transportation accounts for over half of our region's greenhouse gas emissions. The average Northwesterner uses almost four times as much gasoline as a citizen of Britain, Germany, or Japan.[5] James Howard Kunstler was writing about us when he said, "Ever-busy, ever-building, ever-in-motion, ever-throwing-out the old for the new, we have hardly paused to think about what we are so busy building, and what we have thrown away. Meanwhile, the everyday landscape becomes more nightmarish and unmanageable each year."[6]

o o o

IT SHOULD COME AS NO SURPRISE that our habitat of heart and mind also tends to constrict in the presence of such a throwaway landscape. Here in the Northwest, at least, we can still drive to the wilderness when the stress of driving around the city becomes too much. As a last straw, we can use our cars to get away from cars for a brief time. I am well aware that my long walk into the kingdom of sprawl has a slightly preposterous ring to it in a region where hiking is a religion that is practiced exclusively in the temple of wilderness. As a member in good standing of this outdoor recreation sect, I would ordinarily think nothing of driving for hours to engage in the prescribed ritual communion of hitting the trail, usually arriving in an SUV filled to the scuppers with recreational equipment—the climbing gear, skis, bicycles, backpacks, and kayaks that are the lifeblood of affluent Northwest lifestyles.

The problem with all this expensive recreational gear is that it is just so much dead weight sitting in the garage without the king of all recreational equipment—the sports utility vehicle. Ironically, the age of SUVs kicked off right about the time we first got the word from scientists about global warming. It almost seems as if the two have grown up together and are trying to figure out how to live with each other now in the same squabbling household.

Somewhere along the way, our affair with cars turned into an addiction, and our cars now drive us. What was intended as an accessory to life has turned into our culture's primary organizing principle, just when we can least afford to stay on this course. Most people I know honestly believe they have no choice left in the matter, that living without their cars is basically unthinkable, even as they acknowledge that the benefits of their independent mobility have long since been overtaken by its costs. Climate change is only the most recent measure of the scale of this dysfunction.

o   o   o

If there is a lifeblood to a place, then Puget Sound flows in my veins. Situated midway in the long arc of Northwest coastal temperate rain forest, Puget Sound is the second-largest estuary system in the lower forty-eight (behind Chesapeake Bay). It has over two thousand miles of shoreline, draining ten thousand rivers and streams that flow from the two mountain ranges that form its east and west shoulders—the Cascades and the Olympics.

The Seattle I grew up in stitched itself into the glacier-carved hills, gullies, and inland channels that spread east from Elliott Bay. The city emerged from boomtown status during the early twentieth century, transforming the surrounding forest of climax Douglas fir into Scandinavian wood frame houses that were built out of old-growth fir studs that carpenters today would die for as the choicest finish material. The early neighborhoods of many cities around Puget Sound were built by skilled Norwegian tradesmen drawn to the region by its resemblance to the old country. These workers brought into the growing city a culture of no-nonsense working-class competence devoid of many East Coast urban pretensions. This unpretentiousness persists today, even as the ethnic character of the city has grown broadly more diverse. Traveling east and west against the grain of the hills, Seattle still dishes up charming, unorthodox niche neighborhoods that each have their own distinctive flavor and identity.

The same cannot be said for the vast new "in-between" that cars have built, stretching over the Puget lowlands from Olympia to Bellingham, and from the shores of the sound far into the Cascade foothills. Seattle's voters turned their backs on mass-transit options in favor of a sprawl-inducing freeway system in the 1960s and have been trying to figure out ever since how to shoehorn credible mass-transit options into the quirky geography of the city without breaking public coffers. The result is that you can no longer get there from here. A regionwide traffic congestion has hamstrung Seattle's commercial flow and injected a uniform frustration into the basic act of moving from one place to another.

A million and a half new residents are expected to join the four million people who call Puget Sound home over the next two decades.[7] These new arrivals will touch down on a physical landscape altered almost beyond recognition from the region of my childhood. Over two million acres of forest around Puget Sound have been cut, paved, and developed in less than one generation. The flow of expatriates from other parts of the country and the world may be attracted to the sound's compelling natural beauty. But the reality they find on the ground as a baseline measure of ecological health leaves them no way of gauging how much has already been lost.

Puget Sound's surface persona still conjures up images of Ecotopia.* The sound is a poster child for the Northwest's iconic beauty, selling itself to tourists and new residents alike with stunning vistas from just about any vantage, urban or rural. Look west across the sound's waters on a clear day, and you see the spectacular Olympic Mountains, or east from any ridge in the city to see the snowcapped wall of the Cascade Range. Look south for a full-frontal of Mount Rainier's massive dome or north to Mount Baker's volcanic buttress, which set a world record for annual snowfall, with 1,140 inches in the winter of 1998–1999. With three major national parks in the Puget Sound area alone and twenty-five wilderness areas totaling 3.5 million acres (an area the size of Connecticut), this part of greater Cascadia contains arguably more intact ecosystems than any other industrialized region of the planet.** Much of this splendor lies inside my home circle.

But such comparisons tell only part of the story. Dive down below these surface images, and the picture gets cloudy fast. If anything, Puget Sound's picture-postcard beauty obstructs a more realistic assessment of how imperiled the sound's ecology has actually become. Efforts to rally citizen concern and action, especially in response to the federal listing of Puget Sound's chinook salmon under the Endangered Species Act, are hamstrung by the public perception that what *looks* healthy must *be* healthy.

---

*The concept of Ecotopia was introduced by Ernest Callenbach's popular novel of that name (London: Pluto, 1978). The book posited a radical new nation of environmentalists seceding from the United States in a territory that stretched along the coast from Northern California to the Canadian border. Among other things, the nation of Ecotopia outlawed all internal-combustion engines.

**Cascadia* is a bioregional designation for efforts to build more sustainable cities in the urban corridor west of the Cascades. It extends from Vancouver, British Columbia, through Puget Sound and the Willamette Valley of Oregon.

This tendency is compounded by the influx of newcomers who are often content to believe that what they see is what they get. A rainforest ecology that produced the greatest mass of living matter per acre anyplace on earth (the nearby Hoh Rain Forest in Olympic National Park actually holds this distinction), and annual returns of salmon historically in the millions, have been rendered into one of the most toxic marine environments anywhere in the country in little over a century.*

o   o   o

A MERE FIFTEEN THOUSAND YEARS AGO, Puget Sound did not even exist. Its Pleistocene river valleys were buried under three thousand feet of ice from the Vashon ice sheet. When that great lobe of ice retreated north thirteen thousand years ago, the waters of the Pacific Ocean surged into the deep-cut valleys that the glacier left behind. A new inland sea was born.

As the ice peeled out of the river valleys one by one, the salmon moved in, bringing nourishment from the sea back into the mountains and setting the ecological table for a profusion of life that followed them up the new river valleys. Snake River sockeye salmon (before dams pushed them to extinction) climbed as high as eight thousand feet into the Bitterroot Mountains of Idaho. Chinook salmon made it a thousand miles inland along

---

*Seattle's Duwamish River watershed was designated a Superfund site five miles long in 2003. The Puyallup and Snohomish Rivers of Tacoma and Everett hold nearly comparable toxic loads. Thousands of acres of commercial shellfish beds are now closed because the clams, mussels, and oysters are unsafe to eat. Many beaches are so contaminated with bacteria that they are unsafe for swimming. Puget Sound's much-loved orcas have become living toxic waste dumps, testing among the most contaminated animals on the planet—a beacon at the top of the food chain indicating high levels of toxicity throughout Puget Sound's web of life. (Data from Puget Sound Partnership, www.psp.wa.gov; and People For Puget Sound, www.pugetsound.org/.)

tributaries to the Columbia. As the land thawed and the coast became ice-free, humans were not far behind.

New York Times correspondent Timothy Egan defined the region this way: "The Pacific Northwest is simply this: wherever the salmon can get to."[8] Another bioregional frame defines the Pacific Northwest as the original extent of temperate old-growth rain forest, which at the time of European contact stretched all the way from San Francisco Bay to Alaska's Prince William Sound, and from the crest of the Rockies in Montana and Wyoming to the Pacific Coast. Overlay these two maps charting the original domain of salmon and trees, and their boundaries are almost identical.

Every year, urban development and the combined impacts of industrial logging, fishing, agriculture, and dams further constrict the territory that "salmon can get to." And every year, there are fewer salmon left to attempt the journey. With 95 percent of the Northwest's old-growth forest now fallen to ax and chainsaw, and many Northwest salmon runs either threatened or extinct, Ecotopia's beleaguered prospects begin to come into a more realistic focus. By both definitions—salmon and forest—the Pacific Northwest is shrinking fast.

I grew up during the explosive growth of suburbs around Seattle, when the notion of ecological limits was only beginning to enter the cultural vernacular. During the 1960s and 1970s, the region's identification with natural resource extraction turned into an identification with natural beauty for its own sake.[9] How to protect this beauty from further inroads of growth and "Californication" became the cultural preoccupation of the new Northwest. As a college student at the University of Washington in Seattle, with the wilderness movement in full swing, I jumped on that first wave of environmentalists determined to build the new nation of Ecotopia here on Puget Sound's shores. To this day, when I look out at the sound's jaw-dropping beauty, I forget for a moment how deep the divide has become between the image of Ecotopia still lodged in my heart and the harsher reality that now hides in its depths.

o   o   o

MY ANNUAL MIGRATIONS north to Alaska each summer to fish commercially and guide sea kayaking expeditions—a practice I've suspended temporarily during this year in circumference—have kept alive my connections with an earlier, more self-reliant, resource-rich Northwest. These deep annual dives into Alaska's primal landscape do a lot to sustain my spirit in the face of so much loss closer to home. They also foster a certain frontier mystique with my friends—a mystique that I exploit and embellish every chance I get. And I get a lot of chances. I have to search hard these days to find others who were born in the Puget Sound region.

This creates an interesting set of quandaries. While there are many cultural benefits to the growing cosmopolitan character of the region—benefits I enjoy and routinely indulge in—they come at the cost of a de facto rootlessness that is now nearly taken for granted. Nationally, one in five Americans moves every year, and about half the U.S. population has moved in the last five years. Local ecological literacy and cultural continuity are not among the fruits of this demographic roulette.

Apart from its original Native inhabitants, the new Northwest has never been a place where people are *from*. It is a destination that people migrate *to*, usually to start a new life. As additional waves of settlers pour into Puget Sound from other regions of the country, they arrive into a cultural framework that celebrates the Northwest's natural beauty as an increasingly abstract backdrop for economic pursuits that have little to do with anyplace in particular. Seattle's transition into a postregional city has cut most of its economic ties to the land, even though these ties were its original reason for being. It is a telling irony for a region that so celebrates its natural heritage that Puget Sound's two leading homegrown employers, Boeing and Microsoft, are icons of the new flat-world economy.

o o o

BY LATE AFTERNOON, the rain has eased off to showers and I've dropped down from the bluffs of Mukilteo into Everett's working-class neighborhoods. As the city spills out onto the industrial flats of the Snohomish River delta, I find relief from the heavy traffic along residential side streets of modest clapboard houses that have mostly seen better days. Everett fans out over the delta like a pioneer garment that is tattered at the edges, but still hints at things of value hidden in its pockets. There was a time in the late nineteenth century when Everett vied with Seattle and Tacoma for a railroad terminus that would link Puget Sound with the East Coast. Seattle won that shoot-out and now dwarfs its rivals in size and economic clout, as well as cultural vitality. But I hold a special affection for Everett's gritty character as Seattle's smaller cousin to the north. A haven for labor organizers in its youth and a staging ground for a surging immigrant population today, Everett remains staunchly working-class, even as it catches the draft from the new tech economy wafting up from Seattle's East side.

With darkness coming on, I keep an eye out for lodging as I trudge past the Naval Carrier Base, past the massive Kimberly-Clark pulp mill with its sulfur plumes and mountains of sour-smelling wood chips, past the marinas, the fishermen's wharf, machine shops, and boatyards that are draped like decaying ornaments along the dredged channel where the Snohomish River carries its load of silt into the sea. The vestiges of a seafaring life melded into the city's industrial belly strike a resonant chord with my own split personality as an Alaskan fisherman who still divides his time between the wilderness and the city.

Each of the three river deltas that lie in my path during the long walk ahead drains fertile floodplains that roll out like emerald blankets from deep in the flanks of the Cascade Range. Each has played host in the near past to legendary salmon runs that now hover near extinction, as the long arm of urban development spreads its fingers over the land. Last year, forty-three chinook salmon returned to the Stillaguamish River to spawn. The South Fork of the Nooksack near Bellingham fared even worse, with a total return of twenty-nine chinook.

Each of these rivers is the ancestral home to Coast Salish tribes that still bear their names and that refuse to be dislodged from their watersheds. Each river has been altered almost beyond recognition. Yet however much we may have molded these rivers to our economic whims, they seem content to wait us out. We humans cannot win more than a temporary truce with the wildness that flows in their veins. This thought gives me solace as I turn upriver. Here in the Northwest, it is the rivers that are delivering the headline news about climate change, as altered patterns of rainfall and shrinking snowpack reshape their destiny, and ours with it, flushing our illusions of control out to sea like so much dross in a five-hundred-year flood.

Here on the Snohomish, my experience as a salmon fisherman in Alaska helps me fill in the blanks. I can see this place whole through the lens of Alaska's still-teeming salmon rivers. But I also know that none of this is safe from our human reach anymore. Not even the most remote wildlands in Alaska. In the words of Alan Weisman, "Homo sapiens didn't bother to wait until fossilization to enter geologic time. . . . By tapping the

Carboniferous Formation and spewing it up into the sky, we've become a volcano that hasn't stopped erupting since the 1700's."[10]

As I walk through the margins of this Northwest city, wet and bone-tired, my mind shorts out in the effort to imagine a solution. My old friend despair muscles his way into my path so suddenly that I almost run him over. I find him leaning against a cracked concrete wall, casual as can be, as if I should be surprised and happy to see him. He throws his arm around my shoulder in a friendly way, as he's done so many times before, echoing all my reasons for why this world is going to hell. It's an old litany, and I can see exactly where he is taking me. It's not where I want to go. I've spent too much time there already.

I turn my eyes back to the sidewalk in front of me, aware of each step I am taking, letting myself feel the weariness in my legs, the measure of how far I have come today. I let go of my effort to solve every crisis at once, to take on burdens that aren't mine in this moment. I am suddenly aware of my own breathing, the puffs of steam coming out of my nostrils, the fading light on the water. Life climbs back out of the smallest cracks in the sidewalk to greet my passage. When I turn to look behind me, I see that my old friend has already departed. He was never there in the first place.

I don't have to worry about whether life will take care of itself. Life always finds its own way forward, regardless of the obstacles any of us might place in its way. Even the ugliest parts of this city pose no final threat to the long-term prospects of nature. As Weisman has pointed out, "The notion that someday nature could swallow whole something so colossal and concrete as a modern city doesn't slide easily into our imagination. . . . Nevertheless, the time it would take nature to rid itself of what urbanity has wrought may be less than what we might suspect."[11] From where I now stand it is hard to see a compelling way forward. I don't know how to look past the ugliness to a wholeness I may never live to see. But as the light fades from the river, I stand to watch the beauty of its leaden march to the sea.

I am ravenous for a place to stop and rest. I could sure use something to eat as well. No lodging has presented itself among the warehouses along the riverfront. So I cut up over the hill and drop down onto old Highway 99. I grab a room at the first motel I come to on Broadway, run by a family of Korean immigrants. The motel is way past its prime, but I might as well have scored a penthouse in the finest hotel as I slump my heavy pack to the floor of my room. The carpet is badly worn. The linoleum is peeling off the bathroom floor. The air is stale, and I notice patches of mold on the ceiling as I fill the bathtub with hot water. But as I ease myself into the steaming tub, releasing the tension I have accumulated in a long day of walking, I don't believe I can remember a time in my entire life when a hot bath ever felt so good.

CHAPTER 2

Walking the Rivers of Home

o   o   o

What's wrong with the horse? Or the burro? Or the bicycle? Or
even, God help us, the human foot? Why should not Americans especially learn to walk again? There is this to be said for walking:
it is the one method of human locomotion by which a man or
woman proceeds erect, upright, proud and independent, not squat-
ting on the haunches like a frog.

—EDWARD ABBEY[1]

I n the morning, I wake up well before dawn. My mind gropes
for handholds on the unfamiliar surroundings of this back-
water motel room. As the recollection of yesterday's long
walk comes into focus, my eagerness to push on trumps my
weariness. I feel a rush of excitement knowing my adventure is
finally under way. Going back to sleep is not an option.

I roll out of bed and do my usual morning rituals of a few
yoga stretches, some tea, then sitting for a half hour in quiet
meditation. As a climber, I think of this routine as "setting an anchor belay" on my day, sitting in silence before giving myself over
to the day's agenda. This builds a base of stability and confidence
for entering the day that I feel in a visceral way. It is a support

that seems to hold, whether I feel like doing it or not, and I have learned to trust it.

Once I'm done, there is no need to linger in this drab room, so I grab a quick snack, gather my pack together, and head out the door. I'm greeted by the first glimmers of a crimson dawn over the Cascade Mountains to the east and by a clear morning sky. The air is crisp and cold, washed clean by yesterday's rain. There is a thick frost on the ground, and the puddles are frozen. My boots make a crunching sound through the frosty grass as I walk to the shoulder of the highway and turn north again. The Sunday morning traffic is light on this usually bustling highway. I walk through the breaking dawn, feeling my body warm, and my spirits lift with each step.

After a mile, I top a rise over the main channel of the river, and I see the delta looming before me. The estuary is laced this morning with banks of thick fog that soften its industrial edge and give it a primal complexion. The Snohomish is formed by the joining of two great Northwest rivers that drain the primary transportation routes through the Cascades into Eastern Washington. Due east is Stevens Pass, drained by the Skykomish River, which is joined fifteen miles inland by the Snoqualmie River draining Snoqualmie Pass from the south. These rivers flow down from some of the wildest country in the lower forty-eight, with long, fertile floodplains that penetrate deep into the mountains, picking up dozens of tributaries along the way as they cascade down from the surrounding ridges. Only in its final passage to the sea from this confluence near Monroe does the river seriously tangle with our modern urban project.

There is only one passage on foot through the labyrinth of sediment islands and wetlands that form the delta, and that is my current route on old Highway 99. Interstate 5 and the railway bridges rocket by on either side, off-limits to pedestrians. Once the only route north, Highway 99 seems forlorn in the shadow of the immense concrete spans of the interstate, and only local traffic uses it now. A series of outmoded bridges cross these sloughs, linking wildlife sanctuaries and expansive silt islands that have been pressed into service as staging areas for local lumber and pulp mills.

The builders of these bridges must have assumed that no one would be foolish enough to cross them on foot. A narrow concrete parapet hugs the edge of each span with just enough room for a solo walker to pass over the dilapidated marinas, houseboats, and warehouses that seem to huddle like refugees against the steep banks of the channels below. The aroma of mudflats fills the air as the flood tide presses in, reversing the river's current for miles into the hinterland. Migratory waterfowl work the eddies of the river, and a pair of sea lions fish for winter steelhead along the channel.

These creatures, remnants of the river's wildness, escape notice from a speeding car. At a perch in midchannel, I watch the thousand-pound sea lions weaving gracefully between the surface and the river's silty depths. In my work as a commercial fisherman in nearby Possession Sound, there is little love lost between us. We are competing predators vying for a shrinking stock of salmon entering these rivers. The seals and sea lions usually get the prime fish from our nets in a cat-and-mouse game that they are legally bound to win. This is a source of much frustration to fishermen, but the Marine Mammal Protection Act prohibits harming them, and their numbers are rising, adding to the downward pressure on salmon runs. Cut loose from my role as a fisherman on this morning's walk through the delta, I see the beauty of these animals with fresh eyes and appreciate how much more dependent they are on our declining salmon than I am. They have been fishing here much longer than our modern commercial fleet, and for them, there is no other source of food.

I make my way across the wide delta, passing over Smith Island and Spencer Island, Union Slough, Steamboat Slough, and Ebey Slough. In the spaces between industrial yards and the brief silences that punctuate bursts of traffic, I hear the reedy call of red-winged blackbirds in the cattail marshes and the quiet arguments of mallards, buffleheads, and mergansers feeding in the nearby ponds. These are intractably wild species, lovely in their winter plumage, and I feel in them the ancient spirit of a river still tending its own life, oddly unconcerned about the temporary obstructions we had laid across it. I will come back another time in my kayak, to paddle deeper into the wetland's heart and further from the commotion of the highway. From an ecological perspective, this is the heart of my home neighborhood. Yet through five decades of living so close to this river, today is the first time I have ever crossed it under my own power, unaccompanied by the twin barriers of speed and glass, and with my senses fully deployed. It's reassuring to see how many pockets of resilient life are still lurking here just beyond the din of human commerce.

o   o   o

AFTER A FOUR-MILE SLALOM between the cars and the ducks, I cross the final slough into the town of Marysville and head for the first restaurant I can find that is open on a Sunday morning. That would be Don's 24-Hour Café. It is a vintage small-town café, festooned with American flags inside and out, and marked by a conspicuous sign on Main Street declaring, "The Lord is near for all who call on him." After my chilly walk across the delta this morning, I definitely feel the call. The parking lot is full of pickup trucks, a good sign that the food is abundant and does its job well. I walk into a café packed with locals who seem to have their own assigned seats. There is a lull in the conversation as I hoist my heavy pack to the floor, sliding it into the one available stall, where a bustling waitress is already filling my mug with coffee. Tea would have been my choice if I'd been asked, but I wasn't, so coffee it is—the kind of stale, old-style restaurant coffee that would get a person excommunicated from Seattle's Starbucks Nation. My impression is that it is served with pride for just that reason. Antique kitchen implements hang from every beam and wall. A neon sign behind the counter flashes praises to Mountain Fresh Rainier Beer. My eye is drawn right away to the pies in the case, which look grand. Like Everett, this place has a defiantly conservative, working-class aura that recalls my other home in Petersburg, Alaska, at the northern end of the Inside Passage.

I attempt some friendly banter with the waitress, but she takes my order on the fly and is gone. She asks no questions and betrays no curiosity. Nor does anyone else. The conviviality of the place doesn't seem to extend to me, so I sit back to enjoy my coffee and the bubbles of lively conversation swirling around the room. In a culture of hot-wire red state/blue state distinctions, there is nothing purple about this place, let alone blue. My backpack and REI clothing are more than enough to blow my cover in a room full of coveralls and flannel shirts.

What must be even stranger, I'm someone who has obviously *walked* here—a backpacker who took a seriously wrong turn in the foothills. As I survey the crowded booths, I wonder if the thought of walking here entered the minds of any of these patrons this morning. Why would it? Like so many other places, Marysville is up to its neck in sprawl. There are few places within walking distance that would be seen as worth the effort of walking, especially if those places can be accessed more quickly by a car. Walking as an actual mode of transportation has virtually gone extinct in our culture. We have become, in Rebecca Solnit's words, "nothing more than a parcel in transit, a chess piece dropped on another square; [our body] does not move but is moved."[2]

Not that what I am doing on this trip is the wave of the future, even for me. This whole year is a ritual act, not a blueprint for others to follow. A revival of walking as a primary mode of transportation is not likely anytime soon in these parts. There are just too many forces lined up against it. In a geography of nowhere in particular, being passively shuttled and dropped on another square is the new normal. A traveler on foot who is not either (1) on vacation in the wilderness or (2) homeless and destitute is an anomaly. Walking as actual transportation outside our densest city centers does not even appear on the menu of options for most Americans these days.

Still, I can't help but wonder if, by giving ourselves over so completely to our cars, we aren't walking away from some essential part of ourselves. Certainly, we are walking away from what got us around for the first few million years of our existence as a species.

As I devour my breakfast of pancakes and eggs and suffer through my coffee, I contemplate how strange it is that walking itself has come to be regarded as so consummately strange in our culture. How did we arrive at such a distance from the core capacities of our own bodies? These thoughts lead me back to the conviction that sent me on this journey in the first place, that our collective refusal to participate physically in the acts of everyday travel has a lot to do with the unraveling of our climate itself.

It is the unseen psychological impact of this absence from our lives that most concerns me. Solnit shares my view that we don't really see how much we are losing in the bargain. She writes: "Many people nowadays live in a series of interiors—

home, car, gym, office, shops—disconnected from each other. On foot everything stays connected, for while walking one occupies the spaces between those interiors the same way one occupies those interiors. One lives in the whole world rather than in interiors built up against it."[3] The path that led me to this restaurant is stitched together by footsteps that lead all the way back to my front door twenty miles away. The landscape in between is now a verb rather than a noun, folded into an experience of continual arrival. I belong here now in a way I wouldn't otherwise. This restaurant is not simply another disconnected interior that is hooked into the larger world only in the brief space between the restaurant and my parked car.

From this new vantage I'm struck by the bizarre absence that this signifies, the absence of living space between disconnected interiors. It is a state of disconnection that we now mostly take for granted. I'm struck by how quickly the simple act of walking here has begun to bridge that inner absence within my own experience.

Walking, after all, is what made us human in the first place. What could be more basic? Among the tangle of theories put forward by paleontologists about human origins, there are only a few points of wide consensus. One is that we all ultimately originated in Africa. Another is that standing up on our hind legs to become bipeds is what set humankind on its uniquely gifted evolutionary path. Alan Weisman has written: "It is now known that we walked on two feet for hundreds of thousands of years before it occurred to us to strike one stone against another to create sharp edged tools."[4] Walking preceded and made possible our extraordinary abilities to *make* and to *think*, rather than the other way around. Our new bipedal status provided the genesis from which the evolutionary crescendo of human intelligence, technology, and culture all eventually flowed.[5] The eminent paleontologist Mary Leakey summarized the evolutionary primacy of walking by suggesting that "this new freedom of forelimbs posed a challenge. The brain expanded to meet it. And mankind was formed."[6]

What to make, then, of our growing alienation from walking as a means of getting from one place to another? Why should I be so defying convention by walking to this restaurant for breakfast? After all, it was on foot that we humans stumbled into our existence in the first place. It was on foot that we spread ourselves across the globe, finally reaching Patagonia at the southern tip of South America only in the interval since the last ice age, "the farthest place," in Bruce Chatwin's words, "to which man walked from his place of origins."[7] The whole time we were walking our way up the evolutionary ladder, we walked our way into every conceivable surface niche on the planet, from the equator to the poles.

Walking has been a nearly universal fact of life for humankind until the last century and remains so in much of the developing world today. For two thousand years, merchants, pilgrims, and explorers walked the Silk Route, a string of oases strung through the mountains of Central Asia that first stitched together the empires of China, India, Persia, and Rome. Chang Ch'ien crossed the Pamir Mountains on foot from China to open the route in 139 A.D., and Marco Polo followed that same route from Europe back to China in the thirteenth century, to spend seventeen years as a special envoy to Kublai Khan on diplomatic missions throughout the Mongol empire.[8] Prominent Zen temples in Japan traditionally listed their affiliate temples in order of the time it took to walk between them. In the case of Daitoku-ji in Kyoto, these temples lay at a distance of between one day's and four weeks' walk, and monks were expected to make that journey back to the home temple on foot at least once a year. According to Gary Snyder, who trained for a decade at Daitoku-ji, "traces of a vast network of well-marked trails are still found throughout the land."[9] In the era that preceded steam- and gas-powered locomotion, European explorers walked the length and breadth of Asia, Africa, Europe, and the Americas, connecting (and disrupting) cultures that had been ignorant of each other's existence for millennia. In our own mythic American story, pioneers crossed North America on foot in the great Westward expansion of the nineteenth century that closed the earth's last major frontier. Now the remnants of that earlier breed of explorers walk the Pacific Crest Trail or the Appalachian Trail from Mexico to Canada, or climb Everest and Aconcagua in an effort to keep our questing spirits alive in the absence of blank spots on the map. While my current walk is modest in comparison, I like to think that I, too, am an explorer of sorts, a member of this same tribe.

Given that we've been walking for a span of some four million years in our various protohuman forms, waiting for our brains to catch up with our extraordinary capacity for mischief, it seems reasonable that we might still have an evolutionary stake in what is now being called *slow travel*. An outgrowth of the slow food movement that began in Italy two decades ago, slow travel emphasizes the *path* over the *destination*, and the *near* over the *far*, and is rapidly gaining international traction as an alternative to quick-hit, high-speed vacations to distant places.

Carl Honoré tracks the global spread of the "hurry virus" in his book *In Praise of Slowness: Challenging the Cult of Speed*.[10] But what *is* this "hurry virus," and how did we come to feel so victimized by it? It might be worth taking a good walk to think about this question. In fact, walking may be the quickest and least expensive path to a cure for the hurry virus. The growing popularity of slow travel makes a lot of sense when one considers that our minds were shaped on a biological anvil that matched our senses to the world at a speed of about three miles per hour.

In this respect, our love affair with cars puts us quite literally at odds with ourselves, by overwhelming and dislodging the natural connections between our senses and the world we travel through. It is only in the past few decades, particularly with the advent of jet travel, that we have fully given ourselves over to this experiment, unintentionally vaulting ourselves loose from our biologically calibrated, slow-travel perspective on the world. With these connections effectively broken, we now simply apply more and more speed to our pursuit of a constantly receding global horizon. Speed has become the only arrow in our quiver. Even the memory of what it feels like to be connected to place begins to fade. We are left with a vague sense of being out of control, without knowing what it is that we are even missing, all the while treating geography as a mere nuisance to be breached as quickly as possible in our rush between the scattered interiors of our lives.

That this pattern of behavior may have a connection to climate change is a notion that is only now beginning to seep through the fog that has settled over our brains in the wake of all this blinding speed.

o o o

ENTER THE RESISTANCE, which has also been around for longer than most of us might think. I have heard it said, for example, that Thomas Aquinas insisted on walking with the common people rather than riding a horse (which was his due) when church business took him from Paris to Rome. He did this as an act of conscious humility, but one wonders what part these long walks may have played in the development of his seminal thinking. Such walking journeys had been taken for granted by monks and other travelers throughout recorded history, as they were for Native tribes here in the Pacific Northwest, who often moved long distances on foot to summer camps at seasonal hunting and fishing grounds like Celilo Falls on the Columbia River.

By the onset of the industrial revolution, walking had already fallen on hard times in Europe, and the stage was set for a revival of sorts. Jean-Jacques Rousseau, in his *Confessions,* started a whole movement to reclaim walking as a conscious practice at the end of the eighteenth century:

> Never did I think so much, exist so vividly, and experience so much, never have I been so much myself—if I may use that expression—as in the journeys I have taken alone and on foot. There is something about walking which stimulates and enlivens my thoughts. When I stay in one place I can hardly think at all; my body has to be on the move to set my mind going.[11]

Always seen before as a utilitarian necessity, Rousseau enshrined walking as an end in itself, inspiring the modern tradition of walking for its own sake. By making the connection between walking, creativity, and personal renewal, Rousseau drew from a biological well that was already running low in the eighteenth-century Europe of his day. He helped put walking back on the intellectual (and experiential) map for Wordsworth, Kierkegaard, Thoreau, Muir, and a host of other nineteenth-century poets and philosophers who already felt appalled by the ecological destruction and human costs of the industrial revolution.[12] Kierkegaard took long walks daily through the streets of Copenhagen to seed his philosophical musings. William Wordsworth found his poetic vocation during a 2,000-mile walk through the Alpine region of Europe, and Thomas De Quincey later calculated that Wordsworth covered 175,000 miles on foot through the English countryside over the course of his life as a wandering poet. Henry David Thoreau's eccentric rambles across the New England countryside and John Muir's epic journeys on foot across North America and through the Sierra Nevada launched a cultural passion for wilderness. The current popularity of backpacking and trekking can be traced in no small measure back to these same intellectual roots.

Many of these writers influenced my thinking as a young man, so I am in that lineage, too. I walk in their footsteps still, though the urgency of climate change adds a bizarre new twist and argues strongly for bringing the culture of walking down from its pedestal of leisure recreation and back into the marrow of our everyday life. That we are so biologically tuned to walking and hence estranged from our own bodies in this current car-crazed culture only adds to the urgency. Without ways of grounding our lives more directly in the terrain of our immediate habitation, we face extinctions on every level of our being, from the accelerating loss of companion species to the loss of our personal biospiritual connections to the continuity of nature. These are not losses we can long endure, without ultimately losing our humanity itself.

o o o

NONE OF THESE THOUGHTS seem to impress my waitress as she refills my mug with coffee for the tenth time. Whatever else she might be thinking, it is clear she finds little humor in my lame banter, because I can't get her to smile even once. After breakfast, I shoulder my pack and head back onto the streets of Marysville, where the traffic has reached critical mass once again. The only person I know in this town is Bruce, the Unitarian minister, whom I met a few months earlier at a meditation retreat I led. Bruce and I hit it off at that retreat, so I stop at a phone booth to get the address of his church, which turns out to be only a few blocks away. I reach the church just as the Sunday service is about to begin, and though I am not a churchgoer myself, I slide into the rear pew of the sanctuary for a different window into this eclectic small-town culture. It is Martin Luther King weekend, so Bruce's sermon is peppered with quotes and tributes to the great civil rights leader.

When the service has ended, I surprise him among the swarms of parishioners over coffee and pastries in the social hall and compliment him on his sermon. He already knows of my travels and introduces me to a few parishioners, who are less timid about engaging me in conversation than the folks down at Don's 24-Hour Café. These are among the liberals of the town, the other end of the political spectrum from Don's. Yet my declaration of independence from cars seems almost as foreign to them, when push comes to shove. One man shakes his head and says matter-of-factly, "There is no way I could ever give up my car. No way!" A woman asks me, "Do you think you could do this in the middle of raising kids, like I am?" A retired couple point out, "We've waited all our lives for the time and money to travel, and our children live far away. We're not going to deprive ourselves of travel now, even though we know it isn't good for the environment." A younger couple asks me, "What are you doing for a living in the meantime? And do you really think this action will make any difference in the larger scheme of things?" These are fair and obvious questions, yet all I can do is acknowledge that I am wrestling with them too. There is an awkwardness built into this lack of clear answers, and it is hard to find traction. I know well enough how it is to be stuck in the trenches of making a living and raising a family, and how little energy is left over for these big questions when we are subsisting from paycheck to paycheck. This has been my reality, too. I am in no position to judge.

○ ○ ○

I FEEL STRANGELY LONELY as I hit the road again. It is already past noon, and I have a long way to travel. I pass under the I-5 overpass heading west through a slurry of malls and enter yet another world inside the Tulalip Indian Reservation. Where I am going now, I may not have the luxury of lodging to get me through the long winter night that looms ahead. It is a large reservation wrapping the shores of Port Susan for a dozen miles to the north, and I know almost nothing about it. I have never set foot here before, even though the tribal center is less than five miles as the crow flies across the water from my home on Whidbey Island.

Crossing the boundary into the reservation is like throwing a switch, with conspicuous poverty on one side of the line and affluent sprawl on the other. The Tulalip Casino and hotel adjacent to I-5 offers a flamboyant face to the surrounding community, complete with elaborate Native art, palatial architecture, and an inviting air of festive abundance. The parking lot in front of the casino is jammed with cars.

But that is not the world inside the reservation. The two could hardly be further apart. I pass two Native men on foot, headed toward the malls off the reservation, and I ask how far it is to the tribal center. We chat for a minute, and they tell me it is seven miles. These are the first people I've met on foot since early yesterday. Farther down the road, a battered car passes me, stops, then circles back to offer me a ride. The Natives in the car seem friendly. I refuse as politely as I can, telling them that I'm enjoying the walk today. Though I have been passed by a thousand cars already, this is the first time anyone has stopped to offer me a ride. Here on the reservation, for all its poverty, the world of cars is giving way to a world of human faces.

The Tulalip Indians are remnants of the Snohomish Tribe that has lived here for centuries, and they received one of the larger reservations parceled out by the treaty settlement. The Tribal Center on Tulalip Bay is nearly deserted when I arrive in late afternoon. There is an impressive longhouse by the shore, or smokehouse, where the tribe conducts its traditional dances and ceremonies. After being banned for seventy years, the longhouse tradition is making a strong comeback in Salish country, and there are over one hundred such longhouses that have sprung up around the "Salish Sea" in recent years, from Puget Sound to central Vancouver Island.*

Raven and Eagle, the first I have seen of either on this trip, are waiting for me at the Tribal Center, too. They are the two prime totem animals of Northwest Coast tribes, and they have apparently not forgotten their link with these people. A mating pair of bald eagles, doing their elaborate courtship dance on the January winds, land in a huge Douglas fir near the community hall. Their high, screeching calls bring a note of irrepressible wildness to the bay. After nearing extinction in Puget Sound during my youth, their numbers have soared in recent decades, and bald eagles are now a familiar sight again among these islands and forests.

On the beach in front of the longhouse, a batch of ravens croak and strut. It was Raven who created the world in Northwest Coast mythology. Raven stole the light of the sun, moon, and stars from the cedar bentwood boxes where they had long been imprisoned and set them loose in the world, then created human beings when he got bored with a too-orderly cosmos.

Salish Sea is a term used by bioregional thinkers to talk about the traditional, transboundary territory of the Coast Salish people as a single ecological and cultural unit; it includes Puget Sound, the Strait of Juan de Fuca, and the Strait of Georgia.

Ever the trickster, he has never run out of mischief to keep himself entertained since he brought human beings into the mix. Traditional Native peoples in this region believed that these highly intelligent birds were their reincarnated ancestors. Why the ravens have chosen this of all places to cluster, right by the ceremonial longhouse, is an irony I enjoy over a late lunch on the beach.

I don't linger for long. A cold wind is blowing off the water, and I'm getting chilled. I chat with a young Native father unloading firewood with his children from a pickup truck at the longhouse, then ask if there is any lodging near the village. The only lodging, he says, is back by the freeway. So with dusk coming on and the temperature plummeting toward freezing, I walk past the tribal marina, which is filled with crabbers and salmon gill-netters, past the Native school and health center, past the New England–style church of early mission days that stands proudly over the bay. I turn north again on the state highway, walking through sparsely settled forestlands with only an occasional car, and when it is almost too dark to see, I veer into the forest and make a light camp. I have no idea where I am and do not want to draw attention to myself, so I build no fire, wrapping myself in the small tarp and sleeping bag that are all I've brought with me for camping gear. It is still early, but it's cold and dark, so I turn in and try to get some rest.

I toss fitfully in an effort to fill the fifteen hours of darkness with something resembling sleep. Warmth eludes me in the sub-freezing temperatures. A full moon passes slowly over the thick canopy of forest, beaming down from a clear winter sky for much of the night, filling the forest with eerie light and shifting moon shadows. I know that Raven has a hand in this. The howling of coyotes and the muffled call of great horned owls make sure that my dreams are well inhabited. As I move into and out of the country called sleep, I am on a fishing boat in an epic, storm-tossed sea, wild beyond naming. An old Alaskan skipper has taken me back on his crew, and the years have fallen away. There are salmon jumping everywhere, filling our nets. The salmon that no longer swim up the Snohomish River have found a new home, for tonight at least, in the unsettled waters of my dreams.

CHAPTER 3

A Pilgrimage of Homecoming

o o o

Two or three hours' walking will carry me to as strange a country as I expect ever to see. A single farmhouse which I had not seen before is sometimes as good as the dominions of the King of Dahomey. There is in fact a sort of harmony discoverable between the capabilities of the landscape within a circle of ten miles' radius, or the limits of an afternoon walk, and the threescore years and ten of human life. It will never become quite familiar to you.

—HENRY DAVID THOREAU, *Walking*

I t feels as if I've been waiting days for the first glimmers of dawn to announce the end of this interminable night in the forest. The great horned owls notice it first, offering soulful, lengthy discourses on the change of light that pull me out of my uneven sleep. Even the soft bed of moss that served as my mattress has gone stiff with the cold. The tarp around my sleeping bag is covered with a heavy frost that pours like sand down a chute into my sleeping bag as I stir myself to rise. My boots are rigid, too, and it is an effort just to tie the laces. I corral my gear as quickly as I can into the pack and leave the forest in the same conditions as I arrived, with barely enough light to see and barely enough clothing to hold the cold at bay.

As pilgrims from St. Patrick to Basho have found, such discomforts go with the territory, so I'm not complaining. Though I'm not traveling to a far-off place, what I share with pilgrims of old is a common desire to find vistas into the depth of the world that have become hidden from view in the day-to-day preoccupations of my life, to reinvest the ordinary terrain of living with a sense of numinous presence. Right now, that path leads to nothing more glamorous than the frozen dirt beside a highway somewhere on the Tulalip Indian Reservation, a few short miles from home, heading north toward the Stillaguamish River delta.

○   ○   ○

I THINK I'VE ALWAYS BEEN a pilgrim at heart, though not according to any tradition I can name from the past. While climate change may top my reasons for embarking on this pilgrimage, the actual experience of being on the road, with a desire to break the set patterns of my life, is proving reason enough at the moment. The golden, liquid sunshine threading its way back into the forest as I walk is compensation enough for the cold and stiffness I'm carrying out of the long night. I'm happy to be here.

My first trip to Alaska as a college freshman to fish for salmon came from a similar impulse. It had the flavor of a pilgrimage, too, though I would not have called it that at the time. It was a journey into an immense landscape that dramatically enlarged my sense of who I was and what was possible in my life. So did my inaugural tour of Europe by backpack as a senior in college, to explore the landscapes of my Anglo-Saxon and Germanic ancestors. My first climb of Mount Rainier and my lengthy hikes down the wilderness coast of the Olympic Peninsula after graduation also felt like pilgrimages, paying homage to my growing devotion to a wild earth. As a child of the Northwest Coast, I had grown up at the gates of nature's cathedral, but it wasn't until my college years, aligned as they were with the first big wave of environmentalism in this country, that I became an active member of that congregation.

As an undergraduate at the University of Washington in the late 1960s, I had a front-row seat on the emerging environmental movement on the West Coast—a movement spearheaded by the first Earth Day celebration in the spring of 1970. It was a terrific time to be coming of age, when the possibility of new beginnings for our culture seemed palpable. I concocted my own blend of inspirational sources during these heady years, often ignoring my academic coursework for the poetry of Gary Snyder, the Buddhist-Christian musings of Thomas Merton, Edward Abbey's bombastic celebrations of wildness, and Henry David Thoreau's pithy discourses on place-based living. By the time I graduated from college, my copy of Thoreau's *Walden* was dog-eared to the max.

Perhaps that will explain why, when I arrived in Cambridge, Massachusetts, in the fall of 1974 as a theology student at Harvard Divinity School, my first public act was to assemble a group of fellow entering students for a journey to Walden Pond. On a perfect New England fall day, I orchestrated a group hike around the pond and a ritual swim in its waters, then read aloud to my companions the entire chapter titled "Where I Lived, and What I Lived For" from *Walden*. It was my way of saying that I was not going to be an ordinary theology student and that the fate of the earth was not going to be left out of my curriculum of study. The Old Testament of my personal Bible included the writings of Thoreau, John Muir, Aldo Leopold, and Rachel Carson, along with Jeremiah and Isaiah. I was on the hunt for additional voices in the wilderness—a New Testament with enough ecological literacy to close the gap between a theology of personal salvation and a theology of collective healing for an earth in peril.

My pilgrimage to Walden Pond may not have been the traditional indoctrination into a course of theological studies at Harvard, but it was something I instinctively had to do, just as hitchhiking across the continent with a backpack was the only way I could imagine arriving in Harvard Square from the Pacific Northwest. Walking in the footsteps of Thoreau established right from the start the essential link I saw between religious practice and ecological awareness, between the well-being of the natural world and our uniquely human quest for meaning. This link only grew stronger during my three years of study at Harvard, fueled by summers of commercial fishing in Alaska that balanced the intellectual rigors of my studies with the physical rigors of long, hard days on the fishing grounds. Maybe it is that balance that I am striving for again now, a resurgence of physical rigor into my quest to find alignment with my convictions on climate change.

o o o

BY THE TIME I REACH KAYAK POINT, the sun has exploded above the forest, turning Port Susan the same cobalt blue as the sky, and the long vista down Possession Sound a tapestry of islands glinting in the sun. The Olympic Mountains swell in the distance behind Camano Island, displaying their heavy coating of fresh winter snow. I drop down a steep, winding road to the beach still heavily frosted in the shade of the forest. A bustling campground in summer, the park at Kayak Point belongs all to me on this January morning. A few Western grebes and Barrows goldeneyes are feeding in the shallows, diving into the mirrored reflection of mountains that travel with them down into the stillness of the water. The graceful arc of the grebe as it splits the water's surface is one of such effortless artistry that I never grow weary of watching it.

I study the weariness in my body with a similar fascination, almost like meeting an old friend again. The stiff muscles that are the cost of coming here also make the day feel more vibrant and alive. I peel an orange and enjoy a breakfast of bread and cheese while the sun reels itself higher into the sky. A pilgrimage like this one does its job by leavening my abstract questions with the fierce beauty of the moment. It returns a measure of balance to the world by helping to pry the senses open.

This desire for firsthand experience is something I also share with seekers of the past. It was during his first solo walks through the Brazilian rain forest, for example, early in the voyage of the *Beagle*, that the young Charles Darwin was transformed from curious onlooker into pilgrim. The depth of the silence he encountered there cut to his core and unleashed deep powers of observation and excitement. The ornithologist Lyanda Lynn Haupt sees Darwin "at this moment beginning his voyage again, not as a tourist this time but as a kind of pilgrim, living an unfiltered, firsthand experience, becoming his own witness to creation's story, putting himself, as is the pilgrim's task, within that story."[1] This was a classic conversion experience for Darwin, like my first trip to Alaska, one that would sustain his devotion to the smallest and most intimate details of the natural world around him to the end of his days. Like Darwin in his later years, I am returning to the world I've always known, but with new eyes that can penetrate beneath the surface of the familiar, finding sources of belonging everywhere I look.

o o o

FROM KAYAK POINT, I continue north along the beach for several miles beneath high bluffs. I'm drawing close to the mouth of the Stillaguamish River, where the bay's shallow waters run razor thin over tidal flats that spread all the way to Camano Island.

There are few places in Puget Sound where I can walk the beach in this way. Private ownership of local tidelands erects barriers wherever a cluster of houses have come to roost. But there is a wide expanse between those clusters on this lonely stretch of shoreline, and I enjoy the freedom of walking this ragged edge where land and sea are constantly remaking each other. The wide rim of salt marsh marks an uncertain horizon around the bay's northern arc, where the river spreads its freshwater fingers over the wide estuary.

The river has encountered no large cities in its brief fifty-mile rush from Cascade crest to the sea, draining a lovely rural valley from Darrington to Arlington before ferrying its load of mountain silt into the sea just south of Stanwood. The deltas of the Skagit and Stillaguamish press together here from north and south, like a rising tide of fertile loam that is slowly building Camano Island into a mainland peninsula. Only a small slough navigable by skiff at high tide now marks it as an island. Between these conjoined deltas is a vast empire of salt marsh, nearly inaccessible by land or by sea. These two rivers have swapped Cascade tributaries over the millennia, most recently when the Sauk and Suiattle Rivers jumped from the Stillaguamish to the Skagit after an eruption of Glacier Peak rerouted them northward from Darrington. The Stilly's loss was the Skagit's gain, making it the largest river in the Puget Sound basin.

Port Susan itself sits on the nautical charts like an upside-down flask that is half full of sand. The upper bay is a wide expanse of mudflats that give way only grudgingly to navigable waters. The absence of deepwater access has been a buffer against development. This is the end of the road, a place apart, mostly ignored by the thriving upland commerce a few miles to the east.

The shallow fingers of tide that push up over these flats collide with four billion gallons of fresh water flowing into the bay from the Stillaguamish River on an average day.[2] Even without the Sauk and Suiattle on board, the Stilly remains the fifth-largest river in Puget Sound. In many ways, what lies before me is the best of the sound's remaining estuarine ecology that gave us such storied salmon runs, such incomparably rich farmland, such a wealth of clean water rolling down from the Cascade snowfields. All five species of Pacific salmon spawn here, although the total number of returning chinook salmon has fallen as low as a few dozen in recent years. While the river's wealth is much diminished by these losses, it is here and in the Skagit that the greatest possibilities for restoration also lie. From my current vantage on the beach, this spacious estuary stretches out before me with a grandly welcoming presence.

At Warm Beach, I climb through a tiered neighborhood of vacation homes to the top of the bluff, where the state highway resumes its northward push toward Stanwood. Almost immediately, I regret the loss of sand underfoot as the pavement takes up its hammering on my tired legs. I walk for several miles through loose-knit housing developments before dropping down into a wide expanse of working farms spread across the Stillaguamish delta.

I can see the gleaming white church steeples of Stanwood on the far rise beyond the river and reel myself ever-so-slowly toward the town. It is barely noon, and I'm surprised by how tired I feel after only a few hours of walking. I carry this weariness like a physical weight, willing myself forward one step at a time. Blisters have opened up on both heels, and not since my days on the halibut grounds in Alaska have I experienced such a deep fatigue. I resolve to take the first lodging I come to in the town, even though I'd expected to push well into the Skagit by day's end.

Slumping to the ground by a side slough after crossing the main bridge over the river, I munch on trail mix and gulp water in an effort to restart the engines. Great blue herons are fishing for sculpins around the muddy shallows of the slough, their movements a study in patient grace. There is no free lunch for them, no package of trail mix waiting in their pack. They cannot choose to buy organic. What they see is what they get, and they are about their business of feeding from dawn to dusk. The pesticides and petrochemicals that run off these farmlands make their way into the fish these birds are now eating and thus into their own bodies. Such pollution from all points around the sound, urban and rural alike, is a quiet crisis that hangs just below the surface beauty of even the most hidden places. I lie back on the grass in a sun now tinged with warmth, and fall into a deep and welcoming sleep.

When I awake, my mind says, "Let's go," while my body insists, "I'm done." Stanwood is still three miles distant. The thought occurs that I could easily hitch a ride, and no one would be the wiser, but I quickly push down this offer from the less-principled side of my brain. I can't even say why, but I will keep to my vow, even though at the moment I feel as if I am walking on stilts.

Already on this trip, my perception of space has been altered, my sense of geography expanded. No transcontinental flight could touch the distance I have traveled to get here. For the first time on the walk, I find myself missing Sally and the comfort of my own hearth. I feel a poignant confluence of emotions as I think of her— this longing for our physical home in the middle of an island forest, surrounded by the spirit of a region that has crafted within me a wider allegiance to place. It is a love that already goes deep, but it has been growing deeper with each step I take.

o o o

THE LONG SLOG across the flats into Stanwood feels like a trek in the desert, the town a shimmering mirage that never gets closer.

When I reach the outskirts at last, I spot a county bus stop. It is deserted except for an elderly woman sitting in the bus shelter. She is the first person I've seen all day who is not on the backside of a windshield driving by, so I figure I'd better seize the moment. I angle in her direction to ask about lodging. It's hard to say just how old she might be. Despite her shock of white hair, much of her age is written in the script of hard living. I lower my pack to the ground, stifling a groan, as she eyes me up and down suspiciously. Before I can speak she gets right to the point. "My ex-husband used to say, when he saw a person like you, 'There goes someone on vacation.'"

This is not exactly the conversation starter I had expected, and it's obvious right away that I can count on straight answers from this woman. I settle into the seat beside her, trying to ignore her barb. "Can you tell me where the nearest lodging might be?" I ask. "The only motel is out by the interstate," she answers, "five miles east of here."

I can feel the last bit of air going out of my tires. It never occurred to me that there would be no public lodging in Stanwood. For the first time, I regret my commitment to serendipity on this trip. The thought of a second night sleeping by the highway in subfreezing temperatures is not even on my worst-case scenario of options, and walking five more miles in the wrong direction is out of the question.

The woman has me cornered now, and is well into her own life story. I hear how hard it was for her to find a place to live near Stanwood when she got released from prison three years ago. I learn that her neighbor in the apartment next door is drunk a lot and can be a real asshole. I learn more than I want to know about her daughter's first child, delivered at age fourteen, whom she is now raising. I nod my head with each revelation while I catch my breath and consider my choices. Her story puts my own small dilemmas in sharp relief. How does it come to pass that some people are saddled with such long odds in their lives, while others have opportunity handed to them from day one by accident of birth?

Then she mentions something that really catches my attention. "My bus to Everett is due in five minutes. Island Transit just added this new run. It's an express bus, and it only takes forty-five minutes to Everett Station." I let this revelation sink in, and I can feel my energy rise. Maybe serendipity will come through after all. The woman has thrown me an unexpected rope, and I grab it. It's a day earlier than I had planned to break off my walk, and I thought I'd be farther along by now. But I have work commitments waiting either way. In two days, I'm scheduled to resume teaching my stress-reduction classes to vets at the VA Hospital in Seattle.[3] I do a hasty calculation and realize that I could be home by dinnertime if I jump on this bus. With such a great transit connection, I can return to this same spot next week, rested and ready to continue my walk. I couldn't have planned it better.

With this decision made, I turn my attention back to the woman, who has moved on to the trials of her daughter. I wonder when the last time was that she had a listening ear. I wonder what she would make of my own story. When she finally pauses for breath, I take a gamble, telling her about my car-free commitment for the year and the path I've taken to get here. To my surprise, she hears me out, then says, "I'm ahead of you on that one. I've gotten by without a car for years. I haven't been able to afford one since my husband left me ten years ago. The truth is, I do just fine on the buses, and I walk places every day. I'm used to it now. I've come to like it this way."

For the second time, her response takes me by surprise. She may not share my convictions about climate change, but she has made her peace with a low-carbon lifestyle. There is no hint of self-pity in her remarks. For a different set of reasons, she has already managed a large measure of the change that I am just beginning to take on. Are her actions less relevant to the crisis we face because they are made under the weight of poverty rather than environmental conviction?

I want to ask her another question, but this time it feels like too much of a stretch. I want to ask where in her life she finds hope. It's a question I've been pondering a lot lately. If *home* is my destination on this pilgrimage, then *hope* is essential survival equipment—not the kind of hope that requires certain results, but a hope that can keep its shoulder to the wheel no matter what happens. Vaclav Havel put it this way:

> Hope is an orientation of the spirit, an orientation of the heart. . . . It is not the conviction that something will turn out well, but the certainty that something makes sense, regardless of how it turns out.[4]

Havel is speaking from solid experience here. He spent six years in prison under the Communist regime in Czechoslovakia before becoming president of that country in 1989. It was a turnaround that no one could have predicted, and his life is a testimony to the kind of hope he speaks of. No one can say for certain what that future will bring, regardless of how discouraging the current trends. That means there is always room for surprise and always reason for hope. We have no idea yet what we are capable of achieving once we turn toward these challenges with our full hearts engaged. That story has yet to be written.

The unexpected camaraderie I've found with this woman at the bus stop is another occasion for hope. Help comes from unexpected places, and we can almost always find common ground with others when we take the trouble to look. When the bus pulls up, we climb aboard, retracing in forty-five minutes what took me three days to accomplish on foot. We wish each other farewell at Everett Station, and I board another bus to the ferry landing. Back on the island I finish where I began, walking the last two miles home from the highway where the bus leaves me off.

These days on the road have been just what I needed, a perfect beginning for my year in circumference. Even the buses have been part of my pilgrimage, part of the essential gear I will need to make this shift a lasting one. Next week I will return to Stanwood and continue my walk with a refreshed body. In the meantime I'm ready to dive back into my life of work and family, armed with my boots, my bicycle, and a bus ticket.

CHAPTER 4

Where Wild Salmon Still Run

o   o   o

Pugh Creek goes into the Whitechuck
the Whitechuck goes into the Sauk
the Sauk goes into the Skagit
the Skagit goes into the Sound.

—GARY SNYDER, *Earth House Hold*

My home on Whidbey Island is a great base for these adventures, a perfect center pole for my circle around the sound. I built my house on a hillside tucked in the woods above a rural valley that is still marked by working farms. A small creek runs through the valley, and in recent years, coho salmon have been returning to the creek with the help of local schoolchildren, restoring an historic run that had been lost. Where the creek enters the sound, an uninhabited beach stretches several miles south beneath high, forested bluffs to the end of the island. Each day when I'm home, I take time to walk these woods and beaches, and now that I'm a month into my year, I use these walks to reflect on my progress.

I had two main fears coming into this year, and I'm far enough along now to take the pulse on both. My first fear was that slowing down like this and cutting myself off from my accustomed independent mobility might stoke the fires of a restless confinement, or worse yet, that I might get caught in an undertow of depression. I am no stranger to either of these unwelcome guests, and I feared that they might use this break in the action to move in on a more permanent basis. This is a particular risk since I've chosen to begin in the dead of winter, when seasonal affective disorder is a common visitor all over the Pacific Northwest. Forty days and forty nights of rain is not the best recipe for a cheerful disposition.

My second fear was that this jolt to established routine might prove unsettling to my marriage. Sally and I are a study in contrasts, and we have striven to build a life together that works for both of us. This year is no small adjustment to the formula, and I've worried that it might unleash some demons of discord. Both of these fears lurked just below the surface in the months leading up to my launch, and there was no way of predicting where the chips might fall. Only the strength of my conviction that something had to give was enough to push me over the precipice into taking these risks.

A month into my year, with the first part of my Skagit walk under my belt, both these fears are fast fading. Getting out of my car—breaking out of the "scattered interiors" of my life generally—has given me a new buoyancy of spirit. It's hard to imagine, in fact, a better antidepressant than simple fresh air and the regular exercise that now accompanies me from place to place. I feel the opposite of confinement. Being out in the world under my own power has put a lot of fresh wind in my sails and is proving terrific medicine for the winter blues. Psychologically, I've broken my deadlock with a lifestyle I can't believe in anymore, and this has also tipped the odds in my favor when depression comes knocking at the door. This new solvency of spirit annoys the hell out of my old nemesis, who doesn't come to visit nearly as often anymore or hang around nearly as long when he does.

And then there is that great force in my life who goes by the name of Sally. I worried a lot coming into the year about how these changes might affect our marriage. This decision was my choice, after all, and not hers. It is no small disruption to our family life. Large changes can send a large wake through primary relationships.

With our kids out the door, travel is an alluring option for us again, especially with so many good friends scattered around the country and the world. My decision puts that prospect on hold, and my wife was not thrilled when I broke the news to her about my big idea. She shares my concerns about climate change, but thought this plan sounded a little over the top. Initially, she suggested that a three-month hiatus from my car and from travel outside my circle might be enough to get the point across. When I refused to budge, she countered with a six-month proposal. But to her credit, she never seriously tried to talk me out of it either. She knew how hard I'd been wrestling with the question of personal responsibility for our climate crisis, and she respected the sincerity with which I was trying to find some resolution.

Sally also knew that this wasn't going to be her way of tackling the problem, and I respected that, too. She has a network of friends around the country that she actively tends, and unlike my own family, her family of origin lives three thousand miles away. Her father is ailing on the East Coast, and she is a loyal daughter who takes her familial responsibilities seriously. Like most people we know, she also enjoys a change of scene from time to time and the allure of exotic places. In short, she is a case study in why it is hard to give up our cars and the luxury of air travel, if we are lucky enough to have the means to enjoy them.

For all these reasons, I never asked her to take on this commitment with me, and she never offered. That was not part of the deal. But neither was I willing, just to ease her anxiety, to back down on my commitment, as I often do in the push and pull of our relationship. Sally can put up fierce resistance when she feels cornered, but I think she could sense that this time, it was best to give ground and let out some scope on my need to explore this new terrain.

Sally is a big-energy person, willful and opinionated, who has no problem expressing exactly how she feels. She is on the go constantly, with a lively mind and voracious social appetite that I don't even try to match. She is a good balance for me that way, tempering my contemplative nature and keeping me more engaged in my community than I might otherwise be. The pleasure she takes in life pours through her in great gushes of laughter, and she can light a crowded room with the radiance of her presence. She is a great person to have on my side, the best friend and advocate one could hope for when our purposes are aligned. Yet Sally's potential for displeasure can reach storm proportions as well.

So this was a high-stakes gamble on my part. It wouldn't be an adventure if I already knew the outcome, and it could be a long year indeed if Sally chooses to dig in her heels, if she meets my efforts with resistance or resentment. I am asking a lot from her to stand by me on such a large departure from our norm. Our income is taking a big hit during this year of self-proclaimed sabbatical, and our daily logistics are more complicated. Nor can I claim to be truly car-free as long as Sally is still doing the driving for me, buying groceries and running errands that continue to support us both. It is not a small thing to ask.

With so many unanswered questions, Sally and I have avoided talking about the tensions this might cause between us. It is not her way to anticipate future problems when there are enough problems already at hand. She is a here-and-now kind of gal. So I've had to take these first steps into my year trusting that somehow, this will all work out between the two of us.

When I arrive home from my walk, Sally greets me warmly. She has prepared a terrific dinner of Skagit River chum salmon from our freezer that I caught during the commercial salmon season in local waters earlier this fall. I'm pleased when she listens to my stories from the walk with obvious interest, asking lots of questions and taking pleasure in my answers. When dinner is over, she gives me an unexpected gift. She asks if she can join me next week, when I resume my hike through the Skagit basin.

This is a bonus I had not expected. I hear in her question the first solid yes to the direction I have taken and a desire to be part of my year in a more direct way. I'm happy to share this walk with her for other reasons, too. She is a resourceful companion on any trip, eager to dive into unfamiliar ground and undaunted when conditions get uncomfortable. She has been on a number of my kayaking expeditions in Alaska, and her can-do spirit is always a welcome addition. We share a common pleasure at traveling without fixed plans, so that we can be playful in response to unexpected twists and turns along the way. Knowing that time spent on these adventures will not necessarily translate into time away from Sally is a reassuring and comforting thought.

o   o   o

WE'RE BOTH ITCHING to hit the road when the morning comes to resume the long walk. Sally catches a ride to the ferry with a neighbor headed for Seattle, while I peddle my bicycle to meet her at the ferry landing. This is our new routine, traveling by different means to the same destination, with Sally making an effort to carpool now as her way of honoring my commitment. In her own way, she seems to be catching my enthusiasm for this challenge, and the support I feel coming from her is feeding into a renewed current of affection between us. It has become a shared adventure, and this has increased the strength of the wind in my own sails.

Back on the mainland again, we continue to Stanwood by bus through terrain that is no longer a blank spot on my map. We get off at the same lonely outpost where I ended my walk last week, and shouldering our packs, we're on our way. I'm traveling lighter this time, because through this part of the walk, we have friends whose hospitality awaits. This next passage is what I've been looking forward to the most. It will take us through the heart of the Skagit delta, Puget Sound's largest and still wildest river.

Today also marks the halfway point between the solstice and the equinox, offering a seasonal waypoint to chart my progress through the year. The change in daylight follows a parabolic curve through the seasons, with a barely perceptible shift for a month on either side of the solstice. Then the rate of change steepens, and by the equinox, we are adding or subtracting a half-hour of daylight each week. Only in the last days have I begun to sense that the days are getting longer. Though we are still in the depths of winter, some inner pull toward hibernation that we share with other mammals has begun to relax its grip as the darkness eases its hold on the land. I can literally feel it happening.

The novelty of being without a car is wearing off, too. I've been surprised how quickly this new routine has come to seem normal. The agitation I usually carry in my body when I'm rushing around has slackened noticeably, and I feel more attuned to the subtle changes in the season as a result. At a time of year when many of our friends are either off to Mexico or "stuck" at home complaining about the cold and rain, Sally and I are hard-pressed to imagine a place we would rather be, or anything we would rather be doing, than setting off on foot into the Skagit on an otherwise dreary morning.

We stroll through the streets of Stanwood, a tidy farming community that has held to its Scandinavian heritage since its founding in the late nineteenth century. Buffered on all sides by open spaces and out of the main currents of sprawl, it remains unabashedly rural in outlook. Like Seattle's early neighborhoods, Stanwood displays unadorned, well-kept wood frame houses that were built by carpenters who knew what they were doing. The dominant view from the upland plateau is across Skagit Bay, where the wealth of farmland rolls down into salt marsh and mudflats that nearly engulf the entire basin. The scale of what is off-limits to human approach gives this expanse a foreboding look under today's heavy overcast. Squalls of rain delivered by a wet wind do little to soften that impression. But we have good rain gear and plenty of experience handling these shifts in the weather. It isn't long before we've left the town behind and are walking through verdant farmland that angles slowly down toward the South Fork of the Skagit River.

Beyond the delta and the shallow reaches of the bay, the geology shifts dramatically from low-lying mounds of glacial till into the trademark granite upwellings of the San Juan archipelago. The first of these upwellings punctuate the delta like giant haystacks to the north. Growing in scale, they spill out beyond Deception Pass into the Strait of Juan de Fuca to become the lovely San Juan Islands. It is as if the Cascade Mountains have lost their balance and veered sharply to the sea, reaching tidewater just north of the Skagit basin. Though the geology is complex, what we see before us is the beginning of a vast Coast Range that piles steeply down into the ocean from here northward along the entire coast of British Columbia and Southeast Alaska.

It is no small change of scene that we are walking into, as a pastoral landscape turns suddenly mythic and wild. This is the beginning of the Inside Passage to Alaska.

For nearly ten miles, Sally and I parallel the river into the interior of the delta, funneling along a narrow two-lane highway that is the only link between Stanwood and the farming communities to the north. The traffic is heavy with commercial trucks, and we tightrope nervously along the edge of this shoulderless highway pinned hard against the traffic. As we pass the Skagit County line, where biking is a growing craze, the shoulder suddenly widens and the going gets easier. The river flows just out of reach beyond a tangle of farm fields and marshlands west of the highway.

Nearing Conway, the river is now corralled between dikes, and we seize our first opportunity to leave the highway and mount the path that leads next to the river. Locals call these diked sections the Ditch, and for almost a century, dikes have lined both the North and the South Forks in an effort to break the river of its periodic tendency to flood the whole valley. It is a cat-and-mouse game that the river still sometimes wins. For now, though, it's a relief just to walk beside flowing water, buffered from the highway by a thick band of cottonwood trees. The white heads of bald eagles stand out starkly in the cottonwood thickets, working the last of the chum salmon run for which this river is still justly famous. The eagles have come from as far away as Alaska, following the salmon south to feed on this late Skagit River run.

The Skagit is a sprawling system, with nearly three thousand tributaries draining a watershed of over three thousand square miles stretching from Mount Baker to Glacier Peak. Ten billion gallons of water flow through the Skagit daily, fed by almost four hundred glaciers, all of them shrinking under the glare of rising temperatures as global warming kicks in. The river is home to all five species of Pacific salmon, and 270 other species of wildlife.[1] Seattle gets most of its electricity from three large dams on the Upper Skagit, so the river is also a focus of intense wrangling over water and other resources between the competing interests of farmers, fishermen, loggers, Native tribes, and electric utilities. With the recent listing of Puget Sound's chinook salmon as Endangered, the Skagit finds itself at the epicenter of a regionwide fight to stem the loss of salmon-rearing habitat, a battle that the salmon have been steadily losing for decades. Crafting a credible recovery plan that passes muster with all these competing interests in a culture that no longer has an economic stake in salmon is proving highly elusive.

Yet these eagles are evidence that salmon still enter this river in substantial numbers. The Skagit has a greater prospect than any other river in Puget Sound for shaping a future that includes both salmon and people. As Sally and I make our way along the river, the spirit of these salmon is reflected back to us in the cold gaze of these eagles that are still standing watch over their ancient watershed. Sally is at her cheerful best searching for a path that is both close to the river and off the beaten track. Seeking that road less traveled is a pleasure we have always shared, one of our earliest bonds of friendship.

We stop for a hearty lunch at the Conway Café, directly across Main Street from the town's grain elevators, then press on across the bridge over the river onto Fir Island, entering the heart of the delta that lies between the two forks of the river. A wet snow is falling as we turn south along the dike, ditching the traffic at last as we enter a network of back roads that cut across the isolated delta. This is a sentimental journey for Sally, who spent a year working as a farmhand at Cascadia Farm in the Upper Skagit as part of her recovery from medical school. She had also worked off her med-school angst as a deckhand on a halibut schooner out of Sitka, Alaska, at the same time that I was working on a salmon seiner out of Sitka in a parallel program as a recovering clergyman. Perhaps it was inevitable that we would eventually meet and find an answering soul in one another.

There is a more immediate reason that I'm grateful we met. Sally has friends scattered through the Skagit delta from her farming days here, so the quality of my lodging options has risen considerably with her on the team. Tonight we will stay with Brad and Eileen, two Mount Vernon attorneys who live tucked away among the working farmsteads on Fir Island. As we press on through squalls of hail and snow, it's nice to know that a warm house and welcoming friends are waiting for us. Approaching their homestead at last, we spot our first big flock of winter snow geese working the farm stubble around their property, washed like a white tide nearly up to their doorstep. Several thousand strong, the geese are a formidable presence, filling the air with their ancient murmur, and the sky overhead with wings.

o o o

WE LEARN MUCH from our hosts about the controversies raging in Skagit country between farmers, Native tribes, and developers over the future of a watershed under threat. Progress is stalled by decades of resentment between farmers, tribes, and growing cities over who is to blame for the loss of salmon habitat in the Skagit delta and who should bear the costs of recovery. And those costs are great. They include a fundamental reassessment about how all parties in the dispute go about their daily business. The depth of these rivalries has turned the Skagit into a regional case study in the elusive quest for a new culture of ecological sustainability. If residents of the Skagit cannot find a path through this thicket of feuding interests toward a more durable future for both salmon and people, it is unlikely that other great watersheds in the sound will succeed either. Threatened as they are, salmon remain a potent regional icon and a prime indicator species by which to gauge the health of local biological systems as a whole. Among those who care about the fate of Northwest salmon, all eyes are on the Skagit to see if a viable spirit of restoration can be rescued from the ashes of a century of steep decline.

o o o

IN THE MORNING, Sally and I resume our long walk across the Skagit delta toward La Conner on the least traveled roads we can find. We are walking through the richest farm country in Western Washington, and undeniably the most beautiful. The weather has cleared this morning, and the white dome of Mount Baker looms over the landscape like the Great White Watcher (Koma Kulshan) that local Native tribes called the mountain prior to European contact.

One of the Skagit's last links to a Pleistocene past is the great flocks of snow geese and trumpeter swans that still winter in the delta. Trumpeter swans are the largest of all waterfowl, majestic birds in flight, and the snow geese that congregate on the flats can number ten thousand or more to a flock. Our desire to experience this vestige of a wilder Northwest is part of the Skagit's magnetism for us.

Since we're traveling across the delta on foot, our range is limited, and we have to rely on the geese to find us, but find us they do. As we walk Dry Slough through the center of Fir Island, we hear the first tremors of goose music building in the east, then rising to a hoarse urgency. Numbering in the thousands, the flocks fill the sky until they've buried the mountain in a storm of wings. Like a living blizzard, they settle onto the fields around us, flock after flock, covering the adjacent farmland in a blanket of white. The geese pile like snowdrifts against the curving edge of the slough, then settle down for a long lunch. We can hardly believe our luck.

Sally and I sink into the grass to eat our lunch, too, in the company of this croaking multitude, bundling ourselves up against the sharp January wind. The flock seems to function as a single organism, obeying signals from a brain they share collectively among them. In the whole expanse of this delta, how did they choose to land here? Who among their thousands led the way, and who will decide when it is time to go? There is an unpredictable, self-organizing quality to the behavior of flocks, a mysterious intelligence that relies on no one leader. Yet a small number of informed individuals can have a decisive impact on the flock as a whole, even if these individuals are not recognized as leaders and do not recognize each other. It is known, for example, that 5 percent of a honeybee swarm can guide the group to a new hive. And for migrating groups of animals, the larger the flock, the smaller the percentage of informed individuals needed to effect a change in direction.[2] The result is that unanticipated shifts in the direction of travel that benefit the whole flock can happen with breathtaking quickness.

It is a spectacle of immense beauty when seen from the outside. Research into flock behavior suggests that no single leader causes this to happen. An informed core of leaders scattered throughout the flock can trigger sudden shifts in direction. It is almost as if the flock is feeling its way collectively toward the goal. A time-lapse view reveals that small individual shifts cascade into a mass shift at the point when a sufficient minority of the flock has chosen a common new direction. In some cases, that minority can be quite small. In real time, it merely looks as if they all turn at once.

Sally and I sit with the geese for nearly an hour while nothing seems to change. We eat our lunch and they eat theirs. It appears that their appetites will outlast ours, and we are about to head on our way when a single goose lifts off, then another, followed by a few more. Geese start leaving in groups of two and four, mostly flying to the outskirts of the flock and settling back down to feed. Some continue on into the distance as a palpable agitation settles over the rest of the flock. Heads start bobbing, and the murmur intensifies. We watch, almost holding our breaths. There is no doubt that all hell is about to break loose.

Then, with a roar that sets our hair on end, the entire flock peels off from the field like a swell rolling across the ocean. One moment they are a quiet blanket of contented geese. The next moment the sky has erupted with urgent striving, and the geese are fanning off across the delta toward an unspecified destination that some small, anonymous core of informed scouts will help them all to discover. We watch until the geese are a thin cloud on the northern horizon. The silence left by their absence surrounds us in an almost physical embrace. It is hard to resist comparison, flocks of geese to our human flock, the force of long habit set against the stark necessity of survival.

Maybe we don't have to *all* get it before the *flock* gets it. Maybe nature's design has anticipated just such a conundrum, and we can look as reliably to nature for guidance now as ever. If we share any part of the wider biological legacy of flocks, may it be this: that in times of great need, a few individuals acting boldly on their convictions can trigger a shift toward collective survival that is both swift and widely shared. We are never acting alone when we do this. It only appears that way. When we seize upon a strong conviction to change, it is the wisdom of an entire species that may be acting through us, and none of us will ever have to carry this burden alone.

○ ○ ○

AFTER OUR RENDEZVOUS with the snow geese, Sally and I continue on our way through a landscape of almost fantasy proportions. Our goal for the night is the iconic port of La Conner,
where we will stay with our old friends Lauren and Billie. We
cross the North Fork of the Skagit just upstream from Fishtown,
a collection of weathered river shacks connected by boardwalks
that serve as an outpost for hunters and fishermen. The river
flows dutifully seaward here through the Ditch toward its rendezvous with Skagit Bay, whose waters are visible now above the
distant marshes, with the long, rolling ridges of Whidbey Island
enclosing the bay from behind. It is nice to have a glimpse of our
home island, which is now within the reach of another long day
of walking. We stop for coffee and homemade pie at the Rexville
Café, basking in the nostalgia of an older Skagit Valley. We
choose winding back roads through the Dodge Valley, another
hidden jewel of the Skagit, where Lauren and Billie join us to
walk the last miles into town. We pass farm fields decked with
trumpeter swans, while dusk settles over the valley where wild
salmon still run.

La Conner sits on the perimeter of the delta like a postcard
from the edge, proudly claiming the south entrance to the
Swinomish Channel a world away from Puget Sound's prevailing
maritime commerce. It serves as a backdoor entry into the Inside Passage to Alaska, a protected route to Canadian waters
when winds in the Strait of Juan de Fuca make travel treacherous for the smaller fleet. As we walk through its polished neighborhoods, I can't imagine a finer day than what Sally and I have
just shared. I'm struck again by how different it feels to arrive at
a destination on foot after days of travel, rather than blasting in
by car or jet. The speed engulfing our culture has reordered my

perception of the world in ways I didn't fully appreciate until I slowed down long enough to bring my mind back into alignment with my senses.

The Scottish explorer David Livingston, who was the first European to cross the width of southern Africa in 1856, wrote in his journal: "The effect of travel on a man whose heart is in the right place is that the mind is made more self-reliant: it becomes more confident of its own resources—there is greater presence of mind."[3] Livingston, of course, was talking about a very different pace of travel than what most Americans are familiar with, a more ancient pace that matches our human senses to the world. The Zen master Thich Nhat Hanh locates the source of this inner confidence closer at hand: "The path around our home is also the ground of awakening."[4] There is a greater wholeness to the fabric of a landscape we have walked through, a more considerate quality of approach, that makes both the path and the destination feel more alive as a result, and we don't experience the same separation between where we are and what we are.

Sally and Lauren met as farmhands working on an organic farm in the Upper Skagit Valley, and their friendship is rooted deep in that shared soil. Dinner becomes a celebratory act that we all prepare together, drawing upon the last of Lauren's stock of local fall fruit and vegetables. Having walked so far to get here, we've brought this place into that "path around our home" in a more direct way. Arriving on foot, Sally and I have a deeper sense of what it means to be *inhabitants* of this place. Tomorrow, I will continue the walk on my own, and Sally will return home by bus and train. But tonight Lauren and Billie have become neighbors in a new way, and the stories we share over dinner are happening right in our own neighborhood.

An Island Four Days Long

o o o

There are perfect places everywhere on earth,
      and part of their perfection
is in belonging exactly where they are.

—Richard Nelson, *The Island Within*

L a Conner's upscale neighborhoods cut a sharp contrast
with its immediate neighbor, the Swinomish Indian Reservation, which lies directly across the narrow shipping
channel. Here, conspicuous rural poverty and genteel affluence
stare each other nervously in the face, caught in a riptide of cultural disparity that time has yet to heal. My fascination with
Native culture and what it has to teach us has led me to straddle
this divide as often as I am able, and this is a place where I feel at
home on both sides of the water.

In the morning after breakfast, Sally catches a bus for home
while I hoist my pack to continue on my way. A traveler's itch is
in my legs now as I circle back around toward my home island.
The day has dished up another clear and frosty morning as I
climb a wooded rise to the bridge that will carry me between
high granite buttresses onto Fidalgo Island. Technically, this is

the first of the San Juan Islands, the gateway to the archipelago. Mount Erie's billowing granite frame dominates the center of the island, rising thirteen hundred feet from the sea to announce the stark shift in geological character. Today's walk will be a long one, ascending the eastern lobe of the island through the Swinomish Indian Reservation, then skirting the flanks of Mount Erie southward to a stunning entry back onto Whidbey Island across the Deception Pass bridge.

The tranquil view from the height of the bridge gives little hint that I am crossing a cultural fault line too. As I enter the Indian reservation on Fidalgo Island, I pass the Native cemetery where totem poles mingle with Christian crosses in an un-self-conscious alliance of the old and the new. Freshly tended offerings of flowers and memorabilia adorn the graves, revealing a thinner veil between the living and the dead in a place where lines of ancestry arc back through centuries on this same piece of land. I wander through the cemetery, studying the well-kept graves, suddenly uncomfortable with the fact that I don't even know where my own grandparents are buried. This absence stirs a small twister of loneliness in me, a fresh glimpse of how rootless I have become.

The Swinomish longhouse inspires awe even from a distance. It is a cavernous building on the hill, supported by massive cedar house posts—the "spirit tree" of Native tribes along this coast—carved in totem figures that tell the legends of the tribe. Old-growth cedars form the beams and rafters of the building as well, with an open ridge to vent smoke from the ceremonial bonfires inside. I have been honored to witness longhouse ceremonies here on special occasions when nontribal members are invited to attend. It is a gateway into another world. The dances can last all night, with drums and chants hammering at the margins of consciousness. Painted dancers in full tribal regalia circle the enormous bonfires, slicing in and out of a thick smoke haze that hints at parallel worlds beyond the realm of our immediate sense experience.

I stop by the longhouse to pay my respects, then continue on to the home of my friend Marvin, whom I met at an environmental justice rally in Seattle a few years ago.* Marvin and I have spent time together on several occasions since. He is a humble man with a warm smile and a great generosity of spirit, one of the most consistently open-hearted people I've ever met. Every time I am with him, I learn something about what it means to be present with others, to slow down and listen, and to extend a sacred regard toward the places we stand and the people who have come before us.

It has been two years since I last saw Marvin, and I've missed him. It's early when I arrive, and I have not been able to reach him ahead of time, so I have no idea if he is even home. When I knock on the door, his wife answers. Marvin has been up most of the night at a longhouse ceremony and is still asleep. She offers to wake him, but I decline to interrupt his sleep. She catches me up on news before I head on my way. Marvin is giving more of his time to the longhouse these days, she tells me, and is not traveling off the reservation as much as he used to. He is feeling the pull of the old ways and has less time to give to outside causes. I am genuinely sorry to miss him as I leave the tribal center and head across the reservation toward Deception Pass.

An hour later, a car pulls alongside me on the lonely road and rolls to a stop. It is Marvin, and with a beaming face, he invites me to drive back to his house for a visit. I refuse the ride, telling him about my car-free vow and the purpose of my walk through the Skagit. He pulls over to talk on a rise above the Swinomish

*Not his real name.

Channel that has a grand view of the Skagit Valley sprawling away to the east across the water. In spite of the cold, we talk for a long time, catching each other up on the news of our lives.

As I tell him more about the purpose of my explorations, his eyes brighten and he gives an enthusiastic nod. This is a good thing I am doing, he says. All of us were indigenous once. It's not just the tribes who have a stake in the land. The whole culture is out of balance. The ancestors can feel it when someone is taking steps to restore the balance. It brings them joy. They have been waiting a long time for us to wake up, and they are eager to come to our aid. It's not only for Natives that this is true.

Then Marvin offers some more specific advice. What I'm doing this year will not be easy, he says, and I will feel discouraged at times. He tells me to leave the road when I feel burdened and to walk through the underbrush of forest. Let the sticks and branches sweep against my body to pull off the heaviness. Cedar boughs are especially good for this, he says, and when I cross a stream, I should stop to wash my hands in the water and splash a little on my face to show the waters that I have remembered to be grateful.

I know that Marvin is telling me these things because he trusts me and he values my friendship. He doesn't want me to walk alone, and he has a deep conviction that the spirits in the land are there for all of us. It is part of his own generosity of spirit that he doesn't withhold this tribal wisdom from me. In *The Practice of the Wild,* Gary Snyder describes the value of these teachings from the perspective of the wider culture:

> There are tens of millions of people in North America who were physically born here but who are not actually living here intellectually, imaginatively, or morally. Native Americans to be sure have a prior claim to the term native. But as they love this

land they will welcome the conversion of the millions of immigrant psyches into fellow "Native Americans."[1]

A Crow elder had put it to Snyder this way:

You know, I think if people stay somewhere long enough—even white people—the spirits will begin to speak to them. It's the power of the spirits coming up from the land. The spirits and the old powers aren't lost, they just need people to be around long enough and the spirits will begin to influence them.[2]

I'm sure that Marvin is acting out of his own love for this land when he shares these things with me. While some of his words defy the narrow logic of the culture I grew up in, my heart tells me that what he says is true. His people have remained on this land because generations of their ancestors passed along the highly refined and specialized knowledge that enabled them to survive within the limits of this particular place. That knowledge has included elements of reverence and respect for the powers of the land, as well as hardiness of character and a profoundly ecological literacy. While much of that special knowledge has been lost even to the tribes, Marvin is committed to doing what he can to bring it back, and he recognizes this need within the wider culture as well. It is a mark of his care for our collective future that he does not withhold these teachings from me.

In an era of climate change in particular, the value of these special repositories of local knowledge will only go up. When the abstract values of stock portfolios and commodity futures have vanished like a morning mist in the heat of ecological limits, such local, indigenous knowledge of place will once again become more valuable than gold.

o   o   o

AFTER MARVIN AND I part ways, the road crosses the reservation to Skagit Bay, past Snee-oosh Point and Kiket Island, where several Native families are digging for clams on the tide flats. Climbing back into second-growth forest along Similk Bay, I decide to take Marvin's advice and leave the road through an opening by a large red cedar stump. I can still see high on the rotting stump the notches that held planks on which loggers of an earlier era stood to bring this tree down with a double-end crosscut saw. The stump testifies to a time when thousand-year-old cedars were common here. The grove I enter is filled with scrawny newcomers like me, mere youngsters a half-century old. But they have the same sonorous foliage as their elders, and the thick, sweet aroma of pitch that can be mistaken for no other tree on earth.

From my years as a carpenter, I know how gifted and versatile this wood really is and what a joy it is to work with. I understand why red cedar was the most valuable tree in the forest to Native tribes and why early loggers and timber barons put a special price on its head. No other tree could meet so many human needs at once. With a single old-growth cedar, a person could build an entire house of split planks and shake roofs that weathered the rains far longer than other trees, yet also harbored the strength to span wide spaces and bear great weight. The butt of one tree, split in half, could yield two fifty-foot dugout canoes, capable of braving ocean storms and traveling a thousand miles from home. One could braid strong rope and fishing line from its vertical strands of bark, weave clothing, baskets, rain hats, and totem masks for mimicking animal spirits. And perhaps no other tree is as responsive to the knife of a skilled carver. The monumental totem poles that are emblematic to this region, and the patient process of their creation, evoke stronger emotions in me than any other art form I have ever encountered. They carry the soul of the region in a way that has come to transcend culture. It was this tree in the hands of these people that led to arguably the highest artistic expression of any hunter-gatherer culture the world has ever known.

In a recent interview with *The New Yorker* magazine, Gary Snyder echoes Marvin's call to leave the beaten path from time to time:

> Throughout human history and prehistory the trail was only to get you somewhere. What was important was what was off the trail. Food, roots, berries, dye plants, glue plants, poisonous plants, recreational drug plants, squirrel nests, bird nests, everything you might think you need. What's way off the trail are the places you go to be alone and have a vision . . . and then you come back.[3]

As I move through the forest, I pass clusters of young cedars and aim for the branches hanging low to the ground. I let them slide thickly over my face and clothing, then I thread through the salmonberry thickets with their thorn-covered stalks. When I come back to the road, I carry with me the smell of cedar pitch on my body for the rest of the day, a scent that reminds me why I am here as much as any sight or sound ever could.

By late afternoon, I've rounded the shallow waters of Similk Bay and picked my way south along the cliffs and villas of Fidalgo Island. My path leads now into the narrow canyons of Deception Pass, where tidal currents of up to eight knots can churn between granite walls. All the outflow from Skagit Bay must pass through this narrow gorge with each cycle of the tide, creating a tidal rapid that reverses directions twice a day. Only an expert kayaker would enter its treacherous swirl at maximum current.

Crossing the Deception Pass bridge onto Whidbey Island, I feel a wave of homecoming elation. Even though I still have fifty miles to go, these familiar cliffs and currents have come to symbolize the northern gateway to my home. With four thousand acres of old-growth forest preserve spanning the pass, and fifteen miles of shoreline with its wild character intact, it is easy to picture what Joseph Whidbey and his shipmates from the Vancouver expedition might have seen when they first braved these currents and assigned the place-names that have endured to this day. Dropping below the bridge, I take a footpath east along the cut, grateful to leave the highway again. I turn the corner into Cornet Bay, where I keep my salmon gill-netter moored during the winter months. The boat will provide fine lodging for the night, and from the cliffs opposite the marina, I can see the *Martina* illuminated at her mooring by the last, slanting rays of an evening sun, soon to set. It is a sweet and welcoming sight to behold.

Darkness has fallen when I reach the boat, and though I'm spent from the day's walk, it is a weariness that carries deep satisfaction within it. I'm feeling stronger by the day. I light the galley stove and sip my favorite microbrew while the stove's heat slowly gains ground on the night's frigid cold. This boat has been my home for six weeks every fall during the chum salmon run on Puget Sound, which I work with my partner, Dave Anderson, a lifelong Northwest fisherman. After decades of fishing in Alaska, I've brought this part of my life home, too, learning the local rivers and salmon runs from the close vantage of working on the water. This boat is my link to a life that has anchored me within the Inside Passage for almost forty years.

o o o

IT HAS TAKEN ME SIX DAYS of steady walking to cover the wide estuaries that lie in this island's embrace. What remains on my circular path is the island itself, stretching from the San Juans deep into the interior of Puget Sound. Crossing the bridge at Deception Pass has begun the homeward arc of my journey, and it feels good to be on more familiar ground.

Yet is it so familiar? An hour's drive by car will carry me the length of the island along the state highway that bisects its center. On foot it will take four days to cover that same distance, and I will be on unfamiliar ground most of the way. I have entered a brand new island, four days long.

I wake well before dawn. The purring of the diesel stove is the first sound I hear, orienting me in the darkness from the fo'c'sle. The teapot is still steaming on the stove. I rig a cushion on the galley floor to do my morning meditation. The gentle sway of the boat at its mooring and the hum of the stove stir into my meditation a thick soup of memories drawn from this coast. I can feel in my bones how much I belong to the whole reach of it and how the Pacific Coast arcs far beyond the temperate forests of home, ending in a landscape that mirrors our own at the southern tip of South America. It is one continuous coast, one shape-shifting mass of continental drift, one precious film of living biosphere in endless varieties of form.

Living at this center point of the Northwest Coast, I still carry the signature of all the places I have been, all the cultures that have touched my life. There is nothing so human as the desire to explore our world, to cross the horizon, to see a different night sky, fresh landscapes, other ways of being human. It is not travel per se that I am protesting this year. Yet travel, if we let it become an end in itself, can be a way of actually running from our lives, in the vain hope that we will eventually find ourselves in the guise of other places. It can become just another addiction, which only separates us further from the actual life we have been given.

My old friend Charles Darwin surfaces out of this meditative brew as I sit on the galley floor. In spite of the epic scale of his own travels, he would not disagree with what I have just said. I identify with Darwin on several fronts. Both of us were, for example, mediocre theology students and ultimately abandoned ministerial studies for the call of the wild. Both of us were shaped by the infusion of fierce landscapes into our formation as young adults. The mountains of Tierra del Fuego and the stunning tidewater glaciers of the Beagle Channel that lanced Darwin's heart could easily swap places with the landscape of Alaska that so scoured its way into my soul when I was a young man. Like me, Darwin was inspired more by the visceral magnetism of the natural world than by the abstract theological dogmas by which conventional religion has so often attempted to tame these wild unknowns. Only a spirit of open and unfettered curiosity had the power to bring him fully into the presence of these mysteries, and by this approach, he saw into those mysteries in a way that no one before him had succeeded in doing.

But there is another, stranger kinship I feel with Darwin as well. We both eventually found that wild edge waiting for us in our return to the terrain closest to home. Mostly, Darwin is remembered today for his legendary five-year voyage that circled the globe and for the theory of evolution it ultimately engendered. But what interests me most about Darwin's story from the vantage of my year in circumference is how he pulled it all together once he got home. Upon his return to England, Darwin retired to his country manor at Down House to live in seclusion with his family, and he never left. It was there that he spent the rest of his life mining the data he had collected on the *Beagle*. It was there that he concocted his revolutionary theories that would turn the Western world upside down. Curiosity and bold intelligence, rather than endless additional travels, gave him all the leverage he needed. Nothing in his self-encapsulated world escaped his notice, and nothing was deemed unworthy of noticing. Consequently, the material close at hand was more than enough to do the job. Lyanda Lynn Haupt summarizes Darwin's later sense of wonder in the nearby: "It's always a bit startling to remember that, while Darwin gathered much of his initial inspiration in the tropics, for the last forty years of his life he didn't go anywhere. He walked his sandwalk, circled about on the strange wheeled chair in his mind-office, and grew so close to his home landscape that he very nearly sank into the earth itself."[4]

We all stand on the shoulders of our ancestors in ways we often aren't conscious of, lines crossing lines that weave an ever-shifting fabric of nature and culture. Thoreau received the *Origin of Species* as a revelation that confirmed his own radical devotion to the natural world, especially that which lies closest at hand, as the essential wild Text behind the text.[5] These are parables I gratefully take to heart as I continue my own pilgrimage home. By comparison to Darwin's later years, my own local explorations are a flamboyant extravagance of travel, a locomotive binge. As a way of accurately seeing our world and responding appropriately to it in an age of climate disruption, travel may have carried us over one horizon too many. Increasingly I draw inspiration from the mature Darwin, especially the way he turned a single epic journey, coupled with decades spent on a small piece of home ground, into one of the great intellectual adventures of all time.

o o o

SIX WEEKS INTO MY YEAR of local living, I can begin to feel the pace of my body slowing down. The inner residue of hurry and restlessness is gradually seeping out of my nervous system. It is a subtle shift, and it has taken this long to begin registering in my conscious mind. I am able to sit still for longer periods, not because I am more determined to do so, but because I just want to. My mind is more available to what I am seeing. With less wanting of things to be different, less pursuit of external stimulation, I simply see more of what is right in front of me.

One of the most obvious manifestations of this shift is the way I can literally feel the geography around me growing in scale and stature. A circle I drew on the map that felt small to begin with, and potentially confining, seems huge now, since it takes an entire day on foot to cover a small portion of it. Fifteen miles of walking is about what I am good for, yet such a day is filled with far more sensory input than a comparable day of driving that could take me halfway to San Francisco. I end my days physically tired, but emotionally full, with a sense of having transited a whole world of hard terrain. Curiously enough, I can end an equally long day of driving or flying almost as tired physically, but emotionally exhausted at the same time, not sure that I have connected with anything real beyond my desire to cover as much ground as fast as possible.

The landscape around me falls upon my senses differently now, working its way down through my perceptions and into my bones at a rate that my whole being can participate in, every step of the way. Already, I look out on a very different Puget Sound and a very different map of the region hanging on the wall of my office. I see nuances of landscape, identifiable landmarks, cultural niches, and relationships between them that were invisible to me before, and I am only just getting under way. Where there are blank spots remaining on the map, I have a new urge to explore them. My prevailing experience of a shrinking and flattening world has reversed course, and the geography around me has begun to expand again, right before my very eyes.

Gary Snyder touches on this dynamic in his story of riding in a pickup truck through the Australian outback west of Alice Springs with a Pintubi elder named Jimmy Tjungurrayi. As they

speed along the road through his ancestral territory, Jimmy begins telling stories at a very rapid pace about what had happened
in the dreamtime in each of the places that are flying by. Puzzled
by this staccato accounting, Snyder later recalls, "I realized after
about half an hour of this that these were tales to be told while
walking, and that I was experiencing a speeded-up version of
what might be leisurely told over several days of foot travel."[6] The
writer David Abram, in reflecting later on this same story, points
to the inseparable bond between landscape and language within
oral cultures. "We might say that the land, for indigenous, oral
cultures, is the very matrix of linguistic meaning. So, to force a
traditionally oral people off of their ancestral lands . . . is, effectively, to shove them out of their mind."[7] It is worth wondering
what kind of mind we can hope to sustain—what level of
sanity—when the landscape upon which we dwell has been sep-
arated from its stories, when we must piece together our meaning from generic sprawl, usually transiting the landscape at a
pace far faster than our stories can get a purchase on.

o   o   o

IN THE FOUR DAYS it takes me to walk the length of the island, I
realize that I am rewriting the script of a once-familiar story,
working the land back into my mind and new stories back into
the land. Sally meets me in Oak Harbor for the walk along Penn
Cove to Coupeville, where we spend the night in an historic inn.
We pass lost village sites of the Lower Skagit people (the current
Swinomish tribe)—sites that once dotted the shores of Penn
Cove. In this protected bay, every wide shelf of beach that had a
decent landing for canoes was used by these Skagit people. The
present town of Coupeville, Whidbey's earliest pioneer community, was built atop the largest of these Native villages, called by
the Lower Skagit people *bah-TSAHD-ah-lee.* I marvel at how

quickly the evidence of such Native presence has been erased from the land, driven into a small corner of their original territory on the Swinomish Reservation. A few historic markers are the last evidence of this lost world, whose absence burns through my own vast ignorance in waves of unaccountable grief.

Sally and I walk the full sweep of the bay as it slices the island almost in half, pressing deep into the crescent of Ebey's Prairie. The bay's shallow waters are home now to an aquaculture industry of floating mussel pens and ornate Victorian mansions that offer lodging to tourists in this idyllic town. We push on nearly to Coupeville, where we stop for the night at the Capt. Whidbey Inn, enjoying again the satisfaction of having arrived at a familiar destination in an unfamiliar way, after a long journey on foot. The more I walk, the more my body thanks me for doing what it was always designed to do. We settle back for a dinner of fine wine and local seafood while dusk closes its curtain over the bay.

In the morning, Sally and I part ways again, as she heads home by bus while I continue west for a solo walk across Ebey's Prairie, whose rich soil attracted the first Euro-American pioneers to the island in the 1850s. Stepping through the still-frosty landscape, I think of Thoreau's musings in *Walden:* "To walk in a winter morning . . . Who would not be early to rise, and rise earlier and earlier every successive day of his life, till he became unspeakably healthy, wealthy, and wise?"[8]

From a grand vista on Ebey's Bluff looking out toward the Pacific along the Strait of Juan de Fuca, I drop to the beach and walk south past Fort Casey, past the Keystone Spit tidal rips that mark the entrance to Admiralty Inlet, the beginning of Puget Sound's protected waters. The shallow entrance to the inlet is set off by the opposing shores of Whidbey Island and the Olympic Peninsula, with turbulent tidal upwellings that signal its guardianship of Puget Sound waters. I walk these secluded beaches for fifteen miles under a full-frontal of the towering Olympic Range to the west. These high bluff beaches are not wild, exactly, but they feel remote, and I encounter only one other person on the beaches all day. I walk until the salt marsh at Lake Hancock blocks further passage and sends me bushwhacking back to the highway near Greenbank Farm.

I have covered twenty miles, my longest day on the walk, when I finally reach Lagoon Point and turn up the hill to the home of my friends David and Cynthia for the night. Cynthia greets me with my favorite dinner of broiled black cod, a delicacy from the North Pacific that I've passed on to her from my days as a commercial fisherman in Alaska. David is a physicist and an amateur astronomer, a retired Microsoft scientist and fellow Zen student. After dinner, on this clear night filled with stars, David takes me to his backyard observatory for my first look at Saturn with all its rings. At his computer, he zeroes in on an errant star he has been researching, the telescope grinding slowly around on its mechanical arms beneath the retractable roof of the observatory. We spend our lives under "day-blind stars," as Wendell Berry has said, forgetting what a tiny shard of rock this fragile planet really is, spinning around its sun in some far corner of the universe.[9]

Entering the orbit of my home ground again, I walk south past Bush Point in the morning, and along the shores of Mutiny Bay to Double Bluff, keeping to the beaches wherever I can. Foul Weather Bluff and the entrance to Hood Canal lie across the main stem of the sound, with a steady line of tankers and barges steaming close to the Whidbey shore in the deep waters off Double Bluff. I spend the last night of my journey at a small Zen monastery on the bluff where I often come to practice, enjoying a scrumptious vegetarian meal and a night of rest to go with some welcome meditation in the zendo hall. It is an exchange from which I emerge feeling focused and refreshed. In a few days, I will come back to the monastery to sit a weeklong *sesshin,* or intensive meditation retreat, joining Zen students who have come from around the world to train here. That our island community now harbors such places is a measure of how much things are changing in the eclectic new culture of Puget Sound.

I am on the road again at 7:00 A.M., fresh from a morning of meditation, and eager to cover the final ten-mile walk home. I feel the excitement of completion that all pilgrims must feel arriving home after a long journey as I walk the shores of Useless Bay, crossing the dike over Deer Lagoon to Sunlight Beach, and climbing the ridge to Bayview Road. I drop down into the welcoming arms of Maxwelton Valley, past the old dairy farm on Ewing Road, and the valley wetlands now filled with migratory waterfowl. On impulse, when I cross Maxwelton Creek, I stop to splash some of its cold water on my face as Marvin suggested. I arrive home just in time for our traditional Sunday breakfast of sourdough waffles. Doug and Rick and Steve are here to join Sally in welcoming me home.

It is a sacramental moment. During the Passover, observant Jews like to say *dayenu,* which in Hebrew means "It would have been enough." It is an expression of gratitude for all the gifts bestowed on the Israelites, each gift complete and sufficient unto itself. I love this sentiment, expressing a willingness to be satisfied with whatever one receives, even as we press on into the next stages of our journey. This trip has brought new strength to my body and a new currency of belonging to the place I call home. I have many more adventures planned for the year and I'm brimming. But if I get no farther down the road than this one extraordinary walk among the rivers of home, then *dayenu,* it will have been enough.

The most efficient animal on earth in terms of weight transported over distance for energy expended is a human on a bicycle. The most efficient machine on earth in terms of weight transported over distance for energy expended is a human on a bicycle.

—BIKEWEBSITE, "Bicycle Trivia"[1]

CHAPTER 6

Tracking the Elusive Mechanical Horse

o   o   o

Man is a locomotive machine of Nature's own making, not to be improved by the addition of any cranks or wheels of mortal invention.

—*MECHANICS* magazine editorial, 1832[2]

Already the spring equinox has arrived, ending the first quarter of my year in circumference. Though not all days are warm yet, the longer daylight and the general arc toward spring are in my favor for the plans I've made on my bike. I've not only survived the winter without a car, but I rarely even think of my car anymore. Drawing this line in the sand has yielded a shift in perception that still surprises me. Winter itself has come alive in a new way and has failed to bring with it the usual component of seasonal affective disorder that I've come to take for granted. I've had my down days, to be sure, but I haven't gotten seriously depressed once. On the contrary, I genuinely feel better—better about myself, better about my physical capacities, better about my relationships, and better about the overall tone of my life. Oddly enough, I'm finding that it is easier to outdistance the winter blues on a bicycle, and even on foot, than it ever was in a car. If my experience this winter has any merit, then depression seems to have an aversion to bicycles and boots, but loves the comfort and convenience of automobiles. So far this year, my old nemesis has lost interest in me and caught another ride.

This year, spring is the season I'm devoting to bicycle explorations around the sound. Though I will be traveling at a modest pace by my usual standards, it feels luxuriously fast after spending much of the winter on foot. For the first time in years, I have a bad case of spring fever, and the prospect of extending my range for local explorations has my foot tapping. To reach the outer limits of my circle in a single day's travel feels like a grand call to adventure.

○ ○ ○

THERE ARE COMPELLING REASONS why my bicycle spent so many years rusting in the garage while I became ever more dependent on my car. I've built a lot of distance between the major components of my life—home, family, leisure, and work. My house is miles from the nearest shopping center or public gathering place. Only a handful of buses pass near my home daily, and no buses at all come by on weekends. Going car-free where I live has left me with few of the advantages of rural life and minimal access to the advantages of the city, all of which my wife patiently explained to me before I began this experiment. With no recourse to my car, I have left myself temporarily helpless without a bicycle.

Which means that I suddenly find bicycles very interesting.

I can remember with perfect clarity the day, when I was five years old, that my father removed the training wheels from my first bicycle and gave me a shove on the sidewalk in front of our house. I remember how frightened I felt and how astonished I was when I kept right on going without falling. For the first time in my life, I felt powerful, like I imagined big kids must feel. In an instant, the world that had been my neighborhood grew suddenly larger.

Oddly enough, I have no such recollection of when I stopped riding my bicycle as an adolescent. Certainly by the time I got my driver's license, at one minute past midnight on the morning of my sixteenth birthday, my bicycle had disappeared from my memory like a dream at waking. Within the youth culture of the time, bicycles belonged firmly in the domain of childhood, and I was no longer a child. I came of age when cheap gas, cheap cars, and an open road defined what freedom meant in an America that could not yet see any limits lurking on the horizon. It was a time when one could still actually find an open road from time to time, before traffic gridlock became the norm from sea to shining sea.

I awoke from that cultural amnesia quite suddenly during the ten-speed-bike boom of the 1970s. I could hardly even remember having had a bicycle before that. It was as if I had personally discovered the bicycle when I bought my first Peugeot ten-speed in 1971 with hard-earned money from fishing in Alaska, and it quickly became my most prized possession. Before that, as far as I knew, there had been only cars going all the way back to the stone age. The sense of freedom and physical release I found on my bicycle felt almost illicit, and living without a car became a new mark of distinction among my college crowd.

For the next decade of my life, bicycling was my near-exclusive form of transportation. In graduate school at Harvard, I lived without a car for three years, making do handily with my bike and the Boston subway. After divinity school, I moved to Eugene, Oregon, one of the most bike-friendly cities in America, and I continued to thrive on my bicycle. It might have gone on like that except for two things that intervened: work and family. With stacks of lumber now to carry and a young family to ferry around, I used my bicycle less and less, finally hanging it in the back of my garage, where it languished for nearly twenty-five years.

That's where I found my old ten-speed, rusted and forlorn in the back of the garage, when I began to gear up last fall for my automobile fast. And that's when I discovered that bicycle technology during the interim had left me completely in the dust.

○ ○ ○

WORLDWIDE, THERE ARE 1.6 billion bicycles on the road, double the number of cars, and most of them are a source of primary transportation. Here in the United States, 5 percent of the world's population drives 30 percent of its cars, and bicycles have occupied a recreational niche in the American transportation spectrum from the beginning.[3] But with our growing dependence on foreign oil and a high-carbon economy that is now firmly linked to climate change, Americans are beginning to reconsider the merits of the two-wheeler.

It's easy to forget how revolutionary the bicycle actually was when it first arrived in our three-mile-an-hour world, which was the standard human speed limit prior to the bicycle's invention. It's no surprise that people dreamed of liberation from the confines of human-powered locomotion for much longer than we've had the technological means to pull it off. A human on a horse could manage about twelve miles an hour until the horse ran out of steam, but that was in the fast lane. So the quest for a "mechanical horse" that led ultimately to the bicycle's invention is one of the most fascinating stories to come out of the industrial revolution.

Some scholars have claimed that Leonardo da Vinci left us tantalizing evidence that the dream of a mechanical horse predated the industrial revolution by several centuries. A sketch attributed to the *Codex Atlanticus* popped up during the manuscript's restoration in 1974. It was a small, offhand sketch in the margins of his notebook from around 1493 bearing an uncanny resemblance to the modern bicycle, complete with pedals, chain drive, and two in-line wheels. While its authenticity is still in question, other Leonardo drawings with chain-drive cranks make it a plausible discovery. Either way, there is no evidence that the contraption ever went beyond the drawing board.[4]

The first real breakthrough came in 1817, when the German baron Karl von Drais unveiled his *Laufmaschine,* or running machine, later known as the *velocipede.* Two in-line wheels connected by a cushioned seat allowed a person to walk or run while gaining additional ground between strides from the rolling of the wheels. As one enthusiast at the time described it, the rider "pushes the wheels along when they won't go alone—and rides them when they will."[5] Drais's great discovery was that with enough velocity on a good road surface, one could lift the feet off the ground and coast without falling over, accomplishing what amounted to a giant step with no exertion.

The velocipede—also called a *hobby horse*—arrived in America in 1819, the same year as the first steam-assisted trans-Atlantic crossing from New York to Liverpool. Steam-powered carriages, the precursors to the steam locomotive, were making their inaugural trips between American cities at the time, and the velocipede never advanced beyond novelty status by proving its utilitarian value. It required too much work while providing too little benefit, and it was also dangerous. There was no way to brake on a downhill slope, and it had to be pushed or carried uphill by hand. The dream of a practical mechanical horse would languish for another fifty years before real progress was made.

Still, attempts to revive the mechanical horse came and went for another half century, until an obscure blacksmith in Paris named Pierre Michaux attached foot cranks to the front wheel of a velocipede in 1867. It was such a simple solution, yet it changed everything. Michaux's bicycle was an overnight sensation. Within days, cyclists balanced on two wheels could be seen in Paris "cutting across the capital's great arteries, passing like whirlwinds, leaving behind pedestrians, carriages and horsemen." Within months, *Scientific American* was on to the new bicycle, noting how the addition of pedals "completely changes the character of the vehicle. . . . [I]t glides along as though it were alive, and with a smooth grace alike exhilarating and beautiful to behold."[6]

Even in its most primitive form, the newly conceived bicycle could approach the speed of a horse and soon was winning races head to head with top-ranked steeds. The age of the mechanical horse at long last had arrived in the form of a "democratic" little machine that made wider travel accessible to ordinary people. It also reinvigorated an urban population that had become sedentary, setting off a fitness boom. The bicycle proved a boon to women's independence as well, and ultimately to women's rights. Its popularity quickly spread worldwide.

But the dream of independent mobility was just getting started. The bicycle boom of the 1890s corresponded with another invention that ensured that this boom would soon go bust. After the gas-powered motorcar made its appearance at the turn of the century, bicycle production in America fell by three-quarters in just four years.[7] The first bike boom had paved the way for automobiles by sparking a movement for better roads and the means of mass production. It also reordered the public psyche in the direction of independent, long-distance travel on public highways, a demand the railroads could not supply by themselves.

The rest is history—the history of the car, that is. By the time I came along as part of a different kind of boom following World War II, the automobile was a middle-class given across North America, spreading suburban sprawl from our cities like a West Coast wildfire. Worldwide, the bicycle remained the twentieth century's most popular vehicle for personal transportation, but here in America, it receded to the status of child's toy. And while it has revived itself numerous times in a variety of recreational incarnations, the bicycle has never challenged the supremacy of the automobile as a source of primary transportation in the United States.

o o o

But the bicycle has too much going for it to be written off that easily, and climate change is turning a lot of heads back in its direction. While my old ten-speed was rusting in the garage, the bicycle industry was in the midst of an innovation binge, pumping out a host of new subspecies with wide recreational appeal and a growing utilitarian bent. Dave, our community bike shop maestro, gave me a guided tour of his stock, and almost nothing looked or sounded familiar. I certainly knew about the mountain biking craze, mostly as a concerned parent, and the refinements to the road-racing machine that took place in my absence were dizzying to behold. I used to think bicycle mechanics occupied an arcane niche in the transportation world, but their stature has been going up fast as I make my way into this brave new world of human-powered transportation. This is, after all, a time-honored profession. Henry Ford and the Wright brothers were bicycle mechanics before they parlayed their skills with the two-wheeler into the automotive and aeronautical ages, neither of which has slowed the worldwide spread of the bicycle itself.

After several passes at the shop, I started to dial in the differences between utilitarian, road racing, and off-road biking models. I test-rode bikes representing each type, so I could see how it actually felt on the road. For my year in circumference, I wanted a model that would cover the bases of all three, with an emphasis on utilitarian road travel. I wanted a bike that was light and responsive, but not so light that I couldn't pack some gear when I wanted to go touring or commute to work with the essentials on board. I also wanted to be able to leave the road if necessary, but felt no desire to ride my bicycle off mountain cliffs, as my son and his friends seem to think is a really awesome thing to do.

In the end, I settled on a cyclo-cross design, which is basically a road bike beefed up slightly for carrying a modest load, with thick enough tires to occasionally go off road. I picked a bike in a middle price range, without too many frills, but with a carbon-fiber front fork to help ease the shock to my arms and shoulders on rough roads.

I am prone by nature to stick with what I have as long as it still works, so when I do spring for something new, it's a big deal. I could hardly have been more proud riding my new bike home from the shop.* The first thing I noticed was how smoothly it

---

*If, like me, you're mounting an expedition into the bicycle wilderness for the first time or after a long hiatus from the Kingdom of Cars, I recommend using your local bike shop rather than a superstore or mail-order catalog to purchase your next bicycle. There are just too many models to choose from and too many technical considerations and new equipment options to navigate on your own. By buying local, I paid a little more up front, but have benefited enormously from the expertise of my local bike mechanic in helping me make the initial choice, sort out supplementary equipment needs, and stay on the road when I've run into mechanical difficulties.

handled compared with my old bike, how light it was for hoisting onto a bus rack, and how responsive the shifting mechanisms have become. This ease of control and quick responsiveness is a big step forward in technological tuning. In spite of my Luddite nature, I had to admit that I'd deprived myself for too long of a much-improved source of transportation independence.

The second thing I noticed, within a day of bringing my new bike home, was that the technological mechanisms of the bicycle may have improved, but the biological components of the rider had gone seriously downhill. My first bike trip was an eight-mile round-trip to a business appointment, and I had to climb a long hill to get there. Under my own power, that hill loomed suddenly much larger than I remembered. I was a wreck the next day.

It would have been tempting to put my bicycle back in storage at that point, except that I now have no car to rescue me. This is where a line in the sand comes in handy. I had my vow to live up to, a deeper motivation to hold my feet to the fire, which left me no real choice in the matter but to keep riding. Shifting my bicycle orientation from occasional recreation to primary transportation was a big adjustment. But with my car effectively off the table, I got through the logjam of psychological habit and physical discomfort fairly quickly, riding a little more each day. The pleasure I remembered in riding was not far behind, and the basic five-mile trip to town, which used to seem like a major expedition on my bike, started to feel routine.

I noticed other things, too. For example, the time differential between biking and driving on an average trip close to home was no great obstacle. At about four minutes per mile by bicycle, trips of three to five miles do not involve nearly the expenditure of time that I had been inclined to expect. As I got in better shape and factored in the benefits of greater health against the perceived costs of "lost" time for daily errands, my resistance to using the bicycle diminished further.

In addition to the personal benefits, this adds up to real savings in carbon emissions. For most Americans, the majority of automobile trips are within three miles of home, anyway, usually involving one person to a car. But these short, solo passenger trips burn a third of all gas pumped at our service stations.[8] Switching to a bicycle for daily errands close to home is low-lying fruit in the battle against climate change, and knowing my carbon-footprint facts has given me new incentive to stay on track, whether I feel like it or not.

A century and a half after its invention, the bicycle remains the most efficient machine ever invented in terms of weight transported over distance for energy expended. The modern bicycle achieves this efficiency by allowing a rider to average 10–12 mph for extended periods while exerting only the same energy it takes to walk for a comparable duration of time.* Shifting to my bicycle for short, local trips, once I'd greased the bearings of a rusty body and settled into a regular routine of riding, has turned out to be easier than I expected, and much more rewarding. It doesn't hurt that those rewards have included a little more peace of mind. Della Watson has written in *Sierra* magazine: "We've entered an era of change, and when the new world emerges from the cloud of carbon irresponsibility and

---

*Bicycling does in fact involve carbon emissions, when one considers the food needed to fuel the rider. The average carbon footprint of an American meal is significant, when the concept of "food-miles" and energy-intensive modes of food production are factored into the equation. A typical bite of food eaten here in the Northwest travels 1,500 miles from production to table. Add to that the high-carbon modes of industrial food production, fertilizers, and energy-intensive processing and packaging, and even the most environmentally conscious cyclist has probably been fueled on food that was "marinated in crude oil" (see Michael Pollan, *The Omnivore's Dilemma: A Natural History of Four Meals* [New York: Penguin, 2006]). What we eat is as important as how we travel in the fight against climate change.

reckless spending, the bicycle, in all its strange and glorious in-carnations, will still be there to take us where we want to go."[9]

o o o

IN THE MIDST OF THIS QUEST for a clearer conscience, other ben-efits have been accruing as well, benefits that I have not been able to achieve in a lifetime of New Year's resolutions. Within three months of ditching my car, I'm back to my college weight of thirty-five years ago, and I no longer have to rush to the gym in my car to pull this off, pumping more carbon into the atmo-sphere in the process. I find myself eating more sensibly, and snacking less. As my body gets in better shape, I'm less inclined to eat for its own sake. The more I ride, the better it feels, and the farther I can comfortably go. Even the cold and rain of the North-west winter months have been less of a challenge than I ex-pected. I've come to welcome this contact with the elements, which are rarely as daunting in fact as they appear from the backside of a set of flapping windshield wipers. I am less "con-fined" by the weather as a result. The act of travel has become *lived* time rather than *lost* time, part of the normal fabric of my life, bringing a greater sense of wholeness and continuity be-tween formerly disconnected points on the map.

These personal benefits to my health and well-being have flowed naturally out of the larger scope of my purpose for the year, without my having to make them the object of a special ef-fort. I'm not trying to "get in shape." I'm just going about my business now on a bicycle, and one result of that fact is that I'm getting into shape. I was reminded of this irony when I recently ran into a friend I hadn't seen in some months. She took one look at me and said, "Wow! You're looking really buff."

CHAPTER 7

Hooked by Salmon

○ ○ ○

The bottom of the little lake was covered with sockeye salmon in their spawning colors, brilliant blood-red bodies with bright olive-green heads . . . All at once I was wrapped around by the miracle of natural provision in all its profligate abundance. What a welcome the planet has laid out for us! How easy to gather from its bounty what we need to survive! And I understood at the same moment, free-falling and abandoned, how bereft, how orphaned from its sources of sustenance my own species has become.

—FREEMAN HOUSE,
Totem Salmon: Life Lessons from Another Species

When I was twenty-eight years old I rode my bike from Eugene, Oregon, to Port Townsend, Washington, for the only serious road trip I ever took. I was moving back to Puget Sound after six years away from home, and this bicycle trip up the coast seemed like the perfect way to commemorate my return to the sound. It took me four days to pick my way north through the farming communities of the Willamette Valley, the mill towns of the lower Columbia, and the back-road timber towns of Southwestern Washington. When I got my first whiff of salt water and tide flats in Olympia, I knew without a doubt I was home.

It has taken me thirty years to manage a sequel to that first bicycle adventure, but my year in circumference offers the excuse I've been waiting for. I couldn't be more excited if I were a kid again. My son Alex will join me on the first trip I have planned for the spring. I've timed it to correspond with his spring break from college, and we have lots to catch up on as we sort our gear and outfit the bikes for the trip. The fact that he already spends a lot of time on his custom road bike at Western Washington University in Bellingham leaves little doubt in my mind about who will be bringing up the rear.

I'm still trying to get used to looking up at my son, who now has a three-inch height advantage over his old man. His lean and muscular frame is topped these days by a bearded face and a thick Mohawk haircut that makes him appear taller still. He would look intimidating if I didn't know what a gentle nature he has. Like my daughter Kristin, Alex has followed in my footsteps as a crewman on salmon boats in Southeast Alaska and Bristol Bay. He knows what it is to put in long days of work, and he shares my lust for the wild edge. We've climbed some Cascade volcanoes together and gone camping and fishing since he was knee-high to a mosquito. But his striking new demeanor as a young man tells me that there is a stranger lurking in his new body—a person whom I have yet to meet. Luckily, he is not a stranger who is shy about revealing himself. Alex does most of the talking while I do most of the listening, as he spins out enticing new clues to the man he is becoming.

The route I've planned covers two hundred miles of the inner sound in four days, with multiple ferry crossings needed to navigate the maze of islands and peninsulas along the rural west side of the sound, and a seventy-mile plunge back through the industrialized urban corridor from Tacoma to Everett on the return portion of the circle. It will be a study in contrasts, from the wilder stretches of the sound to the belly of the industrialized beast.

The weather is cold and the forecast marginal as we head north on the island toward the ferry to Port Townsend. Though spring is officially here, a big Pacific weather system still has winter on its mind, moving onto the coast with plenty of rain and wind and unseasonably cold temperatures. We consider delaying our departure, but I've been waiting too long for this trip, and Alex has only a short window of time when he can be with me. We decide to go for it, and once we're under way, our doubts disappear. The two-hour ride to the Keystone ferry takes us north to Admiralty Inlet, where the protected inner waters of the sound open their arms out to the sea.

There is a spike in the wildness quotient here at this place of Puget Sound's birth, where the ice dam of the retreating Vashon Glacier finally threw its floodgates open to the Pacific. What a show it must have been! It is humbling to think that the place I now live was buried under three thousand feet of glacial ice a few short millennia ago. The complex inland sea that stole my heart as a child was itself an infant when the first human inhabitants of North America made their way across the Bering Sea land bridge. The veiled mountains looming over the Olympic Peninsula are also geologic youngsters, children of the Cascade subduction zone, where the Juan de Fuca Plate is sliding under the North American Plate to send the earth's crust buckling skyward in a fresh binge of mountain building. As we set off today, they offer only brief glimpses of their jagged heights between shards of thick clouds. A stiff gale has turned the tide rips into a frenzy of combers as we cross the Midchannel Banks. Alex insists that we stay outside on deck to catch the storm's energy at this exposed confluence of the sound, and we watch our bikes take a drenching of spray on the car deck below as the ferry tacks hard into the swell.

In Port Townsend, we ride west past the shipwright shops and marinas of this wooden-boat haven, then push on through the pungent sulfur plumes of the pulp mill in Glen Cove, angling south along the inner shore of the Olympic Peninsula from Port Hadlock to Port Ludlow. Stiff headwinds and hilly terrain make for slow going, and Alex has to wait at the top of the longest hills for me to come puffing up behind him. He offers me high fives and encouraging words. "Geez, Dad, you're doing really great!" The pleasure he takes in this reversal of roles is not lost on me as I slap his hand and stop to catch my breath.

From Port Ludlow we enter the neck of Hood Canal, riding south past Whiskey Spit to the floating bridge that will carry us across to the Kitsap Peninsula. The canal forms a separate lobe of Puget Sound, a long and sheltered fjord that articulates the geologic shift between the Puget lowlands and the Olympic Peninsula, with mountains rising sharply from its western shore. The Kitsap Peninsula stretches east from the canal to the main lobe of the sound, harboring its own tangle of sheltered bays and passageways that make Puget Sound a world of so many hidden places. We are entering the landscape of my childhood, a place apart that hovers mythic in my memory and one that I have never shared with my son in this intimate kind of way.

We earn our passage over the Hood Canal bridge traveling at right angles to the blistering winds blowing up the long reach of the canal. The winds throw us off balance on the thin shoulder of a congested bridge that was never intended for bicycles. It is a sober two-mile crossing, a reminder that bicycles do not yet enjoy equal citizenship in this country built for cars, and I feel both rattled and relieved when we arrive safely on the other side.

From Port Gamble we continue south another ten miles along the shores of Hood Canal, angling inland through Big Valley to Poulsbo—our final destination for the day. It was near this settlement of Norwegian immigrant fishermen on Liberty Bay that my love affair with Puget Sound was first ignited as a child. And not until we enter the town's Nordic-bannered streets do the day's leaden clouds finally uncork their burden of rain, drenching us with a full deluge in the final minutes of our ride. We pedal past the historic Sons of Norway Hall into the sheltered basin, where we take refuge in the first restaurant we can find overlooking the boat harbor.

I had forgotten how much I enjoy Alex's company, especially when we can slip away from our complicated family dynamics for a one-on-one adventure. We order dinner and settle back with mugs of beer to watch the rain slash at the harbor like a whip brandished by the wind. There is a Scandinavian influence in many of the pioneer towns around Puget Sound, with its terrain and climate so reminiscent of the southern Norwegian coast. But no other town in the region (except perhaps Seattle's Ballard neighborhood) has held so stubbornly to its Norwegian heritage. The quiet, rural character I remember from my youth now strains under the congestion of the city that has grown up to meet it, but the beauty of its natural setting still holds a solid piece of my heart.

There is pride in Alex's voice as he describes today's sixty-five-mile bike ride to our waitress, who actually does seem to be impressed by our accomplishment. She keeps coming back to fill our water glasses and ask more questions. Alex's good looks may have something to do with her interest, but I think she is also drawn by the pleasure we are taking in our day's adventures and the unmistakable bond we have as father and son.

This is a poignant homecoming for me, and I have lots of stories to tell Alex. I spent the first twelve summers of my childhood in a beach cabin that my grandparents owned on Liberty Bay, not far from here. This is where my strongest early memories were wrought. Winters were passed in the confusion of the city. But with school's ending each spring, our family made a beeline for the cabin, and life began again. From earliest memory, the waters of the sound pulled me to them as inexorably as the tide.

There is no doubt that on these docks, I became a fisherman, though I never imagined that my passion for fishing would grow to become my primary livelihood. You could also say that this is where I learned how to meditate, though no one I knew at the time would have called it by that name. Long days spent perched by these waters, yearning to see what surprises it might yield, was a mind-altering experience. While I could not verbalize it then, I could certainly feel it, this connection to something vastly more complete than my own small life—something that ties us all to the power of the natural world and carries us beyond even that, outside of time and into the deep refuges of self-forgetting.

From my earliest memory, nothing held more power in my imagination than the elusive salmon. My first real encounter with a salmon took place near here also, and was a seismic moment in my life. I was eight years old when it happened. Dusk was coming on and the dinner bell had already rung, but I couldn't tear myself away. It was high tide, with an evening stillness on the water that rang to the core of my being. I was fishing for sea perch, which had been the outer limit of my aspirations as a fisherman until that night. Gazing from the pier into the deepening darkness of the water, I was startled to see a shape moving toward me. The creature was so out of scale with anything I'd seen before that I thought at first I was imagining it. I knew instinctively by its regal grace and enormous size that it had to be a salmon, and its sudden appearance shot like an arrow to my heart. I was nearly frantic with excitement by the time the fish was directly under me, but it ignored the bait on my hook, passed serenely under the dock, and was gone. Though I failed to hook it, the salmon had thoroughly set its hooks into me. I would never look at these waters with the same eyes again.

I never did catch a salmon in Puget Sound as a child. Nor did I suspect how many had already been lost. No one was there to tell me about the Elwha River kings that could reach one hundred pounds, now lost to a dam, or the Fraser River sockeye that were the prize of the commercial fleet in Puget Sound. I didn't hear tales of Stillaguamish pinks, Nisqually coho, Snohomish steelhead, Skagit chums. I had only my own accidental encounters to go on. I knew little, and understood less, about the true stature of salmon in the ecological and cultural heritage of Puget Sound. But I knew my own yearnings. And the tenacity of my efforts to catch a salmon, however futile, was testimony to the intrinsic power of this iconic creature.

Only years later, as a college student working on a salmon seiner in Southeast Alaska, did I finally witness the spectacle of wild salmon returning in huge numbers to spawn in local streams. In a place far to the north, I caught a glimpse of this dying legacy of my native Puget Sound. Year after year, through college and graduate school, I left Puget Sound to fish the salmon-rich waters of Alaska "just one more time." Somewhere along the way, this annual migration became my life, and not merely a prelude to an inevitable job in the city.

In a recent adaptation of his poem "Hunting Season," Gary Snyder puts a telling spin on the question of who is really fishing for whom:

Every summer, Salmon lure Homo sapiens
toward their home streams.
They do various things which irresistibly draw fishers near
them—leap, surge, swim, stir memories
that make mouths water, that drum adrenalin
into hearts—each one selects a certain person.
Looking up through the water, the Salmon hooks this
human, who is then compelled to reel it to the surface,
clean it, carry it home and eat it.
Then, the Salmon is inside this human being.
He waits and hides in there, but the fisher
doesn't know it. When enough Salmon have occupied
enough people, they will strike all at once.
Those who don't have Salmon in them will also be
taken by surprise, and everything will change some.
This is called "takeover from inside."[1]

It was here on Liberty Bay that my heart was hooked by salmon, and I made sure this "takeover from the inside" happened to my own children as well. Unlike me, Alex and Kristin grew up catching lots of salmon during their youth in Alaska. Both of them saw the streams around their Petersburg home clogged with spawning fish and learned early how to catch them on hook and line. Both watched their dad head off to the salmon grounds in the summer, returning with full fish holds, and both have continued in my footsteps as crew on salmon boats themselves, holding to this contemporary version of an ancient way of life. This bond we share in our family is rare in contemporary America, where the people we hire to grow and harvest our food are so few in number now (0.5 percent of the population) that they don't even warrant their own category in the U.S. Census Report.

o o o

AFTER DINNER, as Alex and I make our way in the rain to the inn where we will spend the night, I continue to spin stories from a youth spent outdoors on Liberty Bay. The stories are now flooding my memory: fishing tirelessly from the docks, hunting for beach agates, building a raft for swimming and a tree fort in the woods, sleeping outside in a covered shed every night because there were no extra rooms in the cottage. My mother flatly refused to be our chauffeur, and we were shooed out of the house every morning, rain or shine. We came to expect that we would spend our days outside on foot, and our range grew steadily wider as we got older. I am proud of my son for his good-humored ability to do the same and for his deep love of the outdoors that we have always shared. This is not a love that can any longer be taken for granted.

Recently, as sales of laundry detergents plummeted, a leading detergent company conducted research to find out why their product sales were dropping so fast. In exploring the habits of parents and children, they discovered a surprising source of the problem. It turns out that children are playing much less outdoors than they did even in the 1970s. Children no longer soil their clothes, because they no longer have contact with the soil.[2] According to the National Household Travel Survey, in 1969 some 40 percent of students in the United States walked to school; by 2001, it was 13 percent.[3] In my neighborhood, I have witnessed children driven by their parents to the foot of their driveway to meet the school bus. In *Last Child in the Woods: Saving Our Children from Nature-Deficit Disorder*, Richard Louv points out that by the 1990s, the radius around home where children were allowed to wander had shrunk to one-ninth of what it was in 1970:

Not that long ago, summer camp was a place where you camped, hiked in the woods, learned about plants and animals, or told firelight stories about ghosts or mountain lions. As likely as not today, "summer camp" is a weight-loss camp, or a computer camp. For a new generation, nature is more abstraction than reality.... Yet, at the very moment that the bond is breaking between the young and the natural world, a growing body of research links our mental, physical, and spiritual health directly to our association with nature—in positive ways.[4]

Childhood obesity has quadrupled since the 1960s, and children are six times more likely to play video games than ride a bike today. Sales of children's bicycles fell 21 percent in the four-year period between 2000 and 2004 alone. Research has also shown a strong correlation between time spent in nature and the incidence of attention-deficit hyperactivity disorder (ADHD) among children.[5] Louv reminisces about his own childhood experiences in nature: "The woods were my Ritalin. Nature calmed me, focused me, yet excited my senses."[6]

The current epidemic of nature-deficit disorder in our children is a societal concern not only because of its implications for their personal health, like obesity, ADHD, and the development of basic empathy and psychological resilience. Children who grow up in an exclusively indoor, technologically mediated environment are also at risk of maturing into care-less adults in the face of wider threats to our living world. Robert Michael Pyle has observed: "People who care, conserve; people who don't know, don't care. What is the extinction of the condor to a child who has never seen a wren?"[7]

Getting our kids outside early and often—and accompanying them as their guides and fellow explorers—is cheap therapy and good medicine for this part of what ails us. Anyone can do this with the children in their lives, whether in a city park or a remote wilderness area, and the benefits are immediate.[8] One day on a bike with my son Alex has cut through months of absence to bring us closer together. I feel his strength and youthful exuberance flowing into me, and I listen with fascination to the ways he is learning to make his own sense of the world. Having shared this adventure with me, he in turn seems more open to receiving the wisdom I have to offer as we rebind our story into a common one that stretches beyond our personal lives and into the natural world that sustains us both.

CHAPTER 8

Hidden Temples of Silence

o   o   o

Like secondhand smoke or elevated mercury levels, dumping noise into the air damages the well-being and health of the many, in order to benefit the few—a violation of the ethic of the commons.

—Kathleen Dean Moore, "Silence Like a Scouring Sand"

In the morning, Alex and I bike the shore of Liberty Bay to the small cove in Lemolo, where I spent those idyllic summers. I show him the dock where we fished, our favorite tide flats for digging clams, and the small creek near our cabin that seemed so much bigger to my child's eye. Where our cabin stood, a large residential house now holds court. My love of this place has passed through to Alex in the passion he feels for that wilder place up the coast where he spent his own first years of childhood and where he still goes every summer to renew that bond. The first salmon that set its hooks into me here played me all the way up the coast to Petersburg, Alaska, where Alex was born and where he got hooked, too. We are both Salmon People now, at home anywhere on the coast where this majestic fish can still get to.

Having shared so rich an adventure already, I'm greedy for more time with him and reluctant to part ways. But Alex has other fish to fry. He will ride across Agate Passage and Bainbridge Island to catch the ferry to downtown Seattle. I was lucky to get the time with him that I did, and we part with a big hug, setting off along opposite sides of the bay. For the next three days, I will travel solo, covering terrain that is mostly new for me as well.

I continue south on the Kitsap Peninsula along the protected passages of Port Orchard Bay. The road signs bear Norwegian names for miles south of Poulsbo—Lundquist, Nilsen, Edvard, Haugen. I pass quiet coves and hidden farmsteads that carry the scent of an earlier Puget Sound. Today's round of sparring seasons yields another unanimous decision for winter, which continues to dish up spurts of rain and a chill headwind all through the morning. A maze of contrasting worlds has tucked itself into these rural back roads. Organic farms mix with rural compounds decked with American flags. Wealthy shoreside neighborhoods vie with pockets of rural poverty tucked back in the forest. The opulent homes lining the beach sit mostly empty and shuttered during the off-season, with owners who winter in the city and the Sunbelt.

South of Brownsville, I hit a road washout from the recent rains. It blocks my way farther south along the water, and I backtrack around Burke Bay to find an inland passage. By early afternoon, I've crossed the bridge over Port Washington Narrows and Dyes Inlet into Bremerton, passing the naval shipyard through a spare and austere downtown. I catch a vintage passenger steamer across Sinclair Inlet to Port Orchard, then ride the arc around Rich Passage through a landscape both familiar and strange, passing endless new variations on the consistent maritime theme that is Puget Sound. At Manchester, I get my first glimpse of Seattle's dominating skyline and urban expanses across the water, while Blake Island counters with a full-frontal view of its forest preserve in the sheltered waters outside Yukon

Harbor. Tonight I will visit a fellow Zen student and friend who is caretaking a private temple complex on Vashon Island.

When I reach the Vashon ferry landing at Southworth, the far hills of West Seattle have disappeared into a Chinese scroll of thick and menacing clouds, which open fire during the ferry crossing in a repeat of yesterday's late-afternoon storm. There is no possibility of escape today as I depart the ferry onto Vashon Island through a torrential downpour that is here to stay. I ascend a killer hill through this deluge to the top of the headland, like a salmon swimming up a steep waterfall. The highway levels off at the top as it winds south along the island, and I pedal the last few miles to my lodging in this downpour, amazed by the sheer magnitude of airborne water. At the prescribed turnoff, I angle west, following directions to a dead-end dirt road leading seemingly nowhere. I turn into a nondescript driveway, following a long dirt road down through second-growth fir and scrub alder. The road bottoms out suddenly at the foot of a massive temple gate. I stare in wonder, thinking, "Only in America."

Inside the gate, an ornate temple with majestic, curving lines rises from a sloped field beneath Douglas fir giants. The temple has been dismantled piece by piece in Indonesia, shipped across the ocean, and reassembled here on this remote, private land on Vashon Island. Granite monoliths and pillared stone walkways shipped in crates from China grace the temple grounds like exotic glacial erratics.* I walk my bike up the steep hill to Jo-san's house wondering if I've fallen through the Looking Glass. A smaller gate at the top of the hill leads to an unheated teak house—also imported and reassembled from Indonesia—where Jo-san is preparing a gourmet dinner of homemade nettle pasta.

---

*A *glacial erratic* is a large boulder that has been dropped by a receding glacier in a place it doesn't belong geologically.

The rain continues to fall in steady sheets from the leaden sky, and I'm soaked to the skin when I arrive. I change out of my wet clothing while Jo-san chops vegetables in the kitchen, wrapped in a heavy wool jacket and scarf. A small electric heater is parked fruitlessly next to her ankles. She makes a pot of green tea from her special stash of premium Japanese sencha, and I wrap every inch of my hands around the hot mug as I wait for a measure of warmth to return to my body.

Jyl "Shinjo" Brewer is an ordained Zen nun who spent ten years in full-time Zen training in Japan. She is an accomplished Butoh dancer as well, with a feisty intelligence, a gusty laugh, and a fierce commitment to the rigors of Zen training. She has returned to her roots on Vashon Island at the invitation of the temple's owner, and her assignment is an intriguing one: to establish a daily meditation practice at the temple and to host small retreats and seminars that will open this treasure to the wider community.

Jo-san and I study with the same teacher, a Rinzai Zen master who travels from Japan twice a year to lead intensive Zen retreats on Whidbey Island. I met Jo-san at our teacher's home temple in Japan, and we reconnected earlier this winter at the Whidbey retreat. A *sesshin* with this teacher is a full-immersion experience—a week of strict silence and long, grueling hours on the cushion. Such a regimen of training is not for everyone, but Jo-san is a serious practitioner who has taught me much about my own sometimes-halting experience with Zen. My daily rounds of *zazen,* or "sitting meditation," have proved a great support during this year, helping to steady my mind and anchor me more firmly in the immediacy of my home ground.

o o o

IN THE MORNING, I'm up before dawn to join Jo-san for meditation in the temple. To our surprise, the rain has turned to snow during the night, lacing the temple grounds with a generous resurgence of winter. We wrap ourselves in extra layers of clothing and make our way through the slush-filled darkness, lighting candles in the temple and settling wordlessly onto our cushions as we have a thousand times before. Every piece of wood in the temple is hand-shaped with intricate joinery and dances in the candlelight. It is a feast for the senses just to enter the building. With the temperature hanging just above freezing inside and out, we chant familiar Zen sutras with puffs of steam billowing from our mouths, then fall into a silence made deeper by the heavy blanket of snow. No sound touches the morning stillness except for the steady drip of meltwater from the temple eaves and the prosaic song of a few hardy robins as light comes on, who stand by their conviction that spring has actually arrived.

More than anything else, I treasure the islands of silence that meditation offers to my wearied mind, hounded as it is by a culture of excessive noise and distraction. Such a discipline of practice may be challenging on a cold morning like today, but it offers a refuge that I would not trade for anything, a chance to drop below the mind's interminable self-preoccupation to a deeper bedrock consciousness that is part of our universal human endowment. The Romanian historian of religion Mircea Eliade posited that the source of religious awe arose when conscious humans first looked up and saw the stars. I think it may have happened when those same early humans looked inside for the first time and saw the stars reflected there.

This capacity for interior silence is a legacy that all human beings share, not just those who consider themselves religious in the modern sense. It is a needless reduction of the human spirit to think that one must be a monk with robes and shaved head to access this domain of our human nature. All the better when our immense hunger for inner spaciousness can be met and heard by the silence emanating from the natural world, each one echoing down into the other. That is why I have led contemplative kayaking retreats in Alaska for the last fifteen years. We can still approach something like the source of religious awe whenever two such vast silences flow together as one. To be present at their meeting is to rejoin ourselves. It is a basic biological inheritance, available to all, and absolutely independent of culture or religious affiliation.

Many environmental activists, for example, even if they define themselves in purely secular terms, can name moments of profound awe in the presence of nature—moments that launched their passion to work for ecological restoration. Whenever we stop to see our world through the lens of its greater wholeness, we cannot help but fall back in love with the possibility of wholeness itself, and we become naturally inclined toward acts of restoration.

I teach meditation to activists, among others, because I am so convinced that our efforts to save the *external* environment will lead to burnout and despair if we do not include adequate attention to our own *inner* habitat restoration. The two are not separate and never have been. Our failure to understand this connection, emotionally as well as intellectually, can overwhelm even our noblest efforts as change makers. This is also why I have increased my time on the meditation cushion during this year in circumference, as an expression of care for my own depleted inner wilderness areas of heart and mind that bind me together with all other life.

o   o   o

THESE VASHON TEMPLE GROUNDS sit on a high wooded ridge with a beautiful view westward over Colvos Passage and the Olympic Mountains. After breakfast, I walk with Jo-san to the top of the ridge, where Mount Constance and The Brothers are displaying their fresh garments of snow from last night's visitation of winter. These mountains lie within the bounds of Olympic National Park. With nearly one million acres of protected wilderness, the park is justly famous for some of the wildest habitat anywhere in the lower forty-eight. But it has a newer claim to fame that gives a different twist to the meaning of *wild*. In his book *One Square Inch of Silence*, the acoustic ecologist Gordon Hempton tells the story of his cross-country journey to record endangered American soundscapes and the thoughts of ordinary Americans about the importance of quiet in their lives. His mission is to mount a defense of natural quiet, and in the process, he has tracked the last strongholds of silence to the Hoh Rain Forest in Olympic National Park, a short jump over the mountains from where I now stand. It was in the Hoh River valley that he found the "widest diversity of soundscapes and the longest periods of natural quiet of any unit within the National Park system." He is working now to have the Hoh designated as the world's first "quiet sanctuary." Ironically, the only invasions of mechanical sound that routinely enter this rare outpost of quiet in the lower forty-eight are the Alaska Airlines jets that drag wide cones of noise across the park on their way up the coast to Alaska, the same jets that have ferried me to my own outposts of solitude in Alaska so many times over the years.

Says Hempton: "Silence is like scouring sand. When you are quiet, the silence blows against your mind and etches away everything that is soft and unimportant."[1] It would be difficult to find a better argument for the contemplative arts as well. From an evolutionary perspective, the human mind is a direct off-spring of just such scouring silences, and it was in their embrace that human beings first learned to gape in dumbstruck awe. It was this same scouring silence in the Alaskan landscape that alerted me to the power of contemplative awe within myself. In a profoundly visual culture, we lose more than we realize when the soul-filling sounds of nature no longer come into our direct experience. We lose a core part of ourselves, a major tributary of our capacity for joy.

Such defections from the soundscape are a further cause of nature-deficit disorder. According to Hempton, sixty decibels is the typical sound volume of a river like the Hoh, and one can hear changes in the pitch of the river by moving a single stone. One gets a similar reading from ocean surf in a storm. But when he placed his sound-level meter on the traffic noise outside the Fifth Avenue entrance to the Seattle Public Library, he got a reading ten times that high. Virtually no natural sound can make it through so thick a wall of mechanical noise. True silence is becoming an extinct experience, with major consequences to our human health. Kathleen Dean Moore poses the question this way:

> What does [this] do to the human being whose ears evolved as a warning system? In daylight, our eyes can warn us of danger in front of us. But our ears alert us to opportunity and danger twenty-four hours a day, from every direction, even through dense vegetation and total darkness. . . . In the cacophonous city we are always on edge, always flinching. . . . People continuously assaulted by high levels of traffic noise have suppressed immune systems and significantly increased risk of high blood pressure and heart attacks.[2]

Yet as Moore also points out, "it's not noise in the cities that most concerns Gordon [Hempton], but the extinction of silence in wild places." Hempton figures that his campaign to gain legal protection for the sanctity of One Square Inch of Silence in the Hoh Rain Forest would protect the equivalent of a thousand square miles of surrounding terrain from the invasion of human sound, setting a legal precedent for other quiet sanctuaries around the country. Such sanctuaries of silence in the natural world will remain important, among many other reasons, for their contribution to the ongoing integrity of the human soul.

Our very hunger for contemplative silence is thus a natural resource that is built into us, a basic feature of our human emotional intelligence that doesn't go away just because we are removed from its sources. With practice, we can learn to reinhabit our inner sanctuaries of silence, regardless of what surroundings we find ourselves in or what faith we claim. This is not as small a part of our global environmental quandary as it might at first seem. The recovery of our capacity for *presence* is essential survival equipment in our efforts to know where we stand and how to "hold our ground." Without rebuilding this *inner* capacity, no advance in green technology or climate policy by itself is likely to achieve the momentum needed to turn this great ship of human culture toward the refuges of deeper and safer waters.

o o o

THE SNOW HAS TURNED TO SLEET by breakfast and back to rain by the time I continue my ride south through Vashon Island's rural landscape. Most of the snow has melted from the roads when I ride out through the temple gate and climb the long dirt driveway to the opposite ridge. I drop to the shore of Colvos Passage through a steep and winding gully, then ride south through a lichen-encrusted forest. The road's twisting rise and fall among steep ridges keeps my blood flowing, and the squalls bring a cooling freshness to the ride. The island's landscape seems molded to the rain that has shaped it, inhaling and exhaling the lovely fingers of mist moving in off the water. The damp fragrance of alder, bracken fern, cedar, and salt stirs memories that slice straight to my childhood on Liberty Bay, bridging a divide of decades that vanish with the intake of a single breath.

At Lisabeula, the road tops out onto a wide agricultural plateau above Quartermaster Harbor, cutting a straight line south through pastured horse and cattle ranches before descending again to the ferry landing at Tahlequah. The small ferry from Vashon to Point Defiance will bring me quite abruptly into Tacoma's industrial heart to begin a different kind of adventure. It is a shift in the character of my journey that I anticipate with a mixture of curiosity and apprehension, a journey unlike any I've taken before. Once I make the short crossing by ferry over Dalco Pass into Commencement Bay, I will chart a path back north to Seattle through an industrial corridor fifty miles long.

CHAPTER 9

Riding Through
the Lost Heart of the City

o   o   o

Some people might say, how tragic. But in a lot of ways, it's not
tragic. All of us are still in the middle of a rich area where things
change. The old teaching says, "It is the place that is important."

—JAMES RASMUSSEN, Duwamish Tribal Council member[1]

The tangled neighborhoods of Ruston rise steeply from the
ferry landing in Tacoma and could hardly be more of a
contrast to Vashon's rural tranquility. They drape over the
Point Defiance peninsula in urban residential streets and mixed
ethnic neighborhoods that drop sharply again to the shores of
Commencement Bay, like a tarnished wreath around the remains
of the Asarco Tacoma Smelter. To the west is the forested peninsula of Point Defiance Park, making the contrast more vivid still.
It is a long slog up the hill on my bike, and when I finally reach
the top, I cut east toward the smelter to ride past clapboard
houses that hover near the ghost of the smelter's stack. My biking circuit through the inner sound turns back toward home now
as I enter an exclusively urban terrain. Today's ride to Seattle be-

gins and ends in Superfund sites that contain the worst toxic legacies in the Puget Sound region, and I've chosen a route north that will take me directly through the heart of its industrial core. It is a journey, for me, into the very depths of the wilderness.

A composite satellite photo of Puget Sound from space gives a more accurate account of these contrasting worlds than any conventional map ever could. The west side of the sound appears as a maze of green islands and peninsulas, with a few modest touches of gray representing the towns scattered about the region. The eastern shore, on the other hand, shows up from space as a solid, wide swath of gray for eighty miles from Olympia to Everett, with only a few modest touches of green still visible inside that corridor of concrete.

By now it's no secret which side of this gray/green line has the biggest hold on my affections. My love of wild places is well-known, as is my conviction that this love has deep biological roots. My choices of residence and livelihood both reflect this bias, as I continue my lifelong campaign against nature-deficit disorder.

I would make no apologies for this bias except for one small problem. It ignores the reality that most humans live with every day, a reality that is becoming more decisively urban all the time. In my tendency to avoid these realities, I risk turning a blind eye toward the places most in need of my care, the places most in need of restoration. I divide an indivisible world into two—one part "wild" and the other part "spoiled," one part "beautiful" and the other part "ugly." It is a common enough bias, and a human one. But it puts me at risk of perpetuating the very causes of this false division, of failing to acknowledge at a deep enough level that our wounded landscapes are part of my own life, too. Our fates are bound together.

So today, I'll be riding my bicycle through places that, frankly, I've avoided all my life, places that are not on anyone's tourist brochure. I am a prodigal son, returning, hat in hand, to the cities of my birth, hoping to see them with fresh eyes. But I am also a one-man truth-and-reconciliation commission— self-appointed—here to confront the darker side of our urban heritage and to begin a long process of reconciliation within myself that can only come from having contended with the truth.

The Harvard biologist E. O. Wilson has said: "We will not work to save that which we do not love." This is a sentiment I've long shared, but when it comes to the most degraded parts of my home, I feel caught between a love in theory and a love in fact. Finding a greater well of compassion within myself for what is broken in the land is part of my homecoming pilgrimage, too. It is not something that can be put off any longer.

I stop on the bluff above the smelter's burned-out carcass before descending to the bay. Its lifeless clay heaps are a sobering sight, offering incongruous shelter for a yacht basin in the lee of Point Defiance Park. For nearly a century, the Asarco Company operated its lead and copper smelter here in Ruston, ending operations in 1985, two years after it was declared a toxic Superfund site by the U.S. Environmental Protection Agency. Air pollution from the smelter deposited arsenic, lead, and other heavy metals in the soil over more than a thousand square miles of the Puget Sound basin by the time it closed, and this toxic load still shows up at above-state-standards across a wide swath of King, Kitsap, and Pierce Counties—toxins that pose a particular menace to young children.[2] The stack itself has been taken down by dynamite to remove a conspicuous symbol of degradation from the skyline. Tidy neighborhoods emanate out from the base of the stack as they have through all the years of the plant's operation, in spite of the toxic legacy that lurks heavily in the soil. Grassy fields and upscale restaurants now line the reclaimed waterfront among the decaying wharfs of Old Tacoma. A new bike path traces the shore of Commencement Bay for three miles from Ruston to downtown Tacoma, and as I ride in from the outer reaches of the bay, I pass throngs of young families, bikers, and pedestrians enjoying the path and picnicking in the waterfront parks.

Spreading north and east from downtown is the sprawling Port of Tacoma, where the Simpson pulp and paper mill dominates in the center of a broad expanse of shipping channels, loading docks, shipyards, and industrial staging grounds that have been retrofitted into the Puyallup River delta. The billowing stacks of the mill still serve up the famous "aroma of Tacoma" as I ride toward the city's downtown business district. Decades of dioxin contamination lace the sediments of the bay, despite recent efforts by Simpson to reduce contaminated effluents from the mill.[3]

Container ships from Asia lie at anchor in the bay waiting their turn to offload as I enter Tacoma's bustling downtown district. I cross the Eleventh Street Bridge over the Thea Foss Waterway and ride along the edge of the mill's massive complex that hugs the river's main outflow into Commencement Bay. I stop to study its maze of stacks and boilers, trying to draw sense and logic from the confusion of its forms. I try to imagine what it would look like to the people who work here, who know its inner logic by heart. The rain has begun falling again, as heavy clouds press down hard on the hills, obscuring the city. I pull on my rain gear to ward off the rain and the chill. The air is laced with acrid smells, and the din of machinery and traffic pulses intensely across the delta. I am left with the image of a river in chains.

I do not feel judgment toward the people who work here. This place is their home. The thrum of machinery is the sound of a paycheck. I know that well. For a fisherman with a family to feed, the whine of hydraulic winches on the deck of a seine boat, the net straining through the power block, can be music from the spheres when the fish are hitting hard. It is the sound of money in the bank, of camaraderie and shared hard work. Even the smell of diesel fumes from the 671 humming in the engine room can carry the pleasing aroma of a livelihood being met. Why would it be any different for the people here?

Still, the questions linger. How did we get caught with this pile of ecological debts? How did we ever come to peace with a life so far removed from our roots in the earth and from our connections to the original vitality of these rivers? To be sure, there are Herculean efforts under way to clean this mess up. The mill has reduced sulfur emissions by 90 percent since Simpson took over the mill in 1985. A new Center for Urban Waters is being planned for this site, bringing together the best efforts of business, science, and public policy to advance the great work of restoration in Puget Sound that lies ahead. A new Shared Strategy for Salmon has crafted an historic plan to restore salmon runs within each of the major rivers in the sound, pulling together all the major stakeholders in an unprecedented collaboration. But implementing these plans will require a huge departure from business-as-usual. It will require a willingness to look far beyond the confines of private, short-term economic stakes—an attitude that is painfully lacking in our present culture.

I look out over the searing contradictions of the port, knowing how little time remains for us to get it right. Will it be the rising sea levels of climate change that finally set this river free? Or will its path back to wholeness run through us, rather than around us? I have no idea, but I suspect the time for finding these answers may be shorter than we currently imagine.

Before heading on my way, I utter a prayer that is part of my daily meditation practice at home. I stand fully facing the river and the mill, and I open my senses to the whole sweep of it: the clouds and the wind, the bay and the river, the hum of the city, all just as it is. I let my impulses toward judgment drain out into the concrete beneath me. Then I offer this prayer, striving with all my might to mean the words that I say: "May the life of this river be free from distress and the causes of distress. May all who live here be safe and free from harm. May they be happy. May they be healthy and strong. May they find their way into a future where all can thrive together in abundance."

o o o

I PICK UP MY TRAIL across the delta on Pacific Highway through the commercial strips of Fife, then cross the I-5 corridor into Milton. Somewhere in this stretch, I pass unceremoniously onto the Puyallup Indian Reservation, but there are no signs to distinguish the reservation from the industrial sprawl that now has the entire valley in its grip. In Milton, I pass beyond the limits of my city map, continuing on by dead reckoning, following the Puyallup valley inland toward its confluence with the White River. This turns out to be a mistake, and before long, I am lost. I stop at a machine shop and a scrap metal yard, asking directions to the Interurban Bike Trail, but no one has heard of it. In the end, I settle on a two-lane truck route heading up the industrial flats. I ride past a progression of warehouses and industrial parks that jut randomly out of the landscape with no apparent relation to one another. I'm sent sprawling into the weeds from the ragged edge of the pavement by a semi-truck passing perilously close to my body. I go down hard on the gravel, scraping my elbows and ripping my pants as several more semis rumble past. This comes as close to Bicycle Hell as anyplace I have ever been.

Junkyards give way to cluttered vacant lots as I move deeper into the valley, until I find myself riding along the Puyallup Levee Road, considerably south of where I had intended to go. I cross a bridge back over the river and follow it upstream to the outskirts of Puyallup, where I stop for directions at a tattered convenience store run by Puyallup Indians. The proprietor is an intimidating man of considerable bulk, surrounded by a cluster of other Natives passing the time together on this rainy afternoon. He leans against the counter and fixes me with an amused grin as I explain where I'm trying to go, then bursts out in a booming laugh. "Man, you are miles away from there!"

Glad to have my own impressions so astutely confirmed, I reward the man by buying a sandwich and a jumbo drink while he offers me a fresh set of confusing directions. I absorb what I can of his instructions, nodding my head knowingly, then exit the store to eat my stale sandwich outside in the rain, sitting on a curb next to a flooded parking lot filled with oil slicks. The downpour creates interlocking rainbow circles on the puddles that entertain me while I eat, and the highway traffic swishes by on a wet river of noise that drowns out all other sound. Where is that One Square Inch of Silence when I need it?

I eat lunch quickly, then dive back into the din of traffic, crossing the swollen river again just downstream from its confluence with the White, where I climb aboard another truck route heading north toward Sumner. I continue my nerve-wracking duels with the semis for several more miles—duels that I have no realistic chance of winning.

At the town of Pacific, I stumble at last onto an access point to the Interurban Bike Trail, which will take me all the way to Tukwila through the industrial fringes of Auburn and Kent. I want to do prostrations by the trail, and for the first time in hours, I'm able to relax and look around me as I ride.

o   o   o

GRANTED, IT'S A CRUMMY DAY. I'm in a hurry, I'm tired, and I have an attitude about the city to begin with. I'm passing through an unknown landscape that feels far from home, and I have only the most rudimentary knowledge of this area to go on. I offer these as honest disclaimers. But almost nothing that I can see across the broad expanse of the valley falls easily on my senses, almost nothing left of the valley seems to belong here, and I am heartsick.

Even Skagit Valley farmers will acknowledge that in its prime, the Puyallup had the best farmland of all. It was blessed with an insular location in the sound, a warmer climate than the Skagit, and broad plains of unmatched fertility. What I am seeing today is this fertility turned upside down, the very best land in the region rendered into the most degraded. As I ride for mile after mile through a paved and scoured landscape, with the last farm squeezed out of an incomparably fertile valley, I can't help but wonder what kind of insanity we have built our prosperity upon. Grief stalks me like a tidal bore up the valley. As I pass across the invisible threshold between the White and Green River watersheds, beginning my long descent into the Duwamish, I remember the prophetic words ascribed to Chief Seattle as he was signing away his Duwamish tribal lands in 1855:

> To us the ashes of our ancestors are sacred and their resting place is hallowed ground. You wander far from the graves of

your ancestors and seemingly without regret. . . . Tribe follows tribe, and nation follows nation, like the waves of the sea. It is the order of nature, and regret is useless. Your time of decay may be distant, but it will surely come, for even the White Man whose God walks and talks with him as friend to friend, cannot be exempt from the common destiny. We may be brothers after all. We will see.*

o   o   o

THE INTERURBAN BIKE TRAIL traces an unbending path along the railroad grade through the baseline of the valley. It seems to have found all the backyards of these industrial parks, the vacant lots that stand in between, and the rear alleyways of remnant neighborhoods that line the edges of our burgeoning industrial project. I stop to rest by a pocket of wetlands hanging off the edge of an industrial fill. Some bufflehead ducks are working the ponds, inhabiting them with no questions asked, unfazed by the harsh lines of separation that we humans have imposed on their land. As I watch them work, their lovely black and white bodies diving down to feed and then popping randomly back to the surface of the water, I notice that the clouds have broken open. The rain has stopped, for a while at least. Nothing ever stays the same for long. The harsh lines of judgment that have been forming again in my mind begin to soften. A Zen saying rises with the ducks out of the hidden places in my own deep memory: "Never forget the thousand-year view." In the unexpected grace of this

*Chief Seattle's grave sits in a small Episcopal Church cemetery on the Suquamish Reservation near Agate Pass, not far from the cottage on Liberty Bay where I spent my childhood summers. I visited the grave with my family and took the words of his speech to heart early on. There are different versions of the speech, and its historical accuracy is questioned. But whatever words were actually uttered by Chief Seattle as he was signing away his tribal land, the speech remains hauntingly prophetic.

moment, the hard certainty that has hammered itself into my perceptions about this place loosens its grip. I am the prodigal son again, aware for now simply of my grief, aware of its potency, aware of its gravitational pull on my body, but aware also that it carries some part of the answer I have come here to find. "We will not work to save that which we do not love."

How does one fashion such a love in the midst of such towering losses? What I see here is only the tip of the iceberg of what is to come, when climate change is factored into the equation. A love that can endure even this must pass inevitably through grief, no less for the land than for the people we have been given to love. This is the way of the world. This is how it has always been. I sit with my grief in the moment at hand as I would sit with any powerful stranger who has come to visit—humbled for a time, and silent.

The valley stretches out the same as before when I resume my ride. The clouds press down as hard as they have all day. But my spirit is no longer so burdened, my heart not so closed. I am no longer quite so blind to the beauty that will never cease looking for a fresh purchase on this land.

o o o

IT IS NEARLY FIFTY MILES between Tacoma and Seattle from tidewater to tidewater, following the inland path of these rivers and the tributaries that span the long valley in between. It is clear now that there will be no respite from the long fingers of industrial sprawl that now weave these cities together, from one end to the other. But the human storm now playing out before me is only one in a long series of changes that have been visited upon the valley. A mere five thousand years ago, the top two thousand feet of Mount Rainier exploded down the Emmons Glacier and White River Valley to cover everything from Enumclaw to

Auburn under the Osceola mudflow.[4] The cataclysm forced the White River north into the Duwamish River system, where it joined the Green and the Black as tributaries. Now an equally large geologic force has sent the White River back south into the Puyallup, in the guise of human engineers replumbing the valley to head off future floods in the heavily settled Duwamish watershed. The White was diverted again to the Puyallup in 1906 as part of a giant flood-control project.

Of the three great tributaries to the Duwamish when white settlers first arrived, only one is left. The White River was the first to go, courtesy of the U.S. Army Corps of Engineers. The Black River went next, when the Lake Washington Ship Canal opened its floodgates to the sea in 1916 through the Ballard Locks, dropping the level of the lake below the Black River's outflow into the Duwamish. Only the Green River is left, cutting the Duwamish to 25 percent of its original flow and leaving the valley shorn of two great rivers.

By the time I pass the unmarked grave of the Black near Renton, I'm running on fumes, thanks to my unexpected detour through Puyallup. It's been a long day of riding, but I still have many miles to go. These are the most poignant miles of the ride for me, because I'm closing in on the city where I grew up. Half of this remaining distance will pass through a Superfund site. That "distant time of decay" that Chief Seattle foresaw in 1855 is now upon us, and the traditional name for this great river (Dkhʷ'Duw'Absh), which once meant "people of the inside," now names a toxic legacy five miles long.

o o o

THE INTERURBAN BIKE TRAIL parts ways with the railroad grade and morphs into the Green River Trail in Tukwila near the old confluence of the Black River, which now masquerades as

Interstate 405 flowing backward into Renton. Shorn of its former limbs, with the Black and White Rivers no longer adding their flow to the river, the Duwamish is a shadow of its former self, technically just a continuation of the Green all the way out to tidewater. Like me at this moment, it is a river running on fumes. The bike trail skirts South Center Mall, then follows the river through a series of meandering curves and greenbelts that serve as the backyard for upscale corporate office headquarters.

I stop at the Hamm Creek restoration project, a short walk from some of the most contaminated sites in Washington, where a Vietnam veteran named John Beal spent the last three decades of his life restoring natural vegetation and a lost salmon run to a ruined watershed. Beal had a bad case of posttraumatic stress disorder (PTSD), and the trash heap that Hamm Creek had become looked too much like the load of garbage he was carrying around inside himself. He decided to do something, with his own hands and on his own time, and his relentless efforts eventually attracted international attention and prestigious awards.[5] But Beal wasn't looking for attention. He was looking for healing. His efforts to restore this small tributary to the Duwamish became his own therapy, and by the late 1980s, he was seeing salmon use the creek again. Native vegetation now abounds in the area. According to Mike Sato, of People for Puget Sound, watching the single-minded gusto with which Beal threw himself into this restoration made "you want to get down next to John and get your hands dirty too, because working with John at Hamm Creek [was] like going to church."[6] I see great blue herons feeding from the muddy banks by the creek's outflow. A pair of ospreys swoop down onto decayed pilings in the river, and lots of waterfowl have found their way back to this part of the river, too, oblivious to the posted signs warning, BOTTOMFISH, CRABS AND SHELLFISH MAY BE UNSAFE TO EAT DUE TO POLLUTION. Part of me wants to warn them off, but I also take solace in the fact that they are here at all—that like John Beal, they refuse to give up their river or to deprive it of their own life, come what may.

When the City of Seattle broke ground for a new firefighter training center, it inadvertently paved over the headwaters of Hamm Creek, and by 2004, Beal saw no salmon return to the creek's north fork—also known as the Lost Fork. He blew the whistle on this illegal wetlands destruction, leaving the city to unscramble the mess, but the damage was done.

"It broke me—morally, mentally and physically," Beal said. "I don't know the words. I was just broken."[7] Saving this small watershed had taken on the dimensions of an ultimate moral imperative for Beal, and no expense was too much to hold the gains he had made. He had come to see in this broken place a full extension of his own life and brought the same fervency of purpose to its healing that most parents would bring to the healing of a seriously sick child.

As I rest in the small oasis of Hamm Creek, I realize that this is the best answer I've found yet to the question I've been carrying all day. What would it look like to truly love this place? Beal's story also casts light on my own work at the VA Hospital in Seattle, where I teach stress reduction to PTSD vets, some of whom struggle with the effects of this trauma four decades after their war service has ended. I think of the new tidal wave of PTSD breaking over our country as young Iraq War vets return from multiple tours of duty in the latest tragic war. The VA Hospital in Seattle, for all its good efforts on behalf of veteran health care, is a place nearly bereft of nature. Efforts to heal that stop at the limits of the human body ignore the vast healing that comes when human nature and wild nature meet. To dress nature's wounds with the heart of a healer, as Beal did, is to embark on a path of healing for oneself. There is no greater symbol of wildness than the salmon, and if Beal could succeed in bringing salmon back to Hamm Creek, here in the very midst of a Superfund site, then no place is beyond redemption. As Beal also proved, no human trauma is beyond the reach of nature's healing alchemy.

o o o

DOWNSTREAM FROM THE turning basin at Hamm Creek, the river disappears altogether, becoming a dredged and straightened shipping channel in the service of heavy industry. At East Marginal Way, the bike trail disappears, too, and I become a bicycle combat soldier again. The wide, looping curves of the old river are now the runways of Boeing Field, and the abandoned World War II B-17 plant by the river is one of the most toxic hotspots in Puget Sound.[8] I am pulled back into a maze of competing commercial arteries that merge and split, the way the river once did, without regard for convenience or gridline patterns. My only glimpses of the river now are from the arterial bridges that cut diagonally across the channel in their race toward downtown Seattle.

I stop on the Sixteenth Avenue Bridge to look at the tangle of commercial wharfs and the rafts of tugs and barges that now claim ownership of the river. As I near the split in the channel that forms Harbor Island, the bike trail picks up again along a side arm of the lower estuary tucked behind Kellogg Island. The last of the lower river's off-channel tidal sloughs are clustered here, and from the Herring House archeological site, I can see traces of the river's past hidden in its muddy arms at low tide.

Across West Marginal Way from Herring House Park is the building I've been looking for, rising between dilapidated houses and commercial offices tucked into the bluffs of West Seattle. It is as unlikely a structure as one would expect to find down the street from a cement factory and a barge line. The building under construction is a new ceremonial longhouse for the Duwamish Tribe, the first of its kind to appear by the shores of this river in 150 years. It rises from a small piece of tarnished industrial land. As I watch, a construction crane lifts a giant yellow cedar house post into place among a row of hand-adzed tree trunks and rafter timbers that will frame the ceremonial space, as this building takes its place among the dozens of other longhouses springing up on tribal lands around the region. More than any of the others, though, I think this longhouse answers the question of what an abiding human love for this wounded place might actually look like.

Though the Duwamish people never did receive their promised reservation or the federal recognition as a tribe that was their due, these direct descendants of Chief Seattle refused to go away. Like other tribes around the region, they took their ceremonies underground, holding on to whatever shards of tradition they could keep alive through generations of government-sanctioned repression, while the wealth of the river itself eroded slowly out from under them. But they never left, and this longhouse is an eloquent declaration that they have no intention of leaving.

Last week, these yellow cedar logs lay outside the shop of my brother Kim on Whidbey Island, a hundred yards from my house. Kim is a woodworker who is passionate about the traditional uses of Northwest wood. These logs had themselves been rejected by a mill, rescued from a scrap heap by my brother, so it is appropriate that their banished beauty is also being made manifest here. And they are indeed beautiful. I took my turn with the adze in shaping these house posts, and I'm proud of my brother's intimate involvement in this act of cultural restoration that is being rightfully celebrated by the whole community, Native and non-Native alike.

I don a hard hat and walk with the construction supervisor through the ceremonial space, feeling the power of this wood to convey traditions of place across time and to root them back home in the present. The ceremonies here will carry that same thousand-year view, transforming a cast-off watershed into a place of possibility again. Even if the Duwamish people never do get their tribal recognition, this longhouse renews their status as prime stewards of the watershed again. According to the Duwamish weaver Mary Lou Slaughter, a descendant of Chief Seattle, the longhouse is "something I never thought I could see." The federal government might deny recognition, "but they can't take away our birthright. We're not going to lie down and die."[9]

o   o   o

THE DUWAMISH CHINOOK SALMON apparently share this view. Of the thirty-two historic runs of chinook salmon in Puget Sound, one-third have already gone extinct and many more are hanging on the brink. Yet like the Duwamish people themselves, the salmon in this river are relentless survivors. Of the original estuary, 99 percent has been lost, and only the Green River system is left among historic Duwamish tributaries for the salmon to spawn in, but this run of chinook has proven surprisingly durable. Six thousand chinook and a comparable number of cohos still brave the toxic residue of the lower river each year on their way to spawning grounds in the Cascade foothills.[10] After a perilous journey lasting several years and covering thousands of miles of trackless ocean, they still find their way back to this one river and will have no other, returning to the stream of their birth for a single and final act of self-sacrifice. They spawn here and die, offering their bodies as precious nutrients flowing back up into the mountains from the ocean. Like the herons and osprey at Hamm Creek, and like the Duwamish Tribe with their new longhouse, these salmon refuse to concede the life of the only river they will ever call home.

Farther downstream, the giant mobile cranes of Harbor Island's port facilities unload container ships from Asia, while the West Seattle freeway arcs like a giant concrete rainbow over the river's entrance to the sea. In the distance, Seattle's downtown office towers hold court over the shores of Elliott Bay. I have to will my tired body through the final miles along Alaskan Way into downtown Seattle.

The familiar streets of the city are as congested as ever at rush hour in the evening. There is the same air of easygoing purposefulness that Seattle is famous for, the same youthful confidence written on the people who throng its busy sidewalks. But it is no longer the same city I have known in the past. I am more sober about its prospects now, more aware of the contradictions hidden in its past. But I am also, strangely, more hopeful about its future as I pedal my bicycle through Pike Place Market and along the shores of Elliott Bay through Myrtle Edwards Park. I feel as though I've visited a dozen countries on this trip, that I'm arriving back in my hometown after a journey halfway around the world. Much more is included in my perception of what this city holds and of what it will take to bring Seattle into a healthy future. Something of John Beal's spirit is in me now, and something of the tenacious people who still cleave to this city's wounded heart as home. I have a new appreciation for the power of small acts of restoration. And I have a new sense of belonging to the stories of these rivers, even in their hour of deepest need. They are my rivers now in a way they have never been before, and I feel an upsurge of commitment to their futures.

Tomorrow, I will finish my ride through the urban corridor of the sound, closing my circle back around to my home on Whidbey Island. But tonight, I will take a much-needed rest with my friends Joe and Lee on Magnolia Bluff. Both of them give their lives to acts of restoration every day. It is their work and their passion, and I can't wait to tell them what I've seen on this remarkable odyssey through the wounded heart of our city.

CHAPTER 10

The Peaks of Circumference, Part 1

∘ ∘ ∘

"Men Don't Get This Far into the Mountains"

Men don't get this far into the mountains,
White clouds gather and billow.
Thin grass does for a mattress,
The blue sky makes a good quilt.
Happy with a stone underhead
Let heaven and earth go about their changes.

—HAN-SHAN, Tang Dynasty poet

It has been an unusually wet spring. Already, the summer solstice has come and gone, the halfway point of my year in circumference, and still it rains. I marked the solstice quietly, in a Zen retreat on Samish Island led by Zoketsu Norman Fischer, a former abbot of the San Francisco Zen Center. I reached the island after a long bike ride across the Skagit flats and Samish River delta. It was my first visit to this island, which rears up from the Samish River delta as a preview of coming San Juan attractions. The island is lovely, rimmed by the Chuckanut Mountains to the east and the high shark-fin ridge of Lummi Island to the north. The San Juan archipelago paints a primal scene to the west across Rosario Strait, while the Strait of Georgia yawns northward into far Canadian waters. It is a place apart, a fine setting for a retreat, and the long hours of daily sitting were a welcome rest from my outward explorations.

I've been amazed how quickly the months have flown by. My year in circumference has already transited from the shortest day of the year to the longest. Already, the arc of daylight is headed back toward its eventual reunion with the winter solstice, the place in time where this all began.

I thought the time might pass slowly, maybe even ponderously, without recourse to my car. But the opposite has happened. I'm as fully engaged in my life as I can remember, and the weeks clip by one after another. It's just framed a little differently now. Not even that much differently. But it is a crucial difference.

I still sit at my computer several hours a day, when I'm not on one of my expeditions around the sound. I've chosen to take a media fast during most of my explorations. But otherwise, I'm absorbed in the same tools of social connectivity as everyone else—daily e-mail and Internet commerce, cell phones, blogging, and wrangling with the tools of digital technology. I'm just not doing it quite as compulsively as before. I'm leaving space for daily contemplation, exercise, and contact with my immediate neighbors. Even though I consider this a sabbatical, I still commute into Seattle once or twice a week by bus and bicycle to teach at the VA Hospital. Working with these vets has kept me grounded in the larger community, reminding me that everyone is carrying a heavy load. Everyone has a story of loss and grief. No one is unworthy of compassion.

A trip to the movie or to a community gathering is a bigger deal than it was before, something that takes effort and planning and therefore something to warrant consideration. I'm not as random in my socializing. I'm learning that small, local activities, entered into mindfully, can bring a lot of satisfaction. I'm not looking over my shoulder, wondering what I'm missing somewhere else.

Last month, I followed my first bicycle trip around the inner sound with a second, longer tour of the region covering five hundred miles, tracing the outer edge of my circle. Where mountains hemmed me in, I pedaled as far out as I could go into the foothills of the Olympics and Cascades, on a route that took me from Victoria, British Columbia, to Enumclaw, Washington, and from Hoodsport to Bellingham. I pushed myself hard physically, and I continue to be surprised by how responsive my body has been to this challenge. In the process, I crossed every major river that reaches the sound inside my circle, weaving myself more consciously into this place where many rivers meet.

With summer coming on, I will be slowing down even more, shifting focus from the spoke to the paddle in a kayaking circumnavigation of Puget Sound. But first, I have one more expedition that beckons, this one combining both the spoke and the boot. From the beginning, I knew I had to attempt the highest points on my circle, from home to summit, under my own power. I could not imagine this year without a pilgrimage to the peaks of circumference.

o o o

WE AMERICANS HAVE a staunchly secular attitude toward our mountains. We love to admire them for their beauty, but it would be a push to say that we revere them. A look at the patchwork quilt of logging scars from any vantage around Puget Sound tells the real tale of where we place the value on these mountains. I've always thought that *sacred* is a matter of scale and that mountains are a hell of a lot bigger than churches. So, do the math. But scale doesn't matter much, anyway, if you take the view that basically *nothing* is sacred, which is a very popular religion these days.

I tend in the opposite direction. I think that basically *everything* is sacred and that our job is to align ourselves with this truth by figuring out what is most sacred and working from there. A smart primate that weighs 150 pounds and has a bad habit of fouling its own nest is a poor candidate, to my way of thinking, for the honor of *most sacred creation in the universe.* I don't care how many titles it has behind its name.

So, in my taxonomy of the sacred, mountains deserve a relatively high level of stature, and humans a comparably lower one. My fellow mountaineers spend a lot of time arguing about which mountains are most worthy of being *climbed,* but that's a different question. I'm talking about which mountains most anchor our sense of place as a culture or offer us the most perspective on our lives, as well as which mountains, when we climb them, offer us the greatest potential for insight into ourselves. Sacred mountains have played a pivotal role in defining cultures and religions for millennia in China and Japan, and even in Europe if you go back far enough. Mountains have always inspired awe with their beauty, defined the boundaries of local terrain, bridged heaven and earth with their heights, and housed the gods where humans dare not go.

But that was before we invented crampons and ice axes and a mechanized view of the universe. Mountains these days are not so much objects of pilgrimage as summits to be bagged. Around here, the most prominent peaks, like Rainier and Baker, are climbed by thousands every year. They are prized for their beauty by all. But *sacred*? I wouldn't go that far. So, I've taken it upon myself to define my own sacred geometry for Northwest mountains that gives them some kind of moral stature, that makes them more than just objects to be conquered.

Imagine my amazement, then, when I stumbled into the uncanny mountain geometry of my own home circle, completely by accident, with most of the obvious local candidates for sacred mountains lying exactly one hundred kilometers from my home. Equally remarkable is that three of these peaks—Olympus, Baker, and Glacier Peak—with the inclusion of Mount Rainier's dominating dome to the south just outside my circle, almost perfectly articulate the four directions on the compass. I challenge anyone, anywhere, to come up with a more compelling mandala of mountains around their home. To find myself exactly centered between these peaks during my year in circumference gave me a boundary that was almost too good to be true. All this puts me in good stead with my Zen ancestors. Zen, as a tradition, seems to have sacred mountains in its blood.[1]

Once I'd made this discovery, I knew right away that I had to climb at least one of these anchoring peaks during the year, from home to summit under my own power. Or more accurately, I had to make a serious attempt. There is no guarantee that even the best-planned climbing expedition will succeed in these mountains, which can dish up harsh winter conditions year-round. That is why they command such respect among mountaineers. Local climbing standout Ed Viesturs, the first American to summit all fourteen of the world's 8,000-meter peaks (26,000 feet and above), has called Mount Rainier the only mountain in the lower forty-eight that provides "the full meal" of climbing. Baker and Glacier are not far behind. These are serious mountains.

o o o

WHEN I WAS IN MY EARLY FIFTIES, some climbing friends invited
me to join them on a mountaineering trek through the heart of
the North Cascades called the Ptarmigan Traverse. It is an expedition of some renown among Northwest climbers, and I was
surprised by the invitation. As with my bicycle, I had not pulled
my climbing gear out of storage in well over twenty years, and my
confidence was shaky. Most of my earlier climbs were in the company of my older brother Kim, who was always the daredevil between the two of us. I had shown a decent aptitude for climbing
in my youth, but also an overly cautious nature, which doesn't
mix well with the sport. There was always a standoff between
my fear of heights and my desire to be part of these adventures.

I had assumed my climbing days were well behind me, but the
invitation gave me pause. Here was a chance not only to renew my
acquaintance with the mountains after years on the water in
Alaska, but also to confront some old fears from a more mature
vantage. If I'd learned anything from my Zen practice, it is that
fear is an enemy of freedom. To live in genuine freedom is to continually question and confront our fears, so that we don't box
ourselves in by fixed ideas of what is possible and what is "safe."
To my surprise I said yes to the offer. I was honored to be included, but also secretly nervous as hell about going. What if I
couldn't pull it off? What if I was the one who froze at a critical
moment on the climb? What if I fell off the sheer flanks of Mount
Formidable or Spire Point, days from any possible help? Even in
my younger years, I'd never attempted anything this challenging.

The trip began with an ascent of Cash Col by way of Cascade
Pass, then clung to a high traverse for forty miles south into the
Glacier Peak Wilderness, threading some of the most exposed
terrain in the continental United States. Our climbing team ne-

gotiated six glaciers en route, all of which had noticeably shrunk from their stated dimensions on our 1970s-era topographical maps. The trip was a crash course for me in every aspect of technical climbing, expertly guided by a local high school science teacher and former Mount McKinley guide named Greg Ballog. It pressed my limit of both skill and endurance, with moments of searing enchantment, and times when I felt exhausted beyond the possibility of redemption. But I made it! My reward was a weeklong immersion in the very temples of earthly awe. It was a revelation to me, after so many summers in Alaska, that I could touch this scale of grandeur so close to home or encounter this depth of solitude a few ridges deeper into the mountains than it was ordinarily possible to go. The trip gave me confidence that I could still handle serious mountaineering, and it blew my love of the mountains wide open again.

I have since climbed some of the local peaks I had coveted since my youth, including Mount Baker and Mount Rainier, and the experience has further anchored my sense of belonging in this place. The mountains surrounding my home in Puget Sound are no longer just two-dimensional walls offering a scenic backdrop to my home in the lowlands. They are individual presences—having revealed some part of their essence to me in my act of climbing them. Some of that depth of perception crosses the visual gap to steady my mind when I look at these mountains now, revealing their many faces across the seasons. When Rainier's massive dome breaks free of the clouds, even at a distance of eighty miles from my home, I can chart the courses I have taken up the Ingraham and Emmons Glaciers on my way to a dawn rendezvous with its 14,410-foot summit crater. When I look at Mount Baker now, guarding the northern rim of my circle, I can see the steep rise of the Roman Wall lifting out of the Black

Buttes for the final approach to its 10,778-foot summit plateau. Each summit reached yields a new perspective on the whole region and a new appreciation for the vast scale of these mountains. From different vantages in the Central Cascades, I can see the profusion of peaks stretching from Mount Jefferson and Mount Hood in Oregon to the Coast Range of British Columbia. Across the wide basin of Puget Sound, I can see the echoing buttresses of the Olympic Range to the west, with the deep channels and shimmering islands of the sound nestled in between. A hundred lifetimes would not be enough to touch on all these mountains. How could I wish for more? From these lofty heights, my life appears on a more realistic scale, both tiny and short. In claiming these mountains as my own, I am really allowing myself to be claimed by them, to be taken more deeply into the marrow of this place I call home.

o   o   o

WHEN ZEN ARRIVED on the West Coast of North America in the mid-twentieth century, it found a welcoming home here in part because of the mountains that define this region and because of the way these mountains had seeded the ground for an emerging counterculture. Led by Gary Snyder and Jack Kerouac, the impulse to reinvest local mountains with some of the spiritual power they had held within Native traditions began to take hold. I caught that virus as a young man myself, and going to the mountains has always been a way for me to reconnect with a personal sense of pilgrimage in a culture bereft of such practices. Mountaineering, for me, is meditation in motion, a rigorous practice of persistence where one has to be ready for anything. Reaching the summit is a worthy goal, but not the primary purpose of the climb. Rather, it is the act of facing the mountain on its own terms. A wrong move at any point on the way can prove fatal. One has to have the courage to turn back when conditions become dangerous, but to continue forward when the going is merely tough. A certain laser focus is called for, a quality that is, frankly, optional on the meditation cushion, yet mandatory on the mountain.

o   o   o

So, WHICH OF THESE three delicious mountains to climb? I spent hours poring over maps, weighing the merits of each. I knew I would probably have only one shot at it. Without a car, just getting to the mountain might prove to be the biggest challenge of all. Each of my circumference peaks has its particular benefits.

Mount Baker is the most accessible of the three and the highest point on my circle. It is a heavily glaciated volcano, holder of the world-record depth of snowfall in a single season (ninety-five feet of snow during the winter of 1998–1999), which translates into massive glaciers that extend far down the flanks of the mountain. It rivals Mount Rainier for grandeur in the Puget Sound viewshed and would be the obvious first choice for my mountain pilgrimage, if I hadn't recently made the summit of Baker via the Coleman Glacier on the north side of the mountain. It is a peak worthy of multiple ascents, however, and I could get there by bicycle without leaving my circle, ascending either the Easton or Boulder Glacier on the southeast face of the mountain.

Mount Olympus lies deep in the Olympic Range, in the heart of Olympic National Park. It is not so lofty in elevation at 7,962 feet, but it is a spectacular mountain, heavily glaciated because of the immense moisture unleashed from the ocean on the west slope of the Olympics. And it is one of the primary peaks that I have yet to climb. Unfortunately for my purposes, it requires a long approach hike from the coast side of the mountains through the Hoh River drainage, taking me well outside the scope of my circle. I conclude that Mount Olympus will have to wait for another year.

That leaves Glacier Peak, which I have yet to climb also, and which is my first choice for this mountain pilgrimage. But there is a problem. You can't currently get there from here.

Unlike the other volcanic peaks in Washington State, Glacier Peak is invisible from most settled areas, buried deep in a half-million-acre wilderness area that bears its name. It is an impressive mountain if you can get close to it, which takes a lot of work in the best of circumstances. At 10,541 feet, Glacier is just 200 feet shy of the elevation of Mount Baker. But it is a long hike in, and there are few places on the urbanized west side of the Cascades from which you can even see it. The bluff above Langley Harbor on Whidbey Island is one of those places, and I pause there often to consider the merits of the mountain. On a clear day, looking east from the island across Possession Sound and the city of Everett, one can see the upper flanks of Glacier Peak tucked far back in the gap between Mount Pilchuck and Liberty Mountain, in a frontline wall of peaks dominated by Whitehorse and Three Fingers. It is easy to misjudge from here the true stature of Glacier Peak relative to its smaller, closer neighbors. The standard route from the west side goes up the Whitechuck River drainage past Kennedy Hot Springs, but a devastating flood in the autumn of 2003 wiped out all access roads and most of the trails into the mountain from the west slope, and it has remained closed ever since. The mountain is still accessible from east of the Cascades, but that would also take me well outside my circle. So I decide to take matters into my own hands and find out for myself if a route into Glacier Peak is still possible from the west side.

o o o

NOT EVEN MOUNTAINS stand still in this transitory life. We eat and are eaten in an endless melding of love and death. The threads of our lives cross and recross, and we can never know what destinies will be woven by them. Most of the connections forged are invisible to us, their genius buried deep in the stuff of everyday life. A few spawn such original creations that they cannot be ignored, and their magnetized lines of intersection pull the very fabric of the future into themselves. Nothing can be the same after.

Gary Snyder is one of those magnetic threads in my own life, a force within the very culture I grew up in that has left an indelible mark on me. This should come as no great surprise by now.

In September 1965, Snyder dragged his fellow poet Allen Ginsberg all the way to the summit of Glacier Peak. Snyder was a seasoned mountaineer, but Ginsberg was a klutz, with no business being that high in the mountains. That trip entered my own mythic imagination as a young man through *Earth House Hold,* Snyder's published journal account of the adventure. When they got to the summit, full sunrise had broken and clear skies unveiled a whole universe of mountains in all directions. "So many mountains, on so clear a day, the mind is staggered," wrote Snyder in his journal, "and so looks to little things like pilot bread and cheese and bits of dried fruit." To Ginsberg he ascribed these few words in response: "You mean there's a Senator for all this?"[2]

My own climbing aspirations are modest ones, but this is one of them. I've always wanted to follow in Snyder's and Ginsberg's footsteps, to make the ascent of Glacier Peak as an act of communion with these legends of the Beat culture. My one attempt on the mountain in the summer of 2003 was beaten back by the weather, and a record flood in the fall of that year closed the door on further attempts. Yet if I could choose one mountain to climb during my year in circumference, this would be it. So I had to find out one thing in advance. Does a way even exist into the mountain from the west side of the Cascades? In seeking an answer to that question, I learned some other things, too. I came face-to-face with the most compelling reason yet why I had chosen to embark on this journey in the first place.

CHAPTER 11

The Peaks of Circumference, Part 2

o o o

"The Sound of Spring Rain"

All my life I have heard rain,
And I am an old man;
But now for the first time I understand
The sound of spring rain
On the river at night.

—Yang Wan-Li[1]

What was I to make, exactly, of U.S. Forest Service notices claiming that Glacier Peak was currently "inaccessible" from the western slope of the Cascades? Such notices can be overstated, in deference to the abilities of the average day hiker. The flood of 2003 was four years behind us now, yet still the Whitechuck River access road was closed nine miles from the trailhead. "How closed?" I wanted to know. There had been additional flooding since, shutting down the North

Sauk River Road also, and thus taking out the last remaining means of access by car from the west side. This business of rain and floods has been getting a bit out of hand lately.

It's hardly news that we get a lot of rain in Puget Sound. But as a rule, it doesn't rain here as much as people think. At least it didn't used to. Typically, it rains a little bit a lot of the time. The grayness is what usually gets to people, more than the rain itself. In fact, Seattle's thirty-seven-inch average annual rainfall ranks forty-first in a recent survey of the two hundred rainiest cities in the United States, based on National Weather Service averages over the last thirty years. Every major city on the Eastern Seaboard gets more rain than Seattle, and we rank far behind the Gulf Coast, where the ten rainiest cities in the United States all reside. But here's the catch. Seattle comes in near the top for the number of days each year that it receives some precipitation (Olympia ranks first).[2] Puget Sound's residents aren't imagining the clouds, but our habitual animosity toward rain could be seen as a problem of perception—a symptom of our wider cultural bias in favor of sunnier climes.

Talk about an exercise in futility. I get bored hearing people complain about the fact that it rains here in rain country. Weather forecasters especially. They instruct us daily to feel miserable if we wake up and find that we still don't live in Tucson, Arizona. What do they expect? Throw a towering range of mountains in front of a thick, moist onshore flow of air, and this is the climate you end up with every time. It is a hydrologic engine that has crafted one of the most beautiful landscapes and productive rain forest ecologies anywhere on the planet. Kenneth Brower captures the mystique of this collision between mountain and sea: "Clouds boil up from the cold cauldron of the North Pacific, white against the high gray. Fogs flow tidally in and out of the inlets. Mist mystifies the forest. Vapors heighten the headlands. White lenticular clouds cap the foothills. The gray inverted sea of cloud decapitates the peaks."[3]

I have to admit, though, this last week the rain has been unusually relentless. Even some of the people with webbed feet have been complaining. A monster low-pressure system out in the North Pacific has been pummeling us, and the rain just keeps coming and coming. It is the kind of weather system that used to happen very rarely, but is becoming all too common these days. A sustained rain like this is more than just a cause for wet feathers. It can also bring deadly floods, and that is just what is happening right now.

There is a lot of precedent in the weather news these days for the word *unprecedented*. It seems we've had a flood of precedent-setting floods here in Western Washington recently. Last fall's flood on the Chehalis River set a new record for destructiveness, topping the record flood on the Nisqually River the year before, which ripped out the highway into Mount Rainier National Park after eighteen inches of rain fell in thirty-six hours. The huge cost of rebuilding that essential road put on further hold plans to rebuild the roads into the Sauk and Whitechuck Rivers. These roads were blown out by—yes, unprecedented—flooding the year before that.

Yet the possibility that a pattern might exist here or that this is exactly the trend we have been told to expect by climatologists in the Northwest as global warming kicks in is something that mainstream news commentators rarely mention in their extensive coverage of these events. Local newspapers and TV coverage of the flood have contented themselves with reporting one disconnected personal tragedy after another, with sensational scenes of devastation and hand-wringing over the anticipated "unprecedented" costs of cleanup. But could all this portend any links to climate change? Apparently not.

Yang Wan-li's ability to finally understand as an old man the "sound of spring rain" suggests a hard-won spiritual awakening to wonder in the presence of rain's bounty:

> *At midnight the cold, splashing sound begins,*
> *Like thousands of pearls spilling onto a glass plate,*
> *Each drop penetrating the bone.*[4]

But his wonder at this revelation presumed a comforting continuity with the past. The rain comes with the season, as it always has. The river in the gorge fills with the sound of rushing water. Crops are nourished. The wells are replenished. The community is held intact. Life can go on as before.

As a Northwest native, I feel a deep kinship across the centuries with Yang Wan-li in the honest friendship I have built with our rainy climate. I find myself the odd person out at times, defending this basic fact of life to acquaintances who seem determined to feel exiled because of a perceived lack of sun. Yet while the rain pounding on my roof tonight is no less evocative of Yang Wan-li's twelfth-century musings, it also carries an edge that it didn't have before. It doesn't feel quite as natural to me as it has in the past. There is an unsettling new aura of danger and threat in the sound, of broken continuity with a past that I have always taken for granted.

I know that changes of this magnitude are themselves not unprecedented, but they have always occurred over much longer arcs of time. Mountains have always been torn down by rivers, as fast as the earth can build them up in the endless, circular convection of our planet's molten core that drives continental drift. Earthquakes and volcanic eruptions continually remodel the earth's surface, forever sweeping away all that came before, if given enough time. Ice ages come and go, possibly spurred by the wobble of the earth's axis across the millennia and its resulting angle toward the sun. From the great seismic convulsions to the slow drip of water on rock, the earth's great natural processes guarantee that nothing we humans consider permanent will actually remain so.

To be sure, periodic floods of epic proportions have changed the course of Northwest rivers since time immemorial. There is no way of knowing with absolute certainty that our recent spate of hundred-year floods in the Puget Sound basin are not just a cosmic coincidence, a colossal run of bad luck. Taken separately, they could be explained in the context of a perfect storm, the components of which could plausibly add up to events of this magnitude without taking global warming into consideration. But taken together, the plausibility argument runs painfully thin. It is difficult to escape the conclusion that we are witnessing the first wave of a dramatically shifting Northwest climate, a local iteration of global trends that are throwing climates into chaos across the globe. While arid regions like Australia and the American Southwest seem headed toward Sahara-like desertification and severe water shortages, climate modeling here in the Northwest points in the opposite direction. We can expect increased rainfall coming in greater concentration during the fall and winter, with harsher weather events and more frequent flooding during the rainy season, and greater periods of drought in the summer. Average annual snowpack in the mountains will decrease by 50 percent over the next half-century and move to higher elevations. Shrinking glaciers that provide stream flow to our Northwest rivers in the late summer and early fall, combined with rising stream temperatures and the increased damage of winter flooding, will put at risk already-beleaguered salmon runs.

Even here in the rainy Northwest, there will be less water in summer to accommodate the fiercely competing needs of farmers, salmon, hydroelectric dams, and burgeoning cities.[5]

o o o

THESE ABERRANT WEATHER EVENTS are kicking in already, exactly as climatologists have been predicting. I know, because I've been watching it. The uncanny series of recent floods is testimony enough. But the true scale of the change under way came home to me last summer, when I took a scouting trip up the Whitechuck River to see for myself if a serviceable way into the Glacier Peak Wilderness might still be found from the western slope of the Cascades. Glacier Peak, the only local volcanic summit that has eluded me, is the obvious choice of the three peaks on my circle as the object of a mountain pilgrimage. But I needed to find a direct route. To stay within the scope of my circle and to make for a feasible trip under my own power, I had to find a way in from the western slope. Even the popular Pacific Crest Trail that skirts the west flank of the mountain through Kennedy Hot Springs was taken out by the flood of 2003, as were the hot springs themselves, forcing a rerouting of the trail around the more arid, east side of the peak. As a result, the western half of this great swath of wilderness has been given an extended vacation from direct human contact. Since my pilgrimage would take place under my own power, anyway, I wanted to see if the damage to road and trail would permit passage by a determined traveler on foot.

Fellow Whidbey climbers Steve Scoles, Joel Shrut, and John Goertzel joined me on the exploratory trip. We came with mountain bikes, packs, and enough gear to bushwhack up the valley beyond the trailhead, hopefully all the way to Kennedy Hot

Springs. If we could make it that far, I figured, Glacier Peak might be within range after all. It had been four years since the flood when we arrived at the confluence of the Sauk and Whitechuck Rivers south of Darrington. We stopped at the ranger station in Darrington on our way out, where I learned that at the peak of that 2003 flood, here near the epicenter of the storm, the Whitechuck and Suiattle Rivers were running at roughly *twenty* times their average volume of flow.

Such a flow is hard to imagine, and the results, even four years out, were stunning to see. The immense steel girders and concrete foundations of the bridge that had crossed the Whitechuck lay slumped and buckled like Tinker Toys, just as the flood left them, with the banks of the river stripped away into the forest on both sides and the shattered carcasses of old-growth trees still piled up and over the collapsed remains of the bridge.

This was not a hopeful sign.

We followed the stem of the Whitechuck road to its barricade nine miles from the trailhead and got our second clue to what we were up against. It doesn't take much to close a road to cars—a small buckle in the pavement or a failed culvert. What we saw instead beyond the barricade was nothing but thin air. The road dropped off like the rim of a canyon, the whole side of the mountain gone, with the opposing rim of road hanging likewise against a chasm on the far side—a new river channel circling lazily through the lost mountainside. We sat with our legs dangling over the rim, weighing our options, and agog at the scale of the damage.

In the end, we dropped down the tattered edge of the chasm into the river bottom, fording the side channel with our bicycles and packs, rather than bushwhacking all the way above the slide through devil's club and vine maple thickets. We crossed two

other major road slides and a number of minor ones in the nine
miles it took to reach the trailhead. Along the way, we had the
eerie feeling that we were witnessing the aftermath of a nuclear
conflagration. Not a finger had been lifted to repair any of this
damage, and the veneer of human control and maintenance was
rapidly being reclaimed by nature. Evidence was everywhere of
wildlife species recolonizing the drainage—creatures that had
shunned this access route before the road was cut off. We saw
fresh bear scat in the road frequently, and twice came upon black
bears meandering up the road in front of us. Blown-down trees
blocked the road repeatedly, and young alders were springing up
in the road bed. The parking lot at the popular Whitechuck Trailhead, when we finally reached it, was already on its way back to
forest. The high-quality trailhead facilities looked lost in these
thickets, having seen few human hikers since the flood.

The trail itself into Kennedy Hot Springs was serviceable for
the first two miles, apart from the litter of downed limbs and
trees across the trail that had to be surmounted. Our goal was to
see if we could reach the old junction of the Pacific Crest Trail at
Kennedy Hot Springs, to assess if passage to the mountain might
still be possible beyond there. All along the deepening canyon of
the river, we saw chunks of mountain caved into a widened
riverbed, with immense logjams at every turn in the river. With
four miles still to go, the forested canyon steepened further, and
the trail along the river's edge disappeared for good. We made
camp at a side tributary, beyond which there was nothing but
sloughed mountainside. There will be no climb of Glacier Peak
during my year in circumference. It's Mount Baker or bust.

After setting up my tent, I left the others to wander out into
the carnage of the riverbed, which had been transformed into a
wide shelf of destruction through which the river now snaked,
confused and rudderless, among piles of truck-size boulders and

the stacked bodies of four-hundred-year-old conifers. It was the closest thing to an apocalypse I had ever seen, and I was awestruck. Standing up close to one such holocaust of trees, I was overcome by the sense that this was no random freak of nature. For the first time, I knew in my bones what the face of climate change looks like. I knew without a doubt that we are the ones who have done this. I myself have done this. The sum total of our human actions has blown this river apart. Out of view of the others, I fell against the shattered remains of a giant red cedar that had been ripped like a toothpick off the flanks of the mountain, and I wept.

CHAPTER 12

The Peaks of Circumference, Part 3

o   o   o

"The Weather Makes Its Own Mountain"

Why is it that when we are hanging from the cliff—beyond the
reach of civilization's safety net, rather than in it—we are most
likely to gain the deepest sense of what it is to be alive?

—GARY PAUL NABHAN,
Cultures of Habitat: On Nature, Culture, and Story

During his exploration of the North Pacific Coast, George
Vancouver recorded these impressions on April 30, 1792,
at first witnessing the solitary visage of a monumental
volcanic peak from far out in the Strait of Juan de Fuca:

About this time a very high conspicuous craggy mountain . . .
presented itself, towering above the clouds: as low down as
they allowed it to be visible it was covered with snow; and
south of it, was a long ridge of very rugged snowy mountains,
much less elevated, which seemed to stretch to a considerable

distance. . . . [T]he high distant land formed, as already observed, like detached islands, amongst which the lofty mountain, discovered in the afternoon by the third lieutenant, and
in compliment to him called by me Mount Baker, rose a very
conspicuous object . . . apparently at a very remote distance.[1]

If mountains symbolize permanence in the human psyche,
then a mountain that towers above all the others must be the
very essence of permanence. Lt. Joseph Baker of the British navy
received a slice of immortality himself by being the first on Vancouver's crew to spy the mountain that day, and he chose well.
What had been the Great White Watcher (Koma Kulshan) to the
local Lummi Tribe would go forward into the future simply as
Mount Baker, though no one ever asked the mountain's opinion
in the matter. Either way, there is no mistaking this mountain's
dominance over its surrounding landscape. My pilgrimage to
Mount Baker puts me in a long tradition of climbers who seek
union with this mountain by whatever name, drawn by its stunning beauty and regal air. That I am traveling all the way from sea
to summit under my own power builds a bridge between the hor-
izontal and vertical dimensions of the world I inhabit. According
to Snyder, mountains symbolize "verticality, spirit, transcendence,
resistance"—the essence of masculinity. Water symbolizes all that
is "wet, soft, dark, yielding, soulful, life-giving, shape-shifting"—
the essence of femininity. The two together make a whole, a con-
joining of the spiritual fruits of wisdom and compassion.[2] If all
goes well on this trip, I will receive an ample baptism in both.

In his *Mountains and Waters Sutra*, Dogen Zenji penned these
astonishing words that reach out to us now from a distance of
750 years: "The blue mountains are constantly walking."[3] What
was he thinking? Could he have possibly known how literally
true his statement would prove to be? Not until the 1960s did our

modern understanding of plate tectonics and seafloor spreading provide a scientific basis that corroborates Dogen's insights into the breadth and scale of our earth's impermanence, and our own radical interdependence with all of nature. The Great White Watcher, we now know, hasn't been watching for very long. The white cone toward which I am about to bend my will is a geologic infant, its summit dome less than 30,000 years old, built on the tattered bones of generations of earlier volcanoes that have long since walked off the world stage, torn down by those not-so-yielding waters. Range after range of mountains has risen up and fallen back into the earth across the Columbia Plateau over the past 40 million years, and that is just the current incarnation of swiftly walking mountains.[4]

o   o   o

IT DOESN'T MATTER if I make the summit or not, I remind myself. The mountain will have the last word, in any event. It matters that I try, that I fulfill my vow to journey to the highest point on my circle during this year in circumference. With the summer solstice behind me and other adventures pending, I can't wait any longer for the weather to break. The time has come for my reunion with Kulshan's high glaciers.

My plan is to bike from home to mountain along the foothills of the Central Cascades, follow the Skagit upriver from the timber town of Sedro-Woolley, then climb the southeast flank of the mountain along the Baker River drainage, ascending by logging road to the Boulder Glacier trailhead at an elevation of three thousand feet on the mountain. The Boulder is my most direct path to the summit from home, one of the steeper glaciers on the mountain, and less frequently climbed as a result. I have already been driven off that route once before by thunderstorms and am eager to give it another try.

I have to fudge the rules to make this work, because there is no way I can carry all my climbing gear on my bicycle. So I will rely on surrogate use of the car that will deliver the rest of my climbing party to the trailhead. I load basic camping gear onto my bicycle, but I leave my climbing pack—ice axe, crampons, harness, carabiners, rope, boots, stove, food, and all—in my garage to be picked up by Steve Scoles and Larry Rohan, who will fill out my rope team. Steve is a seasoned mountaineer who has been my companion on many climbs, a regular mountain goat, and a good friend. Larry is a new friend with less climbing experience, and it will be my first time with him in the mountains. Both are talented woodworkers and neighbors in the Maxwelton Valley.

We've chosen the Fourth of July weekend to attempt the climb. I leave two days ahead of the others by bicycle, with the hope that we'll all reach the trailhead about the same time. The weather forecast is less than ideal, with thunderstorms and periods of heavy rain predicted right up to our scheduled climbing day. But there is sun in the forecast after that. It is often said that mountains make their own weather, inducing storms on their higher flanks even when the weather is more benign in the lowlands. This is especially true of a solitary giant like Kulshan, so forecasts mean little, anyway.

After crossing to the mainland on the ferry, I ride north through Everett, then head northeast from Marysville toward the Cascades, passing into a semirural landscape that takes forever to shake free of its mantle of sprawl. Each of the rivers I cross is swollen to the gunwales with the combination of rain and snowmelt. I stop on the bridges over the Snohomish and Stillaguamish, mesmerized by the high volume of runoff, each river coursing along just shy of flood stage. They charge toward the sound like freighters at full throttle, dark with the flesh of the mountains in their veins, sweeping under the bridges with a bottled fury that sets my hair on edge. From Arlington, I slide north between rims of foothills along Highway 9, past Lake McMurray and Big Lake, riding through hidden valleys, hollows, and dairy farms that hint again at that earlier era of Northwest working landscapes. The traffic is blessedly slim on this stretch of the highway, and the creeks are frisky, cascading off the hillsides with a sudden roar as I pass. The early summer foliage is at its peak. I am awash in an emerald world.

At Big Rock I turn west off the highway toward Mount Vernon, through swollen wetlands and farmsteads toward my lodging for the night. I will stay with my friend Howard Shapiro, a high school teacher in Mount Vernon, who has invited our mutual friends Billie and Brad, hosts on my Skagit walk, to join us for dinner. It will be great to see them again and to build on this rich and growing connection I feel with the Skagit community.

Less than a mile from Howard's house, Swan Road turns sharply left and down, disappearing into a huge lake of flooded pastures. I nearly crash into the barricade that blocks the way forward. The road reemerges on the far side of the valley that is now a temporary inland sea. I have no idea how deep the lake is, but a quick check of the map shows that I will have to backtrack a dozen miles to reach Howard's house by an alternate route. My aching muscles groan at the prospect. I watch as a car drives up, turns, and retreats while I continue to weigh my options. Then a pickup truck with ultrahigh suspension stops to survey the flooded valley. A young man in coveralls gets out of the truck to scan the lake, gives me a knowing look, then climbs back into his cab and plunges into the water. I watch the truck slowly sink down to its scuppers, about three feet deep, reemerging slowly from the other side and driving off.

That's good enough for me. I'm more tired than I am proud, so I strip down to my underwear and start the long, cold slog across the shallow lake, lifting the rear of my bike as high as I can to keep my cargo dry, and balancing it forward on the front wheel. This will be a trip, if nothing else, that acquaints me with the many forms that water can take, from ocean to river, cloud-fall to flooded plains, snowfield to glacial ice. The water is frigid and comes up to my waist at the deepest point, but I feel smug and refreshed as I slowly emerge from the far side. I climb back into my pants and shoes. Within minutes, I am at Howard's house with a cold beer in my hand and a touch of local knowl-edge that I hadn't expected to acquire.

o o o

IN 2004, MY DAUGHTER KRISTIN and I took an intensive four-month course in snow and rock climbing techniques taught by the Everett Mountaineers. At the end of the course, to show our mastery of glacier techniques, we were dropped by climbing rope fifty feet into the bowels of a crevasse on the Easton Glacier of Mount Baker, then left on our own to get ourselves out. We'd heard stories of the climbers who were unprepared, disappear-ing into this cold palace of ice forever. If we couldn't get out of the crevasse by our own efforts using self-rescue prusik tech-niques, we failed the course. It is not an idle requirement. The heavy winter snows that consolidate over these crevasses, con-cealing icy depths, can collapse without warning under the weight of a rope team. Many climbers have been swallowed alive by this mountain as a result.

The volume of ice and snow on Mount Baker is greater than that of all other Cascade volcanoes combined, with the exception of Mount Rainier, so the glaciers here are large and deep. When my turn came, it was a sobering trip into that tomb of blue ice that yawned down into the unforgiving darkness below. The downward journey took me through hundreds of years of compressed annual snowfall, with the ice becoming a more condensed and translucent blue the farther I descended. By the time I came to a stop, hanging from my harness against the narrow walls of the crevasse, the ice was so dense that my crampons could gain no purchase on it. The bewitching beauty of this glacial underworld took my breath away, and as I got my bearings, my initial fear transformed into a crystalline formation of awe. It was a long and exhausting trip back to the surface of the glacier, a few inches to the pull as I slid my prusik knots slowly up the rope with each transfer of body weight from one prusik to the other. I became fascinated by the changing texture and hue of the ice as I worked my way up through the decades toward the present season of snow. Once I knew I was going to make it, I gave myself over to studying the character of the ice that now holds so much of our future human destiny in its frozen grip.

Three percent of earth's water is currently in freshwater forms. All the rest inhabits the depths of the saline ocean. Of that precious film of freshwater, over two-thirds is bound up in glaciers and ice caps, most of it in Greenland and Antarctica. It is now well documented that this storehouse of glacial ice is melting fast because of climate change. All forty-seven North Cascade glaciers are currently experiencing "ubiquitous, rapid and increasing" retreat, according to the North Cascade Glacier Climate Project.[5] That includes the eleven glaciers on Mount Baker, which have all been in retreat since 1984. Orwell would be proud.

A glacier is a frozen river flowing slowly down the slopes of a mountain. The steeper the slope, the faster the ice flows and the more it fractures to form the open crevasses that create such a danger to climbers. Glaciers form when more snow falls in the winter than melts in the summer. The residual snowpack is then buried by successive annual snows, placing it under increasing pressure that changes its crystalline structure until the glacial ice is nine times denser than the original snow that fell on the surface. It is this density that gives glaciers their stunning clarity and blue color. In Greenland and Antarctica, there are ice fields that are deeper than Mount Baker is tall, concealing in their ancient buried ice a history of climate, precipitation, and temperature spanning over 400,000 years. The difference in texture between summer and winter snow creates layers similar to marine sediment. These layers allow for precise dating of the ice. Air bubbles trapped in the layers are time capsules of atmospheric composition as well and have verified that atmospheric CO_2 and methane are higher today than at any other time in the past 400,000 years.[6]

I have more than a mountain's summit on my mind, therefore, as I ride toward the northern circumference of my circle. This mountain has seen ice ages come and go. It will accept without complaint whatever the climate dishes up now. The mountain doesn't care whether it remains clothed in a mantle of ice. It will move into its own future confidently, with or without human witnesses, accepting its ultimate demise with the same equanimity that it now accepts a changing climate. I take solace in this kinship of the long view I have received from these mountains. I am part climber and part pilgrim, hoping some of the mountain's equanimity will rub off on me.

o o o

SEDRO-WOOLLEY IS ONE of the strangest names for a town that I've ever run across. It grew out of the union of two dueling pioneer towns that refused to give up either of their names, coming together where the Skagit River spills out of its narrow upper valley onto the sprawling delta. The town wears its timbered past as a badge of honor, and on this Fourth of July morning, there is no holding back its patriotic fervor.

The annual parade is just getting started as I cross the bridge over the Skagit, then turn east up the valley on my final approach to the mountain. I fall in behind a platoon of flag-waving cowgirls on horseback, and pickup trucks festooned in red, white, and blue banners. The sun is shining through broken clouds as I ease my way through town with the parade, enjoying the sweetness of this unabashed display of affection for country. It is hard to imagine a more iconic expression of American idealism than Sedro-Woolley has dished up today, and I come away smiling.

I have mountain fever now, and a long way to go, so I don't linger with the festivities for long. I break off from the parade, seeking side roads along the river. I stop at a tiny café in Hamilton for the heartiest burger and fries I've had in years, a place decades removed from the busier towns along the highway. Hamilton cleaves to its purchase on the river with the faintest of handholds, as if it will be swept away for good by the next rise of time's floodwaters. Young children playing in the dusty streets approach me on my bicycle with un-self-conscious curiosity, wide-eyed inhabitants of another place in time. As I wend my way deeper into the valley, the surging waters of the Skagit scour at the highest parts of its banks, sucking tree limbs underwater, the river's restless spirit churning past in wide eddies.

At Concrete, I head north up the Baker River drainage, and the grade steepens. I am on the lower flanks of the mountain now. I gain elevation gradually for another twenty miles, then head up the mountain in earnest when I cross the Boulder River Bridge. The last five miles of my ride are on logging roads that switchback relentlessly up the mountain toward tree line, dead-ending where a giant hemlock has fallen across the road just shy of the remote trailhead. My bicycle odometer reads 115 miles when I arrive, almost double the distance from home as the crow flies. No cars are here, and only one other climbing party has signed in on the trail register so far this year, a group that came through two weeks earlier and failed to make the summit. It is the Fourth of July weekend, and I have the entire east flank of the mountain to myself. I slump down, exhausted, on the edge of the roadway to wait for my companions and give myself over to a serious nap.

An hour later, I wake to the sound of a pickup grinding up the steep grade of the gravel road. Steve and Larry pull to a stop with big grins on their faces, two hours ahead of nightfall, and we get right down to business. The weather has been improving all day, giving glimpses of the mountain through breaks in the clouds. As we sort through our gear, Steve and Larry decide to bet on the improving weather, leaving their tents and some extra clothing behind so that they can go light and bivouac on the mountain.

I'm not so sure. I resolve to take a heavier pack, keeping my small tent and more backup clothing on board. We cook a quick dinner on the truck tailgate as we arrange our gear and reconnoiter with the maps. Steve was with me on our failed attempt on this route four years earlier, so we both have a visual picture of the approach to the glacier. There is one fairly challenging rock pitch that mounts the lip of the glacier itself, but otherwise it is straightforward. Tired as I am, I share their eagerness to hit the trail with whatever daylight remains.

It feels good to set out on foot, after so many miles of peddling on my bicycle. Even the heavy pack feels solid and comforting on my shoulders, rooting my body into the ground with each step. Within moments, we have passed the veil into primeval old-growth forest, fast on the heels of the receding winter snows that still linger at this low altitude in patches on the forest floor. Freshly blooming dwarf dogwood and trillium flowers line the trail. I think there is nothing lovelier in the whole world than a thick scarf of dwarf dogwood wrapping the base of an old-growth tree in spring, unless it is the piercing trill of a hermit thrush slicing through the wall of silence in the forest. This evening, we are graced with both. Even at three thousand feet, the conifers are gigantic. We pass stands of hemlock and red cedar seven feet in diameter. In failing light, we prepare a makeshift camp just off the trail, less than two miles into the forest. I am asleep as soon as my head hits the pillow.

o o o

IN THE MORNING, we wake to the penetrating hammer of a pileated woodpecker working a dead snag, the sound echoing across the forest. I feel as if I have traveled a thousand miles through the mysterious country called sleep. A thick and misty fog envelops me as I step outside my tent, sending shivers through my sleep-warmed body. We boil water for a hasty breakfast of oatmeal and tea, packing our gear ahead of the rain that seems sure to follow.

By the time we are back on the trail, the mist has indeed given way to rain, and the trail has given way to snow. We are now navigating by dead reckoning and by compass, without the evidence of a trail to guide us. Our memories from the last time around offer scant assistance in the absence of a trail. We pick our way through ravines that have begun to shed themselves of forest, and we leave the forest behind for good when we mount the final ridge that will bring us up to the lip of the Boulder Glacier. It is raining hard and steady now. We travel in silence, no one wanting to name the discouragement we are all feeling.

The ridge narrows as we climb, falling steeply off to the left into a wide chasm of snow and scoured rock that rises to a far ridge shrouded in fog, the bones of the mountain left naked by the recent departure of receding glacial ice. On the right, we angle toward a vertical rock wall that we must soon ascend to reach the glacier. Steve and I compare notes, confirming that the configurations of landscape add up to the intended route. At the top of the ridge, a small bergschrund has formed where the snowfield has melted away from the rock face, leaving a precipitous gap between opposing walls of snow and rock. This we manage without difficulty. I know we are on track when I spot the climbing rope that has been set in place here by wilderness climbing rangers. The rock face presents a single pitch of Class 5 climbing, made extra-slick today by the rainwater coursing down its face. The rain intensifies as we fasten ourselves to the rope one by one and start up.

At the top, we pull ourselves over a lip of rock and snow that slopes up to the glacier. This is where the real climb begins. We huddle under a tarp rigged from a hummock of gnarled spruce, heating water for soup and tea. The glacier above is lost in deep clouds, and we have seen no trace of the upper mountain all morning. Larry's antiquated leather boots are soaked through. A raw wind has kicked up, and the chill is starting to penetrate. Without a change in the weather, we have at best two or three hours to work with. To spend the night here in these conditions, without proper tents and wet as we are, would mean almost certain hypothermia. *How could we have been so cavalier?* I think. We are ill-equipped for this weather, and the choice is no longer in our hands.

"The weather makes its own mountain," Steve mutters in discouragement, accidentally getting the order of the words reversed. Maybe the chill is starting to get to him. The mountain's capacity to make its own weather is legendary in these parts. But Steve has it right, also. Ultimately, it is the weather that will tear this mountain down, like every mountain before it. Water that flows always downward, seeking the lowest places, following the paths of least resistance, will finally have its way with the mountain. Even the last strongholds of ice hanging on the highest flanks of the mountain will give way to the pull of gravity and the heat of the sun. It is happening as we speak.

Maybe it is appropriate, here at the halfway point of my year in circumference, that I should find myself stranded midway between sea and summit, banished from the mountaintop, and at the mercy of the weather. Maybe it is appropriate that this "failure" should be at least in part due to our own negligence. We were in too much of a hurry. We couldn't be bothered to make the most prudent choices. We wanted to get up and down the mountain as fast as possible. And now our options have been whittled down to one. We have to retreat. Steve and Larry are on tight schedules, so we don't have the luxury of waiting out the weather down below to try again.

We sit out the rain until midafternoon, the latest point from which a return to the trailhead by dark is still possible, and it continues without relent. It is time to let go of my dream of traveling from home to summit under my own power. We quietly gather our packs together and move back to the edge of the cliff. One by one, we fasten ourselves to the rope with the rappel devices on our harnesses and drop over the edge, rappelling down the slippery rock face to the bottom of the pitch. Buffeted by shards of mist sailing on the wind, we retrace our steps down the long snowfield toward a distant canopy of forest.

It is almost dark when we reach the trailhead and load our soaking gear into the back of the pickup. We cook dinner on the tailgate for the second night in a row, eating in somber silence. Then Steve and Larry climb in the cab and drive off. It is strange to watch them go as the darkness closes in, knowing I still have a long ride ahead of me in the morning. I crawl into the tent I've set up in the middle of the road. "I signed up for this?" I think, as the rain pelts against the rain fly on my tent. "I never thought it was going to be easy." With my companions gone, I'm keenly aware of how alone I am on the flank of the mountain, miles from any other human as the surrounding forest slides into darkness.

In the warmth of my sleeping bag, I let myself fall under the spell of the rain, and it soon sings me to sleep. Summit or no, this year is only a beginning. This night is just another night, and the path is more important than the destination. Whatever I accomplish or fail to accomplish during this year in circumference, humility is called for. I am one person doing the best I can to face an uncertain future with honesty.

o o o

By morning, the rain has tapered off to a light mist, though the mountain is still buried in clouds. I'm awake at first light and eager to descend to the warmer temperatures in the valley. I pack my gear and am under way with only a quick snack to hold me through to breakfast. My hands cramp from the sustained effort to keep my speed in check down the miles of steep and rough gravel road. I pass rapidly back through the seasons, from late winter to midsummer. A broadening palette of aromas from the forest clue me in to the growing richness of the understory as I drop in elevation. In a matter of minutes, I pass from the equivalent sea-level ecology of Southeast Alaska to that of Puget Sound.

By the time I reach the town of Concrete, I have cashed in most of the elevation gain and am back on the floor of the Skagit Valley. I stop for breakfast at a roadside diner and watch as cyclists pass by singly and in bunches while I eat. The Skagit's long and lovely flood plain penetrates the North Cascades all the way to Marblemount before it narrows and begins to climb, so it has become a Mecca for road bikers on training runs. I'm surprised to see this much bicycle company so far up the valley.

Well greased with flapjacks and sausages, I head upriver to-ward Rockport, where the Skagit's main tributary, the Sauk, adds its ample volume of flow to the river. I will take a different route home, tracing the Sauk upriver as far as Darrington, then turn-ing seaward again along the North Fork of the Stillaguamish for another twenty-five miles into Arlington. When I reach Rock-port, I stop to rest at Steelhead Park by the confluence of these two great rivers. Watching the currents, I notice an elderly woman with a walker who seems to be making her way ever so slowly in my direction, one determined step at a time. Sure enough, I do end up being the object of her mission. When she reaches me, she pauses for breath, then points toward my tail-light, which is flashing a staccato red. "How does that thing work?" she asks, then runs me through my paces on the gear I have strapped to my pannier, the shifting mechanisms on my handlebars, and how my speedometer measures my speed. Sat-isfied with my answers, she peers back at the parking lot, where another group of cyclists has just rolled in. She gestures in their direction and says, "It's starting to look like China around here."

That draws a good chuckle, and she laughs along with me. "I wouldn't have thought of it like that," I say, "but you've got a point." She eases down onto the bench next to me, and we watch the river go by for a time, basking in the shade of cottonwoods and a cool breeze blowing down through the Sauk Valley. In point of fact, this trickle of recreational cyclists is a far cry from the hordes of bicycles that fill the cities of China today. It is an anom-aly of the Fourth of July weekend. The supremacy of cars here in America is hardly under threat from the original mechanical horse. But even here in Rockport, a stronghold of conservative, working-class America, the culture is palpably changing. While my attention has been elsewhere, a new bicycle boom got under way in this country, and it is gaining steam. This time around, with soaring gas prices and climate instability adding air to its tires, our latest bike boom is showing no signs of going bust.

Sunlight filtering through the forest complements the sound of flowing water as I ride the Sauk's meandering floodplain for twenty miles into Darrington, past its confluence with the Suiattle River. At the Sauk-Suiattle Indian Reservation, yet another new ceremonial longhouse stands proudly near the highway saying, "We are still here. We aren't going anywhere." The Sauk Prairie was home to a thriving Native culture prior to European contact, and I can see why as I cross the naturally open flats at Darrington into the headwaters of the Stillaguamish River. I follow its lovely rural valley west to Arlington for twenty-five miles, beneath the high buttress of Whitehorse Mountain and the Boulder River Wilderness rising steeply from the south bank of the river.

My goal for the night is Arlington, but the motels are all out by the freeway, and I am on a roll. It is a gorgeous evening, and I am feeling a strength I didn't know I had. I decide to push on toward Everett, following the setting sun as it drops toward the far Olympics. Two hours later I am on the ferry from Mukilteo back to Whidbey Island. Mount Baker is still lost in the clouds of its own creation, but here on Possession Sound, it is the full glory of a summer eve. I ride the last four miles from the ferry to my home in a daze of satisfied exhaustion, climbing the long hill that has become my regular companion, then coasting down into my beloved Maxwelton Valley. From the first break of sunrise to the last glimmers of sunset, I have been on my bicycle, working, as the farmers used to say, "from can't-see to can't-see."

I may not have made the summit this time, but I have been to the mountain. I have received as always its good and forthright counsel. Now, with no more fuel than the calories derived from three ordinary meals, I have covered 115 miles of hard terrain in a single day of biking, getting closer to the country that lies between the mountain and my home than I ever have before. That's good fuel economy, and a damn fine use of a beautiful summer's day.

SECTION 3   ○   THE PADDLE

It is hard to devise a definition for sea mammal that does not make the Aleut a specimen. When the naturalist Georg Steller, who accompanied Vitus Bering to Alaska in 1741, saw his first Aleut, a man kayak-shaped below the waist, sea-lioned and bird-feathered above, with sun-darkened face and bone in nose, the naturalist was seeing a new species.

—KENNETH BROWER, *The Starship and the Canoe*

CHAPTER 13

Crossing an Uncharted Sea

o   o   o

The reinvention of daily life means marching off the edge of our maps.

—BOB BLACK, *The Abolition of Work and Other Essays*

I have been three days on the paddle when I reach Hope Island in Skagit Bay. The steady swish and swing of the stroke is gradually taking residence in my body, like a physical chant that pulls my mind to the margins of time. I am too immersed in the repetition to notice how monotonous it is. In the ancient logic of travel across water, reverie seems to win out over boredom in the end. Small things reach out to grab and hold my attention—the pattern of tiny eddies from each paddle stroke as they recede into my wake, the lift and sway of the kayak in the choppy waters, the tide rips that keep my senses alert.

Deception Pass is right around the corner, where Skagit Bay gives out into open water, and the current can clock eight knots at peak tide going through the pass. The narrow neck between Hope Island and Ala Spit offers my first clue that the acceleration of current has begun. The long reach of Whidbey Island acts as a sheltering arm around the shallow waters of Skagit Bay, where the outflow of the Skagit River runs head-on into some of the strongest tides in the Puget Sound basin. These waters are unpredictable and dangerous, and this is my first time through on the paddle, so I am doubly alert. It is a lonely stretch, buffered by the river's wide tidal estuary. It is here that the gently rolling mounds of glacial till from the south sound give way to the dramatic granite topography of the San Juan archipelago. And it is around the corner in Cornet Bay, just shy of the pass, that I will stop for the night, sleeping once again aboard my thirty-two-foot salmon gill-netter *Martina*.

My journey by kayak began at Possession Point on the south end of Whidbey Island, at a launch near my home, and it has taken three days to paddle the full length of the island, dissecting by water the route I took on foot through the Skagit basin earlier this year. Catching the last of the flood tide at first light this morning in its northward push up Saratoga Passage, I rounded Strawberry Point into Skagit Bay right at slack tide, just in time to catch the ebb's northward retreat, working both halves of the tide to my advantage. This opposing pulse of tide acts like an accordion here, flowing in with the flood from north and south simultaneously to collide in turbulent confusion at Strawberry Point, then retreating again toward opposite ends of the island during the ebb. I've timed my passage to get the best of both, and already by late morning, I've covered twenty miles from Daya and Shanti's house at Race Lagoon, where I took lodging for the night. Deception Pass is right around the corner.

I've shifted my focus for the next month from the spoke to the paddle, in a planned circumnavigation of Puget Sound, beginning with this two-hundred-mile journey by paddle from Whidbey to Vancouver Island and back to witness a coastwide Native canoe rendezvous. This morning, I've covered a stretch of water that is unfamiliar to me, and I've had to recalibrate my position in the home landscape yet again. I've been tricked more than once into false assumptions about my position and course. Crescent Harbor beckoned like a siren song in the morning mist, offering a false promise of passage, while my true way forward lay hidden behind Utsalady Point, on Camano Island. There is no marked path here on the water, no road to follow, just the ever-shifting pattern of wind-driven waves and tidal currents on the water. Even the solid line of the island's shore melts hauntingly into the fogbanks before I can be sure of my bearings. Beyond the island's edge, looking east across the Skagit flats, I can discern no shoreline at all, just a distant expanse of mudflats and salt marsh that morphs mysteriously into far mountains with no clear line of demarcation. I can hardly believe that the Tang Dynasty scroll I am paddling through this morning is the same landscape I have inhabited for fifty years.

I've been surprised by the scarcity of waterfowl here in a tidal estuary made just for them. I've passed only a handful of pigeon guillemots, a pair of Western grebes, and a single marbled murrelet. Their absence is unsettling. The numbers of grebes have plummeted around the sound in recent years, and the marbled murrelet is now so scarce that it has been listed as Endangered in Puget Sound. Farther up the coast, where the tidewater old growth crucial to their nesting still abounds, the companionable murrelet is everywhere, its soft, plaintive call a fixture in the soundscape of these inland waters. Today I am keenly aware of how much I miss these birds, how much less alive this place feels without them.

Harbor seals, on the contrary, are thriving here, their numbers growing under the shield of the Marine Mammal Protection Act. Their heads pop up randomly around my kayak, like small, curious periscopes circling warily in my wake. I watch them slant-ways, avoiding the eye contact that makes them slide back beneath the waves. Occasionally, a seal surfaces directly in front of me, ignorant of my approach, only to explode back beneath the water in a cannon shot of shock that leaves my heart pumping, too. A pod of harbor porpoises cruises past my boat, their small bodies emitting soft exhalations as they sound and dive. The silence of my approach that brings me so close to these marine animals and to their elusive voices in the soundscape is one of the joys of traveling by paddle, offering a more direct encounter with the life of this coast.

o o o

THE MAP OF PUGET SOUND that hangs in my office back home contains detailed topographical information about the terrain I have been exploring this year, with one glaring exception. In an effort to highlight the American topography, my map goes suddenly blank beyond the Canadian border, with only a faint outline of the islands and coastline stretching north into British Columbia. My circle cuts over the southeast corner of Vancouver Island, yet the map on my wall offers no clue that the city of Victoria dwells in that place and is part of my circle, too. If this map is to be believed, the terrain beyond the border consists of nothing but flat and featureless ice. What renders it blank in our contemporary American imagination is an arbitrary line drawn on the map in 1846, settling the disputed boundary between British and American territories on the Northwest Coast. The terrain north of that line today is, for practical purposes, irrelevant to many of the people who live south of it, hence the curious amnesia on my map.

The Oregon Treaty of 1846 dealt yet another bewildering blow to the Native people who had inhabited this transboundary region as one coherent homeland for centuries. Overnight, it became illegal for Salish tribes to venture onto much of their traditional summer fishing grounds or to sustain familial ties with extended tribal clans who were now officially defined as illegal aliens.

I grew up on the U.S. side of the border, taking this cultural and geographic amnesia for granted. Even as a commercial fisherman, in my annual migration between Puget Sound and Southeast Alaska, I tend to view the vast Canadian coast as little more than a scenic backdrop, terrain to be merely gotten through on the way to my business that lies always north and south of its broad borders.

I love this map for the intimate topographical detail it offers of the Puget Sound basin, yet its strange demarcation of land beyond the border has wiped the cities of Victoria and Vancouver completely off the map, replaced by a uniform white labeled simply "Canada."

Boundaries can be useful things, giving our lives a scope that we can manage and comprehend. We build fences around our homes, and borders around our nations, to give some sense of order and containment to our lives. But in so doing, we can also imprison our thinking, becoming blind and even hostile toward what lies beyond the arbitrary lines we have drawn. I'm aware that my own home circle this year can cut both ways. It has been a terrific tool for focusing my attention on the place at hand and holding my feet to the home fire. But "home" is never fully what it seems. It is always shape-shifting, spilling over the lines we've drawn, opening new layers of complexity that force us to reexamine its meaning in our lives. The obvious symbolism of exclusion that is written into my map offers clues to the limitations that are built into my thinking as well. For practical purposes, my sense of what constitutes home territory stops squarely at the Canadian border. What was once a continuous cultural and ecological unit, a seamless Salish Sea, now lies sundered into separate foreign countries that have only a limited sense of shared bioregional identity. No doubt, that blank spot on the map lies on the south side of the border, from the Canadian point of view.

My destination on this kayak trip lies across multiple boundaries, including the one that separates past and present. By pure coincidence, I will cross the Canadian border in Haro Strait at the very place where the international boundary intersects with my home circle. By crossing over onto the blank part of the map that hangs on my office wall, I will be passing outside my home circle for the first time this year, even as I am entering a literal foreign country. I will be leaving the waters that are known and familiar to me, entering an almost mythic landscape. The map on my wall would have us believe that this boundary line through the strait is hard and fast. But nothing sticks to the water. There is no trace of it out here in the real world. The Native peoples who were here before us never bought into this definition of home. With extended tribal clans and deep cultural roots still lying on both sides of the border, the Coast Salish people have taken to the paddle once again to reassert their symbolic claim on the full reach of the Salish Sea.

I am crossing these boundaries with them, one paddle stroke at a time, to witness the convergence on Vancouver Island of over one hundred native seagoing canoes that will be arriving from villages up and down the coast, helping to revive an ancient canoe culture that had been given up for dead by the mid-twentieth century. As with the resurgent Native longhouse tradition, the great cedar canoes that once roamed this coast from Southeast Alaska to Northern California are making a comeback, both as a symbolic link with the past and as a living vessel for transporting these cultures into the future. Conceived

as an initiatory rite for Native youth in 1989, these "tribal journeys" have grown in scale and stature, with a different host village each year. This summer, the canoe rendezvous is being
hosted by the Cowichan (Quw'utsun) First Nation on the Canadian side of the Salish Sea.

The fact that this event is taking place outside my circle only
increases its appeal as the object of my first kayaking pilgrimage.
It is in the spirit of the occasion that I should be willing to leave
my home waters, joining canoes that have in many cases jour-
neyed much farther from home than I have, in an effort to stitch
the ancient culture of this coast back together again. While I am
not a member of any tribe and will take no formal part in the ceremonies, I offer this journey by paddle as a gesture of respect for
the resilience these Native traditions bring to our wider culture,
by traveling with them in spirit all the way from home under my
own power.

This is also a chance for me to claim these waters as my own
in a new way. Nowhere is the gap in my local knowledge more
conspicuous than here on the water. Compared with my knowledge of Alaska, where I've spent decades as a commercial fisherman and sea-kayaking guide building a deep, practical
intimacy with its coastal ecology, my knowledge of the Salish
Sea remains superficial, even though I spend a majority of my
time here. Growing up in an already-depleted Puget Sound, I've
taken this gap in knowledge for granted, seeing it as an unfortunate consequence of relative plenty and loss. At the intersection of natural resources and livelihood, Alaska still has what
Puget Sound had in its "youth," but has no longer. The sound's
beleaguered salmon runs, its growing toxic legacy, its urban
sprawl, and its congested waterways do not stack up well against
Alaska by any measure of ecological health. Through all my years

as a migratory animal moving back and forth with the seasons between Alaska and Puget Sound, I've accepted these imbalances as a given.

I can accept them no longer, not without a fight, at least. For starters, I see these losses in my home region more clearly now with the perspective of years. In remarkably short order, the natural abundance we inherited from Native peoples here has been squandered, leaving us groping ever farther up the coast for that stream of natural resources. More to the point, the myth that we can continuously flee from loss to plenty by targeting yet-unspoiled regions is being punctured by our climate crisis. Climate change is the great truth-teller of our age, and Alaska's "pristine" northern ecology is under greater threat from global warming than the more temperate climates to the south. My willingness to separate home and livelihood by a thousand miles, under these old assumptions, no longer feels like an act of reason.

What better occasion than a regionwide Native canoe rendezvous to reconnect with what is most enduring about my own home waters? Again, I am inspired by the refusal of Native peoples here to accept as permanent this degraded status. Something in the audacity of their acts of cultural self-reclamation makes it mandatory for me to attend.

CHAPTER 14

A New Species of
Marine Mammal

o   o   o

What might happen if some of those who now turn inward, apprenticing themselves to all kinds of gurus, therapists, and Web-masters, would turn outward as apprentices to other species?

—GARY PAUL NABHAN,
Cultures of Habitat: On Nature, Culture, and Story

I am a sea-kayak guide part of each year, so I have an economic stake in my craft as a paddler. But like virtually all of my contemporary kayaking enthusiasts, I do it mostly for fun. No one is paying me to go on this trip. In fact, I'm losing precious income by giving time to this exploration. I'm not out hunting, as in ages past, to gather food for my family, with starvation as a consequence if I fail. If anything, the lack of a contemporary connection between the paddle and the hunt reflects a strange new blindness that has crept into our core concepts of craft, leisure, and livelihood.

It is easy to forget, in the heat of our current global commerce, that the Salish Sea long stood at the heart of one of the world's greatest canoe cultures. And it is by paddle that one can still most directly taste the sound's lingering wild spirit. In the words of Steven C. Brown, "the dugout canoe was synonymous with life—a way of life that enfolded the canoe into nearly every aspect of daily living.... Without the development of sea-going watercraft, the peoples of the Northwest Coast would have lived a marginal existence devoid of many of the characteristics that we associate with the wealth and artistry of their world."[1] The Haidas, centered in the Queen Charlotte Islands (Haida Gwai), were the acknowledged masters of canoe building. Even the Tlingit Indians of Southeast Alaska, the fierce and powerful tribe to the north, agreed that it was in Haida Gwai that Raven first taught humans to build canoes.[2] It is nearly impossible from the vantage of our contemporary culture to imagine the level of dependence, craftsmanship, skill, and mythic importance embodied in these vessels.

No part of the Northwest Coast was more populous prior to European contact than the Salish Sea—stretching from Puget Sound north through Georgia Strait and out to the Pacific along the Strait of Juan de Fuca. It was through this stretch of temperate coastline that great stands of western red cedar grew, sometimes reaching fifteen feet in diameter, from which an oceangoing canoe of sixty feet in length could be carved from a single section of tree. The result, in Brown's words, was vessels "that were both beautiful in form and perfect in function."[3] Some have suggested that European exposure to the Nootkan canoe design on the outer coast of Vancouver Island inspired the development of faster, sleeker clipper ships in the mid-nineteenth century, accelerating the expansion of global commerce and trade.[4] The cultures that perfected these superb vessels roamed the coast from Southeast Alaska to the Columbia River and sometimes as far south as Northern California, in missions of trade, warfare, and cultural expansion as well as hunting. It was not unusual to paddle sixty miles out into the stormy waters of the North Pacific on whaling and sealing hunts.

Although Raven might disagree, it is not known when the first canoes were built, or what they looked like, though oral histories among all the tribes suggest that the first human inhabitants on the Northwest Coast arrived by watercraft. Direct archeological evidence in bone and stone from Southeast Alaska confers an antiquity of human habitation at least nine thousand years before the present, and some archeologists push the likely beginnings to well before that, perhaps as long as twenty thousand years ago, as Asian tribes worked their way around the northern Pacific Rim by skin boat or wooden canoe.[5]

The tribes of the Northwest Coast arguably took their artistic culture to a higher level than any other hunter-gatherer culture in the world. In the thin and rocky lowlands squeezed between mountain and sea, these tribes practiced no agriculture at all, which is usually associated with the development of high art. What these people had instead was a staggering natural abundance of food that, with the help of the canoe, made possible a similar kind of leisure-based artistic culture. And the canoe itself became one of the highest expressions of their art, even as it made possible the leisure that could produce such works of art. A summary of the diet of Northwest Coast Native cultures, rendered here by the legendary Haida carver Bill Reid, paints a picture of this astonishing abundance. But it is an abundance that would have been largely impossible without the great canoes:

In a few weeks, men could gather enough salmon to last a year. Shellfish grew thick on the rocks and sandy bottoms; halibut carpeted the shelf floor; . . . sea lion and sea otter, seal and whale and porpoise were everywhere, and all flesh was meat.

In the early spring the rivers swarmed with oolichan, the magic
fish of the north coast, ninety percent oil and, to those who
knew it well, fragrant, delicious oil to enhance the flavor of
dried salmon and halibut, to mix with dried berries, to flavor
stew, and, though they did not know this, to provide most of
the stored nutrients necessary for life in the too-often sunless
seasons. There were nettle roots and water lily roots and sea-
weeds, gull eggs, black bear, grizzly bear, deer, and much more,
right there for the taking. If the sea hunt were unsuccessful or
smoked fish ran out before the new season arrived, mussels
were a dark blue mantle on almost any rock, cockles lay exposed at low tide, abalone and rock oysters could be found
with little effort, tide pools yielded delicate sea urchins, the
octopus could be flushed from his cave, and clams lay under
most beaches. Even today, only a stupid man could starve on
this coast, and today is not as it was.[6]

Canoes connected seasonal food-gathering sites far removed
from each other and carried the clans and needed supplies to
seasonal camps through sometimes extreme ocean conditions.
As Brown has suggested, "canoes were the vital kingpins that
made such an existence possible . . . the bridge between the
wealth of the sea and the reality of life."[7]

As a commercial fisherman and sea-kayaking guide, I like to
think that I'm reasonably well informed about coastal ecology in
this region. But Reid's claim that "only a stupid man could starve
on this coast" has always made me nervous. I wonder what kind
of smarts I would show if I had to survive exclusively on what is
to be found here. Interrupt the global food supply chain for more
than a few weeks, and the ranks of the "stupid" among today's
Puget Sound population would be legion, and starvation rampant. Most of us would not have a clue what to look for, or where

to begin looking, and I'm not sure I would fare much better. As I paddle today past the traditional grounds of the Swinomish people, in a fiberglass kayak imported from Britain and with food on board from Trader Joe's, I wonder what my chances of survival would be if I were thrown back onto this place as a source of complete livelihood. I might find myself standing with everyone else on thin ice indeed.

o o o

So it is with more than a passing interest in the fate of this canoe culture that I have set my sights on the First Nation of Cowichan Bay on Vancouver Island. And it is with more than a recreational interest in kayaking that I have chosen to travel the entire distance by paddle, one hundred miles each way. The days when such a journey was routine along this coast are barely a century behind us. The ancestors of these canoe pullers would hardly be impressed by this feat. I wouldn't impress the growing tribe of extreme kayakers, either, who might see this as little more than a warm-up to a major ocean crossing. But it feels like a big deal to me, and I am actually fairly nervous.

I will be joined tomorrow in Anacortes by my daughter Kristin and two other experienced paddlers, Jay Thomas and Robin Clark, for the crossings of Rosario and Haro Straits through the San Juan Islands and into Canadian waters. Robin, a coastal restoration activist, rowed a small dory last summer all the way from Ketchikan, Alaska, to Anacortes, Washington, a distance of six hundred miles.

Even Robin's epic trip would have been considered routine by the fierce warring cultures of the North Coast. Here on Whidbey Island, for example, the grave of Col. Isaac Ebey tells a grim story of the prowess of this canoe culture. Following the murder of a Haida chief in the Queen Charlotte Islands by whites from Puget

Sound, a war canoe set out from Haida Gwai on a mission of revenge in 1857. According to their strict code of justice, retribu-
tion had to be exacted against a person of equal rank in the
offending tribe. Paddling six hundred miles south to Puget
Sound, the Haida party searched for an appropriate white *tyee*,
or chief, and chose Colonel Ebey as their man. The first permanent white settler on Whidbey Island, Ebey had the unfortunate
distinction of being the prosecuting attorney for the early Whidbey community. That was good enough for the Haida warriors.
On a hot August evening, they beached their canoe at Ebey's
Landing, raided Ebey's home during a dinner party, and exacted
their revenge. They murdered and beheaded the island patriarch
in front of his wife and guests, then took his head in the canoe
as a trophy and paddled the length of the coast back up to Haida
Gwai. Such cycles of revenge and counter-revenge were a fact of
life among Northwest Coast tribes prior to contact, and the sight
of an approaching war canoe from a rival tribe must have been
a fearsome thing to behold.

Our own repressive policies toward aboriginal peoples in both
Canada and the United States in the late nineteenth and early
twentieth centuries were every bit as brutal, stripping tribes not
only of their lands, but also of their languages, ceremonies, and
other traditions. The advent of new economies and engine-powered boats dealt the final blow to this canoe culture, dooming it
to near-extinction. As Brown has observed, "one by one the grand
vessels that helped to make the Northwest Coast cultures what
they were fell before the ravages of time."[8]

o   o   o

THE CURRENT RENAISSANCE in Northwest Coast canoe culture
began when a Makah sealing canoe made the transboundary
trip from Neah Bay on the Olympic Peninsula to Port Renfrew on

Vancouver Island in 1976. In 1989, the "Paddle to Seattle" brought nineteen traditional canoes from as far away as Bella Bella in northern British Columbia and the Quileute Nation on the Pacific Coast of Washington, the first modern revival of a large-scale potlatch gathering by canoe. The Makah Nation's first gray whale hunt by canoe in over seventy years occurred in 1999, generating enormous international controversy and worldwide media attention. The success of this hunt gave a new stature to the Makah Nation among indigenous communities around the world and helped spread the canoe revival to other Northwest Coast tribes. The few remaining canoe builders with knowledge of the old techniques began helping other tribes build the first modern versions of traditional cedar dugout canoes, to go with a growing fleet made with modern materials like fiberglass. Yet even the best modern carvers must reinvent the ancient art of canoe building. None of the modern canoes have yet risen to the level of craftsmanship and performance achieved by a lost generation of master carvers, who took many secrets of construction and design with them to their graves.[9]

Still, the canoe culture in its modern manifestation has made a remarkable recovery, and the international rendezvous that began with the Paddle to Seattle twenty years ago has become an annual event of great significance to tribal communities along the North Coast. This year's "Tribal Journey" to Cowichan Bay will include over one hundred canoes from up and down the coast. A decade into the twenty-first century, the Northwest Coast canoe is back, helping to repower and heal the cultures that originally gave it birth.

o   o   o

IN THE MORNING, I time my departure from Cornet Bay for high slack tide, so that I can catch the first of the ebb through

Deception Pass during a brief respite from its notorious whirlpools and eddies. Even so, there is plenty of tidal current, and I slide quickly through the narrow canyon beneath the high suspension bridge that connects Whidbey and Fidalgo Islands. As I move out into open water, the residual swell from yesterday's high winds out in the Strait of Juan de Fuca stack up against the ebb, making for tough going around Rosario Head and along the exposed cliffs leading up into Burrows Bay. The swells are large and chaotic, with the backwash off the cliff face running head-long into the prevailing sea, complicated by tidal currents converging from multiple directions at once. There is almost no wind this morning, so I can only imagine what this stretch of water would be like under a full gale and during peak tide. I am not among the people who would seek such conditions out.

The kayak I am paddling to Cowichan Bay is as far from the grand seagoing canoes as a paddle craft can be. My tiny boat would have been a complete outlander on this coast in the days of the canoe's dominance. Apart from a fleet of Aleut hunters who passed down the coast in their skin *baidarkas* in the late eighteenth century as far south as California under forced servitude to Russian sea otter ships, the Arctic was the exclusive domain of the kayak. The Aleut and Eskimo cultures certainly took paddle craft to the peak of skill and daring in the harshest of all ocean conditions on earth. The kayak was a big reason the Eskimo culture was able to thrive in such harsh conditions. In its modern recreational incarnation, the basic Eskimo design has proven so adaptable that its worldwide popularity in recent years has rocketed past that of all other forms of paddle craft combined.

The sea kayak is a common sight now in the waters of Puget Sound, as it is in other coastal waterways, lakes, and rivers the world over. Sea kayaking is one of the fastest-growing sports in the world today, and the Salish Sea is one of its great Meccas. There are many good reasons for kayaking's popularity. At a basic level, it is one of the easiest sports to master as a novice, and the rewards are immediate. One can go places in a kayak that no other craft, mechanized or otherwise, can access. Even in heavily urbanized waters, a kayak can open doors into fingers of wildness that one might never suspect were there. Traveling in silence brings one closer to wildlife, and closer to an inward, contemplative rhythm that engine-powered craft can rarely access in the same way.

Yet as with hiking and bicycling, the kayak's modern revival is almost exclusively for sport. It is a popular leisure activity precisely because it is *not* a function of livelihood and certainly not a mode of conventional travel. Sea kayaks now compete with a vast fleet of pleasure boats here on Puget Sound as escape hatches from the world of work, resulting in the same kinds of feuds that exists between cross-country skiers and snowmobilers in the pristine backcountry of the Cascades. The race to find the last uncongested places of solitude is quickly spreading the paddle virus to the outer limits of the world's wild coastlines, from the Arctic to the equator.

The word *kayak*, or *qajaq* in the Inuktitut language, means "hunter's boat," and its purpose was not recreation but survival. Kenneth Brower describes the impact of the kayak on the Far north:

Eskimo kayaks, slender and nearly weightless, were the finest hunting canoes in history. Skin boats made the Eskimo culture circumpolar. . . . The oars of the umiaks and the double-bladed paddles of the kayaks chopped down vast distances, allowing Eskimos to exchange ideas, designs, and genes all around the top of the world. A Greenland Eskimo could follow, haltingly, the speech of an Eskimo from western Alaska. It was not that way in the dugout country. When a Tsimshian addressed a Nootka, he might as well have been speaking Chinese, or Kwakiutl.[10]

Archeological evidence dates the use of kayaks back between two and four thousand years. Constructed by each hunter to conform exactly to his own physical dimensions, traditional kayaks were built out of rare and precious driftwood wrought from a treeless environment, were covered with sealskin, and functioned like an appendage of the hunter's body—extremely light, maneuverable, and watertight. The hunter wore a waterproof hide jacket that was literally sown into the combing of the kayak before he set out. With water temperatures hovering at or below freezing in the Arctic, a "water exit" from the kayak was synonymous with death, so a paddler's life depended on his ability to roll his kayak back upright when rough seas or the battle to subdue a harpooned mammal caused him to capsize. As many as ten different "Eskimo rolls" had to be mastered for different conditions, with or without a paddle in hand, and sometimes, a hunter rolled deliberately to escape the force of a breaking wave. Eskimo paddlers could play in the surf like sea lions. Early European explorers in the Arctic were amazed at the skill and daring of these hunters in their tiny skin boats. In his early-nineteenth-century account, *Narrative of a Voyage to Hudson's Bay in His Majesty's Ship Rosamond,* Lt. Edward Chappell offered this description of the kayak:

> [It was] built of a wooden framework of the lightest materials, covered with oiled seal skin . . . sewed over the frame with the most outstanding exactness, and as light as parchment upon

the head of a drum. . . . [T]he slightest inclination of the body, on either side, will inevitably overturn them; yet in these frail barks will the Esquimaux smile at the roughest sea; and in smooth water they can, with ease, travel seven miles an hour.[11]

H. C. Petersen, in *Skinboats of Greenland,* described the conditions and uses a traditional kayak was built to master:

> The kayak must be able to transport its owner in very rough seas; not just in the swell of the waves but in the churning, choppy seas where the waves break unpredictably from all sides. It must be able to shoot river rapids. It must carry the catch and animals killed, and other goods as well. . . . It must be transportable over large distances resting on the kayaker's head, over ice as well as uneven terrain.

Targeted animals on a kayak hunt included seals, walrus, whales, narwhals, sea otters, waterfowl, and swimming caribou. A whale hunt could involve upward of two hundred kayaks or baidarkas, and the risks were great. Speared whales or walrus would often turn on their pursuers, and the conditions of the hunt were deadly to begin with. It was understood that some of the hunters would not come back alive. But the alternative for the entire village was sure starvation.

All this puts my journey to Cowichan Bay in a rather tame light. To be sure, I know contemporary kayakers who do push the extreme edge, seeking out the worst conditions, crossing long stretches of open water or circumnavigating Iceland. Yet while their actions require daring and skill, their motivations are personal and psychological, a test of individual prowess or a thirst for adventure in a world shorn of blank spots on the map. Such expeditions are idiosyncratic, untethered to matters of collective survival that drove the design and use of these boats in the past. So is my current trip, for that matter. Like the canoe rendezvous that is the object of my quest, this trip is primarily symbolic, an effort to reshape my own imagination to include realities that have fallen off the radar of my culture.

CHAPTER 15

Riding the Long Wave

o o o

Everything is waves. The universe of space and matter is charged
with energy, and this energy organizes into the pulsations we call
waves. . . . The passage of energy through matter organizes matter, and waves pass through everything—steel, stone, flesh and
blood and water and air and space alike. Waves are the imprint,
the signature, not only of life, but of existence itself.

—Drew Kampion, *The Book of Waves*[1]

Robin, Jay, and Kristin arrive at the Anacortes boat launch
in Washington Park soon after dawn with their boats balanced precariously on the top of Robin's tiny car. Robin's
double rowing dory, the *Barbara Goss*, is so outsized for the car
that I wonder how they escaped arrest by the highway patrol.
They are beaming with anticipation as we unload the boats and
move gear to the beach. It is a clear morning, with light winds
and calm seas across Rosario Strait. Jay and I will paddle our
kayaks while Kristin joins Robin in the *Barbara Goss*, which is
rigged as a double racing shell with a wide, stable beam for handling rough waters. We sort through our gear as a progression of

luxury sport boats put out from the launch to troll for coho salmon. Our goal is to make the wide passage of Rosario Strait into the San Juan Islands during the relative calm of morning, before the warming temperatures over land kick up a convection of cooler air rushing in off the water that can stir the already turbulent rips into a dangerous brew. I am grateful for the company and experience of these fellow travelers.

Kristin has recently returned from her year of salmon research in Norway, and I am thrilled that she can join me in this brief interval before she starts graduate school in the fall. From her earliest childhood in Alaska, Kristin has been at my side for every kind of adventure, and she is as fearless as she is good-natured and cheerful. Following the pattern of my earlier years, she balances winters in academia with summers fishing commercially in Alaska. Already, in the few weeks since her return from Norway, she has fished Alaska's Bristol Bay, catching enough Egegik River sockeye salmon to pay her tuition for a year of graduate school. In a good year like this one, at the peak of the run, Bristol Bay's fleet can catch two million sockeye salmon in a single tide. It is a spectacle to behold, and a reminder of what Puget Sound was like in its own ecological prime.

Jay Thomas is an engineering consultant whose professional motto is to "show people what winning looks like," and he approaches kayaking with that same confident gusto. His thoroughness is joined with an infectious enthusiasm that is just right for this trip. Unlike me, Jay does not hesitate to throw himself into extreme conditions, and my own confidence going into these crossings is much higher with him on the team.

Robin is a colleague of Kristin's in the field of coastal restoration. She is a short, gregarious woman whose humble demeanor belies a core of inner strength and self-assurance. Her knowledge of restoration efforts in Puget Sound brings a base of local lore that will enrich our passage. Robin talks about her six-hundred-mile paddle from Alaska to Puget Sound last summer in a matter-of-fact way, as though it is something that anyone with a summer off from work would naturally choose to do. Both of us had made plans independently to paddle to Cowichan Bay for the Native canoe rendezvous and were happy to join forces when she learned of my plans from Kristin. Robin's dory can move fast through the water under skilled hands. Both she and Kristin rowed on crew teams in college, so they will have to hold back on the throttle to match the slower pace of our kayaks. At least that is the reason that Jay and I give for this difference in speed.

The conditions are still excellent as we set out, with calm winds and moderate neap tides.* We leave just before high slack, hoping to avoid the strong ebb current that will kick up in Rosario Strait during peak tide. We set off across Guemes Channel to Reef Point on Cypress Island, passing through the ferry lanes that link the mainland to the San Juan Islands. Then we head for Thatcher Pass on the far side of Rosario Strait.

This is the first of several major shipping lanes that we will have to cross during the trip. The freighters can grow from tiny dots on the horizon into gigantic container ships in a surprisingly short time, steaming by at thirty knots and kicking up ocean-size swells in their wake. These ships do not change

---

*A *neap tide* occurs when the sun and moon are at right angles to each other in their positions relative to the earth (the bimonthly quarter-moon phase), thus offsetting their gravitational pull on the earth's oceans. Because it is so much closer to the earth, the moon's gravitational pull is more than double that of the sun, so the moon is the dominant factor in generating tides. Larger *spring tides* occur during the monthly full moon and new moon cycles, when the sun and moon are pulling in a direct line, compounding their gravitational pull on the oceans.

course or slow down for anyone, and a wayward kayak might not even show up on the radar. So it is up to us entirely, monitoring the visual position and direction of the ships, and the VHF commercial shipping frequencies, to make sure that we do not arrive in the center of the shipping lanes at the same time that a freighter does. Once in the lanes, we pour on the coals, and soon there is no turning back. The conditions range from calm to turbulent and back again unpredictably, with tide rips creating random and powerful eddy lines that swirl around our boats. But the winds have held off, winds that can turn these rips into combers in a hurry. We drive our paddles and oars into the water in rhythmic, heated strokes, with Kristin and Robin pulling slowly away.

Once we've passed out of the lanes, we ease the intensity of our strokes and pull back together as the granite bluffs of Blakely Island draw slowly near. The straits widen quickly to the south, and it is humbling to be on the edge of such big waters in these tiny craft. We slide into the sheltered waters of the San Juan chain, hugging the cliff faces to avoid the flotilla of yachts all vying for remnants of the islands' fabled solitude. The ferry from Anacortes yawns past us in the narrow channel, stuffed to the gills with cars and tourists who are after the same thing.

Crossing to Lopez Island, we stop for lunch at Spencer Spit, taking a swim and a long nap in the sun before continuing on through Harney Channel against the dramatic shoreline of Orcas Island. Crossing the entrance to West Sound beneath the distinctive profile of Turtleback Mountain, we paddle out through Pole Pass and the Wasp Islands into San Juan Channel and our destination for the night at Jones Island State Park. We are late arrivals to a busy campground and have to shoehorn ourselves in among the other paddlers in this special campsite for paddle craft. Luckily, they welcome us as fellow members of the tribe.

The sun sets slantwise over the north end of San Juan Island, casting an intense glow across the water as the evening coolness sets in. We make a pasta dinner with homemade basil pesto, smoked salmon, cheese, and sourdough bread. Cardboard with ketchup would taste good after our twenty-mile paddle today, so this meal is a feast. In the morning, we will travel a short five miles to Roche Harbor on San Juan Island, where a large encampment of Native canoes from the east side of the sound has gathered before crossing Haro Strait on the last leg of their journey.

o o o

IT HAS BEEN FOUR DAYS NOW since I left Possession Point, and watching the slow descent of dusk over San Juan Channel from a bluff above our camp, I can feel the cumulative effect of these long days on the water settling into my body—days stitched together not by clock time, but by the rhythms of tide and weather, physical effort and fatigue, and the slow turning of daylight and darkness one into the other. The compulsive demands of a clock-driven life do not release their grip easily on the body and mind. It takes time, the kind of open, unfettered time that is becoming an extinct experience for many in our culture. As I sit by the evening calmness on the water, I can feel the same inner spaciousness that comes after a comparable number of days on the cushion in a meditation retreat. This quality of inner *presence* cannot be forced or hurried. It is not a function of will; nor is it to be found in books or conceptual arguments. Whether by the path of the paddle or the path of the cushion, a comparable duration of time outside of time seems to be required to throw open these gates of inner presence.

The snowcapped peaks of Vancouver Island and the looming Gulf Islands lie in the distance across the international boundary, messengers from a strange and half-forgotten world. The

wide strait that lies between us will be the most exposed crossing I have yet made by kayak, and the thought fills me with apprehension. Yet how could these islands be alien? Beyond this
artificial boundary are islands in the same chain, scoured from
granite uplift by the same Cordilleran ice sheet, home for millennia to the same tribal peoples who could not have imagined
such a binding separation. It is these people whose journey
across time I am following on this trip. I am leaving the confines
of Puget Sound and going home to the Salish Sea.

o o o

A FEW YEARS AGO, I led a meditation retreat for religious leaders at the Garrison Institute in New York, a former Catholic
monastery on the Hudson River that now serves as an interfaith
contemplative center. Garrison sits nose-to-nose with the im-
posing fortress of West Point Academy directly across the Hudson River, the two centers offering a bizarre contrast of
methodologies for achieving "peace" and "security." The Garrison
retreat brought together an impressive group of clergy, rabbis,
Roman Catholic nuns, religious scholars, and theological students, bound by a common desire to explore the spiritual di-
mension of the environmental crisis. My co-leader on the retreat
was Rabbi Larry Troster of GreenFaith, a good friend and colleague who has been my partner in a series of similar retreats in
New York and Seattle.[2]

My job was to introduce this group of Western religious leaders to some basic forms of Eastern meditative practice, exploring how these practices can reinvigorate Western contemplative
traditions and at the same time spur a deeper inquiry into the
importance of ecological restoration as a moral and religious issue. Rabbi Troster engaged the group in a fresh process of theological and biblical inquiry to get at these same questions.

Among the participants at the retreat was an eminent butterfly expert from the Natural History Museum in London. Dick Vane-Wright, a wiry Brit with a white goatee, looked every inch the field scientist. As an entomologist, Dick did not fit the profile of the other retreat participants, and he made no bones about the fact that he was an agnostic. Yet his career as a field biologist had led him to a conviction that the natural world is alive in a way that his fellow scientists often fail to recognize. Dick was eager to engage in this dialogue with others who are more fluent in the language of the sacred, to see what common ground he might find there. He was also curious to see if meditation might give him some fresh viewpoints into the questions that had pursued him to the edge of nature.

Three days into the retreat, Rabbi Troster and I took the group on a silent hike up Bear Mountain in a nearby forest preserve. I instructed participants to spread out and take their time, approaching this hike as a form of walking meditation, setting aside the need to identify or quantify what they were seeing. Each person was invited to receive what passed into the senses as if seeing it for the first time: the quality of light filtering through the forest, the fragrance of new spring growth, the color and symmetry of wildflowers, the texture of tree bark against the hand. For over an hour, we climbed in silence, then sat on the rocky summit in a brisk wind, gazing out over restored forest in all directions as far as the eye could see.

On the way down from the summit, we stopped for lunch at a mossy overlook and shared some of what we had discovered on the hike. I mentioned my Zen teacher's dictum that it takes the first three days of a retreat just to arrive on our cushions. It takes that long to dispel the clutter in our minds and settle the scattered energy in our bodies. I've found this to be true on wilderness expeditions, like my trips in Alaska, as well. It often isn't until the third or fourth day of an extended hike or paddle that I begin to fall into alignment with my surroundings. It simply takes this long for the soul to catch up with the body.

Hiking down the mountain, Dick and I fell into conversation. He told me about a five-month scientific expedition he had taken through Southwest Africa in 1972 as part of a team of entomologists searching for insect species new to science. As the expedition progressed, he began to notice this exact phenomenon. If the group stayed in a particular camp for less than three days, their success in finding new species was spotty. But if they stayed for three days or longer, their productivity began to shoot up. They started to dial themselves into the place, to find a more relaxed awareness, a greater sense of presence that led to simply seeing more and making a greater number of valuable discoveries. He told me he was beginning to feel that same sense of relaxed awareness after three days in this meditation retreat. Perhaps it is the same experience speaking.

I call this phenomenon the *three-day rule*. Could it be that we are biologically calibrated to need this kind of open time in order to see into the deeper coherence of our lives? Fragmenting our attention into smaller and smaller units, which are dictated by the accelerating pace of modern life and the speed of our computers, risks the extinction of a core part of our intelligence. It places the fruits of wisdom itself on the Endangered Experience List.

The roots of contemplative awe, or what we commonly call *meditation* and *prayer* in today's specialized religious vernacular, are firmly founded in this biological inheritance from the deep past, a capacity that all humans still share for focused reciprocity with the forces of wild nature—a capacity that has been, until recently, mandatory for survival itself. As hunters and gatherers, our predecessors faced constant dangers and routine exposure to the elements in the course of daily existence. Their success or failure in finding food and protecting their clans depended on an intimate knowledge of local terrain, of plant uses and animal behavior, and of subtle cues to changing weather, all monitored directly by the senses on a moment-to-moment basis. Success in the hunt might require hours spent waiting in stillness for the target animal to reveal itself—the Eskimo hunter standing motionless on the ice above a breathing hole for seals, the down feather of a seabird suspended above the hole to signal the animal's transitory presence beneath the ice. If the hunter's attention wanders and he misses that brief movement of the feather signifying breath—and seal!—his family goes hungry for another day.

A focused, unwavering attention, tuned to the immediate conditions of the landscape and wrapped in a thick garment of sensual engagement, is part of the hunter's basic survival equipment, every bit as much as the spear that stands ready for a skilled strike when the moment is at hand. Through all these long hours of waiting, a vast silence "like a scouring sand" is working the hunter's mind, burning into it a different kind of hunger: the hunger for silence itself. Surely such experiences, common across the millennia to all active humans, carried within their very structure a quality of *numinous* awe—the wild wonder and terror that still inhabit the deep corridors of the human heart.

o o o

A SMALL GLIMPSE of that wonder and awe is waiting for us in our crossing of San Juan Channel this morning. The four-knot currents give us an unexpected run for our money on this two-mile crossing, kicking up the kind of heavy turbulence that I habitually avoid. I am usually not a guy who seeks out conflict. But the anticipated winds in the marine forecast today only stand to make the crossing worse, so we decide to go for it. Jay is his usual hard-charging self, calling out encouragement to me as we plow into the swells in midchannel. I can see from the set on Kristin's face as she pulls on her oars that she is not so sure about this, either. Rosario was a piece of cake compared with this, and we are only beginning to test the limits of what our boats can handle. We round Limestone Point into Spieden Channel with the tide running hard against us, picking our way along the beach to Davidson Head and around at last into the protection of Roche Harbor.

From our camp on Posey Island, a tiny rock outcrop reserved for paddlers, we can hear the sound of steady drumming and Native chants floating across the water from a canoe encampment on the inner harbor a mile away. A dozen tribal canoes from the eastern part of the Salish Sea have converged here for two days of preparation before the final push into Cowichan Bay tomorrow. A Native tent city has sprung up next door to this luxury yachting resort, creating a bizarre contrast of worlds. The canoes are an impressive sight lining the beach a short distance from the plush marina filled with million-dollar yachts. We spend the afternoon with friends from the Swinomish "canoe family," playing horseshoes and listening to stories of other tribes—the Lummi, Nooksack, Upper Skagit, and Tulalip, whose route lies with ours through the San Juan Islands. Other subgroups of canoes are staged elsewhere, representing northern, southern, and western contingents of tribes that have come from as far away as Bella Bella in northern British Columbia, and the outer coast of Washington, Oregon, and Vancouver Island. The mood is festive, with a throng of tribal members joining the canoe pullers here to offer support and to share in the excitement. We find ourselves welcomed openly into the circle of Native families.

Tonight we are camped on the far edge of the San Juan archipelago, facing another open expanse of water. Tomorrow I will leave my home circle for the first and only time this year, rising for a dawn passage over Haro Strait. The larger canoes will make the six-mile crossing later in the day, accompanied by a fleet of support vessels. Secure in our own small encampment for the evening, we hear the Native drums pounding late into the night, pulling us across the threshold into sleep on mysterious currents of myth and legend that can never finally be torn from the heart.

o o o

IN THE MORNING, we launch with the sun just as it rises from its mysterious lodging behind Spieden Island. I think of Northwest Native accounts of Raven freeing the sun, moon, and stars from their captivity in bentwood cedar boxes, causing such terror in a people accustomed to darkness that they fled to the far corners of the world, adopting different languages and customs in the process. Now these scattered tribes are coming back together again for a great potlatch, the first of its kind in a century on Vancouver Island. So far, Raven is smiling on the assembled tribes, withholding his potential mischief on the water.

We set off again in calm winds this morning, skirting the narrow channel between McCracken Point and Battleship Island that issues us out into the open waters of Haro Strait. To the south is the yawning expanse of the Strait of Juan de Fuca, with distant alpenglow over the snowfields of the Olympic Mountains forty miles away. Everything about this place feels big and slightly menacing. Forests of bull kelp send their bulbous heads and long, sweeping fronds in the direction of the current, helping us gauge its bearing and speed. Giant barnacles cling to the rocky shores, creations of the ocean conditions that often pummel this exposed shoreline.

The resident pods of orcas that routinely work the waters of Haro Strait are nowhere to be seen this morning, but the tide rips are here in force. We are jolted one way and the other by sharply conflicting eddy lines, beyond which we enter the stream of freighter traffic coming into and out of Vancouver, British Columbia. The ships approach unseen from the north through Boundary Pass, emerging suddenly into view as they make the ninety-degree corner into Haro Strait at Turn Point on Stuart Island. From there they can be on us in a matter of minutes. We take a last good look for traffic as we enter the lanes, then pour on the coals once again, the U.S. shoreline fading behind us while the bulk of the crossing still lies ahead. Jay is a stronger paddler than I am and pulls out in front, while Kristin and Robin have left us both in their wake, leaning hard on the oars of the *Barbara Goss*. It is hard to stay close to each other in this immense wilderness of open water.

Halfway through our crossing, the wind kicks up suddenly from the south, coming up the long fetch of the strait, and a sharp swell is not far behind. Soon the wind is blowing steady at fifteen to twenty knots, and we find ourselves wedged in the narrow trough of the waves. We plant and pull with each stroke, plant and pull, rising and falling like tiny corks, our paddle strokes offering the only traction and stability we have on the water. The swell begins to crest in whitecaps that rise up beside us, but there is no turning back. From my vantage so close to the water, the other boats appear and disappear in the alternating peaks and troughs. Each stroke is a running conversation with the wave at hand, and there are no two waves alike. Braced by the cold, salt wind, we push ahead. There is no resolution to this conflict but the next pull of the paddle. The same wind that blows the lid off these waves blows our sense of time out the window. Almost without realizing it, we pull the distant shore ever so slowly toward us.

When we're sure we've cleared the shipping channels, we converge and angle north toward Halibut Island, running half with the swell now until we can gain the lee of Sidney Island. Though it is little more than a reef with a small stand of storm-gnarled trees, we pass close by Halibut Island, reassured by the sight of something solid in the waves. Haro Strait does indeed look like good halibut grounds. It has the depth and exposure, the up-wellings of current, and the hard bottom that halibut like. I can almost feel these great predators of the deep lurking beneath us in the strange underworld of the strait—behemoths that can reach three hundred pounds and that the Tlingit Indians called "the old woman." I have never felt more linked, here in the Salish Sea, to that greater scope of wildness that I associate with Alaska's rugged coast.

The swell eases off as we slide into the protection of Miners Channel. Every island and landmark here is new to me. It is still five miles across Sidney Channel to Vancouver Island itself, where we will clear customs in the town of Sidney. But these are more protected waters now. I feel like Robinson Crusoe as we pull our boats up to rest beneath the deserted bluffs of Sidney Island. Fresh deer tracks etched perfectly in the wet sand are the only sign of life on the long and lonely beach that stretches off into the distance. I feel certain that we are the first humans to ever set foot on this island.

o o o

As a fisherman, I'm tuned to the subtle varieties of wave action on the water. When halibut fishing in the Gulf of Alaska, for example, along the outer edge of the continental shelf, the direction of the wind has a big impact on the type of sea we have to contend with. A brisk southeasterly wind, like the one out in Haro Strait this morning, breeds a short, steep wave formation that slams continually into the boat, making it hard to keep balance. If a gale blows out of the southeast on the fishing grounds, the sharp swell can put us out of business in a hurry, with most of our energy spent just staying on our feet.

A westerly wind, on the other hand, generates long, rolling swells born in the far reaches of the ocean, sometimes arriving days after the actual storm has ended. Such swells can be quite huge, yet, in the long interval between peak and trough, they still pass through with an easy grace that transfers smoothly into the motion of the boat. Out on the ocean, even in the midst of a major squall, one can detect a deeper groundswell moving beneath the surface turbulence. Dan Kowalski, my longtime partner on the halibut grounds of Alaska, has a great name for this: long-wave modality.

A similar distinction plays out in physics across the spectra of wave patterns. Longer sound waves, like the low rumble of a diesel engine or the deep exhalations of a humpback whale, can carry great distances over the water. They are felt as much as heard and have a primal tone. The longer wavelengths of visible light penetrate a wider, diagonal swath of atmosphere when the sun hangs low on the horizon, giving us the brilliant colors of sunrise and sunset.

These long-wave patterns in nature stir quieter, more contemplative wave patterns in the mind itself. It is this contemplative aspect of mind that is crowded out by the fast-paced, short-wave tendencies that are the building storm of our contemporary culture. In truth, our minds are endowed by evolution with an essential capacity for both. Like all vertebrates, humans are hardwired to notice and respond to sudden sounds and movements in our environment. Failure to do so often meant death to our distant hominid ancestors. Those who responded quickly passed this vigilance on to us in a genetic trait that neuroscientists call the *establishing reflex*.[3] The fast-cut, quick-change patterns of digital media use this reflex quite deliberately to keep us glued to our television and computer screens, changing images many times a second, often beneath the radar of our direct awareness. The establishing reflex is a literal gold mine to advertisers. Many commercial Web sites now shamelessly employ the establishing reflex to surround our quest for information with a constant barrage of pulsing, jumping images that scream out for our attention from the periphery of the screen, and by dint of evolution itself, we are programmed to respond. As annoying as these ads may be, they are there because they work.

The "five-second rule" of contemporary filmmaking, epitomized on the Internet by YouTube, allots just five seconds to filmmakers to capture the attention of their intended audience. Failure to hook viewers during this razor-thin window of available attention means that most of these potential customers will have already moved on to the next.

When I compare the short-wave character of this five-second rule with my own three-day rule, the odds seem heavily stacked against the long wave. It is difficult to make a compelling case for long-wave modality when all of society's winds seem to be blowing hard from the southeast. The tight trough between the waves of our current short-wave media culture may be riveting to our attention, but it is no place to spend the whole of our lives. As we are reduced to a five-second attention span and driven by an obsession with speed in all domains of our life, we have hardly noticed the long-wave storms of astonishing magnitude that have been gathering on the horizon.

As I paddle toward Cowichan Bay, six days now into my journey, I am riding on that long wave again, from whose crest I cannot fail to see these gathering storms. But I can also begin to feel the deeper pulse of a longer wave still, present in the drumbeat of the earth itself, on whose mantle these islands are only temporary bubbles, floating for a moment on the surface of a molten sea.

o o o

THE SOUND OF A CONCH SHELL splits the evening air, bringing the large crowd that has gathered near the mouth of the Cowichan River to silence. Again and again the conch rings out, and I follow the sound to its source—a young Native man standing on the point, dressed in tribal regalia of red and black button-blanket and woven cedar bark hat. Looking out in the direction he is facing, I see a great canoe of the West Coast Nootkan design coming into view around the point. At fifty feet in length, it is a splendid sight, with two dozen paddles beating the water in a steady, unified rhythm. Throughout its approach, the conch continues blowing, and to my astonishment, I find that there are tears running down my cheeks. Turning to Kristin, I see that she also is fighting back tears. I did not expect to feel such a wave of emotion. It comes from a place outside my own experience, from a culture that is alien to my own, yet somehow a part of me. The pride that is evident in these pullers at the end of a long journey is a pride that swells in us, too, having worked so hard to come this far. As the canoe nears the beach, at the command of the canoe leader, paddles flip up in unison and are held erect by the canoe pullers. I can see now that this canoe is from the Sooke Nation on the south coast of Vancouver Island. It is carrying a "spirit pole" erected as a mast in the bow, carved for this occasion, and has been paddled from village to village for over three months to bless each of the tribal communities as they made ready to set out.

Thus begins the formal protocol for coming ashore, kicking off a week of Native ceremonies and games. The canoe leader calls out from the water to his Cowichan hosts, "We are from Sooke Nation and we have been on this journey for ninety-five days! We bring our spirit pole as a gift, and we ask permission of the Cowichan Nation to come ashore!" With permission granted, they move in to the beach, while behind them, the first wave of canoes has already rounded the point. The tribes from the north come first, with the canoe from Bella Bella, which has traveled farther than any others, coming at the front of the line. Then comes the contingent from the south, then the east, and finally the west: canoes of every description and size, some of modern materials, others newly carved traditional cedar dugouts, some with a handful of pullers, others with twenty or more, most dressed in tribal regalia. They raft up along the beach until all 106 canoes have arrived.

Kristin and I volunteer to help steady the canoes, while the growing multitude of pullers pound their paddles against the deck in an outpouring of drumbeat and chant. Thousands of people are gathered along the beach to watch. The faces in the canoes are alert and radiant. Many are young, completing their first canoe journey, women as well as men. Some are weeping openly. The power of the moment is electric. We wade into the throng of rafted canoes, waiting until all have arrived before beginning the landing protocol. The canoe leaders stand ceremoniously among their crew, older veterans of multiple journeys, wearing the totem crests and headdresses of their home tribes as they bear this canoe culture out of its nearly forgotten past.

I steady a canoe whose leader stands with such dignity that I can scarcely take my eyes off her. As the flotilla grows in size, the constant beating of paddles carries over the bay like a thunderous rain. The woman is wearing a thick cape of woven white wool and a headdress of white martin skins. She is an elder, yet seems ageless, her face exuding a radiance that cuts to the heart, a strength of bearing that is riveting. Her canoe is from the Suquamish Nation, Chief Seattle's home tribe, whose reservation on Agate Passage abuts the land where I spent my childhood summers. I feel an unnamable link through her to a part of my own heart that inhabits that same land. I feel as if I have known this woman for a thousand years.

o   o   o

THE COWICHAN TRIBE was the largest tribe on the coast of British North America prior to European contact, numbering four to five thousand people. By the early twentieth century, smallpox had reduced that population to five hundred. These ravages by disease were experienced up and down the coast, killing up to 90 percent of the tribal populations and arriving ahead of the Europeans themselves. Captain George Vancouver was shocked, when he arrived in 1792, to find whole villages abandoned and littered with skeletons. The first place that he came upon was a village site in Discovery Bay on the Olympic Peninsula; it had been recently abandoned and was "over-run with weeds; amongst which were found several human skulls, and other bones, promiscuously scattered about." As the expedition continued, crew member Thomas Manby noted, "we saw a great many deserted Villages some of them . . . capable of holding many hundred inhabitants." A decade before Vancouver's arrival, the smallpox virus had already spread across the continent from tribe to tribe, reaching the Northwest Coast. Vancouver was right in his conclusion that "at no very remote period this country had been far more populous than at present."[4]

These cultures were already decimated by an incomprehensible cataclysm when the white settlers arrived, making the subsequent course of cultural subjugation that much more inevitable. That the tribes have survived at all, and that we are witnessing a cultural revival two centuries after their apocalypse, is testimony to their inherent resilience as "cultures of habitat."[5] The strength of the people remains infused with the strength of the land that bore their ancestors, and one can feel that strength in the events unfolding today.

These people chose well. The Cowichan River flows out of the Vancouver Island Ranges through a long and gentle valley offering abundant spawning habitat for salmon. The surrounding waters of Satellite Channel and Saanich Inlet contain an expanse of sheltered waterways and level beaches for building villages. Even today, one can feel a lingering ecological abundance in the salt marshes that stretch far inland from the head of the bay.

When all the canoes have landed and the welcoming protocol is complete, we are herded onto school buses with the rest of the crowd and transported six miles upriver to tribal headquarters in the town of Duncan. It feels strange to be suddenly traveling away from tidewater in a motorized vehicle. Hoping for the best, we have left our boats tucked away on a private float in the harbor as we head for Duncan with the others. Tonight's ceremonies are not to be missed.

In the spirit of the old potlatch ceremonies, every tribe represented must share its dances and stories before the larger gathering, and with so many tribes present, this will take days, running deep into the night. The tribes that have come the farthest perform first, and the sound of signature Northwest drums and chant is constant in the air. The dancers perform in a large field under the light of torches and stars, taking the guise of their totem animals with movements summoned out of the mists of time.

It is well after midnight when we decide to call it a day. We still have no idea where we will sleep, and every room for rent within miles has been booked in advance for this event. A night chill has set in, and the last chartered buses to Cowichan Bay left hours ago. Our camping gear is with the boats, so there is nothing for us to do but walk the six miles back to Cowichan Bay. Tired though we are, the long walk feels good after so many days confined to our tiny boats. The dark and empty roads of a world shut down for the night add an aura of otherworldly calm.

Soon we are deep in conversation, spurred by the vigor of the walk. This has been a day to remember, and there is much to process—the wave of emotion we all felt at the arrival of the first canoe, the strange language of dance and song that still anchors the spiritual life of these tribes, hinting at a many-layered world inextricable from place. Kristin tells stories from her year working with north coastal fishermen and Sámi tribes in Norway, whose lives are still entwined with the last of the wild Atlantic salmon runs. They, too, are remnant Salmon People who can remember when the annual runs of salmon were the prime sustenance of their lives, as salmon have been for tribes from Hokkaido to Kamchatka, California to Alaska, New England to Greenland and the north coast of Europe.

Robin tells stories of successful restoration projects around Puget Sound; the reclamation of critical salmon habitat in the Nisqually and Skagit deltas, Native land reclamation projects, and historic watershed recovery plans built on new partnerships between old adversaries. The path toward enduring restoration is steep, but there is also much to celebrate and a growing appreciation on all sides of the political spectrum for how important a healthy Puget Sound is to our collective life and culture in the region.

The two hours of our walk evaporate in the heat of conversation, and soon we are back at the harbor in Cowichan Bay. It is beginning to rain, and we are dog-tired. Most of the canoes have been hauled above tidewater on a lonely beach east of town, a haunting sight as we approach in the darkness. The area is deserted except for two Cowichan guards warming themselves by a fire, huddled beneath a leaky shelter for the night. They invite us to warm ourselves by the fire while they tell stories of deadly skirmishes between the Cowichan Tribe and invading Haida war canoes in the nineteenth century, memories still seared with resentment in the minds of their people. Deep roots in the land carry long tendrils of memory. The history of these tribes on the coast is not a peaceful one.

We ask permission to camp nearby, and they point to a rise above the canoes. Who could have written a better script? We pitch our tents in the shadow of these slumbering giants. "Of course we would end up here tonight," Kristin says. "This trip has had a mythic feel from the beginning."

I fall asleep with the sound of drums still pulsing through my body and the vision of wary dancers crouched in fur capes— half-human, half-animal—crossing the borders between spirit worlds as they have done for so many centuries in the past. Raven, Eagle, Wolf, Salmon, Orca, Otter—all the animal villages that used to surround our human habitations: some built beneath the sea, some on the earth, some in the sky; some of them sinister, some life-giving, each of them in full commerce with the human realm. Where have they all gone? What part of our human spirit has departed with them?

Of one thing I feel certain as the rain beats against my tent and I fall across that other permeable boundary into sleep. These canoes are not alone here. We are not alone here. This is not a

stunt. The canoes are spilling over with ancestors. My own ancestors have come to join them tonight. In my dreams they are
talking to one another. They are calling for a great Council. They
are putting aside their grievances of the past. The future of all
our children is at grave risk, and they are not willing to remain
silent any longer.

CHAPTER 16

Homeward Bound

o   o   o

The wilderness pilgrim's step-by-step breath-by-breath walk up a
trail, into those snowfields, carrying all on the back, is so ancient
a set of gestures as to bring a profound sense of body-mind joy. Not
just backpackers, of course. The same happens to those who sail
in the ocean, kayak fjords or rivers, tend a garden, peel garlic, even
sit on a meditation cushion. The point is to make intimate contact
with the real world, real self.

—GARY SNYDER, *The Practice of the Wild*

The darkness is deep tonight not only because of the rain.
Tomorrow is the new moon, so we go to sleep without
moonlight to leaven the clouds. July has come and gone,
ending the "Moon of Deep Waters" in the Salish thirteen-moon
calendar. August will usher in a fresh moon cycle called by the
Salish people "Salmon Coming Home Moon." The great sockeye
salmon run of the Fraser River is now pouring in through Haro
Strait along the Salmon Banks of San Juan Island, and other runs
will soon follow, heading toward every major stream that flows
into the Salish Sea. These salmon will be our companions on a

shared journey home, and in the coming days, all of us will be riding on big new moon tides.

It's still raining in the morning, and I wake early to gusts of wind whining through the firs. This is not the music I hoped to hear as we prepare to head homeward. Crawling out of my tent, I can see a froth of whitecaps out in the bay. The canoes look alive in the morning light, their graceful upswept prows covered with Northwest totem designs, all facing outward toward tidewater for quicker launch, a holdover from the era of warring canoe tribes. Most of these canoes are of the Nootkan design, perfected by the great whaling cultures of the Makah and Nuu-chah-nulth on the outer coast of Vancouver Island. A few are of the Northern design, with high, sweeping sterns mirroring the bows for better performance in a following sea, designed by the great seagoing tribes north of Vancouver Island.

The harbor is hung low with clouds, which press down with their heavy, gray fingers, while the tide has emptied the basin in front of us. Everything is wet and heavy, coated with the aroma of muck and seaweed. We gather our soaked gear and walk back toward town to commiserate over breakfast in the cold outdoor café that is the only place open for business this early. A few local shipwrights and fishermen huddle with their coffee, as they doubtless do every morning, trading news from the docks. Otherwise, the town feels empty and a bit forlorn. Yesterday's throngs of tourists have shifted inland with the Native tribes to Duncan or have gone home. With a gale blowing out on the water, we are pinned to the beach. No sane mariner would be out in Haro Strait today, even on a hefty boat. Picturing the exposed journey ahead with today's winds and tides, I feel very far from home indeed.

In truth, though, we have no grounds to complain. The conditions have been remarkably favorable on the trip so far, and we are due for a storm. Such squalls can persist for weeks during the winter, but usually blow through quickly in summer. I use the time to write in my journal, swap knowledge of the coast with fishermen in the harbor, and chat with the skippers of tribal support boats getting ready to head back across the Strait of Juan de Fuca.

One of the skippers is Ed Charles, a fisherman and cedar carver from the Port Gamble S'Klallam Tribe. We recognize each other from the Jamestown S'Klallam carving shed on Sequim Bay, where he has worked with my friend Nathan Gilles producing exquisite totem poles. I've stopped there often to watch Nathan work, and Ed is usually there, too. A friendly guy with a warm face, Ed wears his experience on the water with an easy shrug of his shoulders. He tells of crossing the Strait of Juan de Fuca during a storm in his Dungeness crab boat last week, accompanying the canoes from the South Sound and Olympic Peninsula. A strong gale caught the group by surprise in the middle of the strait. "Some of the cockier kids in the canoes saw God that day," he says. "They insisted on going in their T-shirts and without life vests, and they nearly froze from hypothermia and fright. We had to tow some canoes out of danger. I haven't seen swells like that in a long time. It was a wild ride, and those kids were different people when they got to the other side. They won't forget it for the rest of their lives. They're not alone against the world anymore. They're part of a team now. They're part of their tribe. And they're not afraid to say they're proud of it."

It is the sea's vagrant disregard for human safety and comfort that makes it such a stern teacher. The possibility of death is folded into every storm, written on every rising gale. Once we venture away from shore, we enter a trackless wilderness with no guarantee of reaching safe harbor again. I love this fact about the sea. It tells the naked truth about our human vulnerability, and therein lies its beauty, too. The sea is never to be taken for granted or controlled. Yet neither can we get free of it. Our own bodies are 70 percent water, echoing the proportion of the earth's surface that is covered by ocean. Water flows through every cell in our bodies. It is the circulatory system of clouds and mountains, the red river of our blood. The sea enfolds us in a permanent marriage between the beauty of an aroused heart and the stark reality of our own sure demise. Whether we turn into the swell or run before it, we are destined to spend our transitory lives at sea.

Ed's departure for home is delayed by the storm today, too. He seeks us out again later on the float to tell us how much he appreciates that we've come all this way by paddle to witness the event. He says he respects us for it, and his words are heartfelt. We shake hands warmly and wish each other a safe crossing home.

By afternoon, with rain squalls still lacing the bay, it's clear that we will not be going anywhere today. A waitress at the café named Erin takes pity on us and offers space on her living room floor for the night, which we gratefully accept. The forecast calls for calmer winds by morning, so we prepare for a departure at earliest dawn. Kristin and Jay are both pressed by tight schedules, but are determined to get back across Haro Strait into U.S. waters with us before they catch a ferry home.

Saltspring Island's beautiful rolling prow is lost in the mist beyond Separation Point when we rise, but the winds have laid down their swords. We have learned to seize the morning calm when we get it, and we seize it with gusto this morning. It feels great to be back on the water, heading in the direction of home. A gentle breeze is at our back, and the air is cool and cleansed by yesterday's rain. The morning ebb is with us, giving an extra push, and we make good time. We are crossing the head of

Saanich Inlet when the crews of the Puyallup and S'Klallam Tribes roar past us in their fancy boats, heading home. They honk their horns and wave as they stream by at full throttle, no doubt enjoying this reversal of traditional roles.

By the time we reach Sidney Spit, the wind has kicked up again. We linger on the spit for a couple of hours waiting for the tide and wind to ease off on their bickering, and then we make a rough crossing out to Gooch Island, the last rocky outpost on the Canadian side of the boundary, to spend the night. Jay and I walk to the outer edge of the island, where the tide makes a churning wake around Tom Point, signaling big forces ahead. We watch a pair of freighters from Vancouver heave into view, making the sharp corner at Turn Point and barreling past our camp in the fading light of evening, a reminder that currents and wind are not our only concerns in the morning. Neither of us speaks on the way back to camp, and dinner is a somber one. I set the alarm for 4:30 A.M., crawl in my tent, and go to bed.

o o o

RAVEN IS LENIENT with us during the crossing in the morning, but he has other mischief in mind. We set off at first sunrise in the direction of Turn Point in blessedly calm waters, before the ebb has a chance to pick up speed. The sky is clear except for some thick banks of fog down the strait. The murky bulk of a tanker slides ominously by in the neck of the channel as we pull out from Rum Island, but no others are in sight. A huge yellow bubble of light builds over Stuart Island, ready to explode out of the eastern horizon at any moment, while the sky transforms into intense scarlet and violet hues, mirrored to perfection by the flat canvas of the strait. I am spellbound.

The *Barbara Goss* pulls ahead with the rhythmic stroke of her oars as if it is sailing into the heart of a furnace. Jay is in front of me as usual when we enter the shipping lanes, and the sun's first rays crest over the island in a brilliant ring of fire that obliterates his body. This display of celestial fireworks ushers us simultaneously back inside my home circle and back into American waters. Each pull of paddle and oar brings us deeper into the heart of the fire. With Turn Point shielding our view of southbound freighters, we lean into our strokes with double abandon, and before long, we know that we are home free.

o   o   o

HOME AND FREE. These two words have not meshed very well recently in the country I am returning to—a country torn by a rising tide of political and cultural divisions and a rampant loss of civility. We are out in the vortex of Haro Strait now, square on the U.S. border. The current is sliding us south at three knots while we push east across that invisible boundary at about the same speed, and we start to hit tide rips almost as soon as we enter U.S. waters. The sum of our forward and sideways momentum adds up to a diagonal trajectory across the strait toward the north end of San Juan Island, right where we want to go, anyway, to clear customs in Roche Harbor. It is a wide exposure that turns from smooth to nasty as we hit the countercurrents of Spieden Channel pouring out like a river into the strait. Accustomed to these dramatic mood swings on the water, we plow through the turbulence in high spirits until we slide back inside Battleship Island and round the corner into the protection of the inner harbor.

The customs office is a small, white shack on the end of the dock at the Roche Harbor marina. We pull up to the pier at 7:00 A.M. in a celebratory mood, knowing that the most daunting part of our homeward journey is already behind us. We are back on American soil, back in familiar terrain, and I am back inside my home circle again. The sign on the door says the customs office opens at 8:00. We have an hour to kill.

This is where we make our really big mistake. Assuming that the cordial reception we received at Canadian customs will be repeated here on our home side of the boundary, we decide to get a cup of coffee. All my life, I have crossed back and forth over the border into Canada with nothing but a few basic questions asked and a polite nod on both sides. But this is the first time any of us have entered the United States by paddle. We are unsure about the protocol, but we are all good citizens, and we don't mind hanging out for an hour waiting for the customs officer to show up. We pull our boats onto the float and walk to the head of the dock to grab some coffee and a donut.

When we return, the customs officer has just arrived and is unlocking the door to his tiny floating office. One look at his demeanor tells us that all is not well. We greet the man, but a hardness to his face quells any further small talk. I will concede that Jay and I look more unsavory than usual. Neither of us has shaved for a week, and it has been some days since any of us has had a shower. But a smile from Robin or Kristin will usually melt an iceberg.

Not this iceberg. The man gestures toward our kayaks and growls, "Those your boats?" When we nod yes, he says, "Get in here! You folks are in a heap of trouble." This is not the welcome we expected as we file glumly into the office.

Clearly, I am the chief terrorism suspect, because the officer ignores the others and addresses his remarks directly at me. I stand meek and contrite across the counter, not sure what I have done to deserve this reception. The man appears hard-pressed to keep his anger in check as he fixes me with a withering look. I prepare for the worst. What comes out of his mouth, though, exceeds my

wildest expectations. "You" he says, thrusting his finger mena-
cingly toward my chest, "have put your country at risk!"

So unprepared am I for this remark that I have to quell a
nearly disastrous impulse to laugh out loud. I am already longing for the hospitable Canadian waters again. He attacks the key-
board of his Homeland Security computer with a bottled fury,
with my passport laid out before him, and as the minutes drag
on, I am left to wonder why Kristin, Jay, and Robin, sitting frozen
in the corner with faces drained of color, have *not* put their country at risk—why this is apparently my singular achievement. He
strikes the keys with a force clearly intended to emphasize how
thoroughly he means business. Meanwhile I work feverishly to
assemble the implications of this mysterious encounter.

Being a confirmed terrorist is a novel experience for me, one
that will take some getting used to. My worst prior offense was
a speeding ticket I got some years back on the highway west of
Winthrop, Washington, so this represents a major jump in status for me. I remember feeling sheepish when I got nailed for
speeding, but I didn't feel that I'd just put my country at risk.

Maybe we weren't supposed to walk up the dock while we
were waiting for the customs office to open, I think. That must
be it. I wonder what the interior of the maximum-security prison
is going to look like. I wonder if I will be allowed to consult a
lawyer or to call Sally before they load me on the next plane
bound for Guantanamo Bay. This will be a hell of a way to break
my airplane fast.

After an interminable wait, the officer seems satisfied that he
has entered the data from my passport onto every blacklist
known to the U.S. Customs Agency. He now recites the list of
dire consequences I have brought upon myself, beginning with
the five-thousand-dollar fine that comes with this offense, and
the possible jail time that is within his jurisdiction to impose.

"*That* was an expensive cup of coffee," I think to myself. He then goes through the same laborious process with each of the other members of our terrorist cell. It takes over an hour before he is satisfied that we all appreciate how serious a risk we've actually posed. When it is over, he waives the five-thousand-dollar fine, but files a warning on each of our passports.

We file morosely out of the customs office, all trace of enthusiasm expunged from the morning. This will be an interesting scenario to explain at our next border crossing, assuming we are ever let out of the country again. We thank the man for his generosity in waiving the fine and promise that we will never, ever, under any circumstances, put our country at risk again by getting coffee while we are waiting for a customs officer to arrive at his post.

o o o

WE ARE THOROUGHLY RATTLED as we straggle away from the dock. This was not the homecoming any of us had anticipated, especially after such a fine crossing of Haro Strait this morning. It leads to a sober conversation about what real national security might look like and how long a shadow fear still casts in the post-9/11 era of the Department of Homeland Security. It seems appropriate, somehow, that we should spend the rest of the morning bucking a stiff tide into San Juan Channel. Exhausted from the effort, Robin and Kristin are sucked away from the beach into turbulent rips as we round Limestone Point. It is a scary moment, and there is nothing Jay or I can do to help. We watch nervously as they fight their way back inch-by-inch against the boomeranging current into the sheltered waters beyond the point. We have been lucky on this trip. The possibility of real danger is lurking in these waters on even the calmest days. It is nothing to take lightly. Only as we angle across to the Wasp

Islands with the change of tide does the tension of the morning begin to ease its grip.

We make Blind Island State Park for the night, grabbing the last available campsite on this tiny rock outcrop in Harney Channel. A heavy rain is falling as we set up camp, and we erect a small tarp to huddle under. This is as far as Kristin and Jay will come. Tomorrow, they must jump back through the Looking Glass into the waiting arms of clock-time. They will take the two kayaks with them on the morning ferry to Anacortes from Orcas Landing, and I will join Robin in her rowing dory for the final sixty miles home to Whidbey Island.

o   o   o

IN THE MORNING, we break camp and cross the channel to Orcas Landing, loading the kayaks and gear onto the ferry along with Kristin and Jay. I hate to see them go and am grateful that Robin is willing to stick it out with me for the duration of the trip.

Not since my years on the lightweight crew at the University of Washington have I taken the oars of a rowing scull. The long, gliding sweep of the stroke is still written in the memory of my body, but that is where the resemblance ends. We barely make East Sound before I've worked up my first blisters, and my legs feel like wrought iron. We stop at Obstruction Pass to rest, then climb into and out of back eddies that slingshot us along the shore, as we vault past the powerboats laboring against the heavy midchannel tides. There is a certain satisfaction in seeing our human power temporarily trumping carbon power in a head-to-head duel.

Again our luck holds, in spite of the threatening winds in the forecast, and we are greeted by a gentle swell in Rosario Strait as we round the corner out of Obstruction Pass. This is our last major crossing, so we seize the moment, stroking out into open water, angling toward the north end of Cypress Island on the far side of the strait. Only when we pass the channel marker a mile offshore do we see what we are up against. The marker is heeled over by the tide, which is running perpendicular to the strait, dead against us. We are rowing against a tidal river that has slowed our progress to a crawl. There is so much to learn about these waters, and we pay for every deficit of knowledge. But we are not going to wait this one out and chance the weather later. Leaning into the oars, I pull until my body is drenched with sweat and my legs are burning embers. The forested prow of Mount Constitution rises steeply in our wake from the shores of Orcas Island, while Georgia Strait billows out into open Canadian waters to the north. We are a fish being played by the tide, reeled ever so slowly to the Cypress shores beneath the majestic face of Eagle Cliff.

I flop myself onto the beach like the spent fish I am, spread-eagled and limp in an act of complete submission to the land. I have not bothered to notice that we have landed on private property. Robin has fared better, and her social graces are still intact. She walks up the long, slanting beach to chat with the landowner, who is busy hammering a new plank into his wooden dory. This beach, it turns out, is part of an old homestead, one of the few such private holdings on the entire island. Cypress is the wildest of all the big islands in the archipelago, 5,500 acres of spectacular rock outcrop and old-growth forest. With 90 percent of the island in protected ownership by the state, and no roads or ferry service for its handful of residents, Cypress Island speaks an earlier vernacular of San Juan history.

Once I come to my senses, I walk up to the boathouse to join the two of them in conversation. Every inch of the man feels rooted in this place. His handsome, weathered face, his ease of bearing, and his obvious skill as a shipwright make him a good candidate for island poet laureate before I've heard him utter a word. He makes clear from the start that he is no fan of the sea kayakers who stop by these days to shit on his beach. But he has rowed his own dory all through the islands, so the *Barbara Goss* piqued his interest as he watched us struggling toward shore from far out in the Strait against the blistering tide. He knew exactly what we were up against. His classic wooden seiner is anchored just inside the point, so I share with him a common history of commercial fishing on this coast. We rest for a spell as he regales us with stories from a long life spent on this same piece of land. Earlier this year, he stood with his father, now almost one hundred, and both of his children, at the same Skagit County Courthouse where his dad purchased the abandoned homestead at auction eighty years earlier. Together they signed a conservation easement that will protect the wild character of their hundred-acre gem in perpetuity. It is a moment of unexpected grace to swap stories with this guardian of the island's wild heritage before we head on our way.

o o o

THE REST OF OUR TRIP HOME is straightforward and fun. There are no more exposed crossings to make, and the weather holds fair. We stop at Pelican Beach on north Cypress before crossing Bellingham Channel to row down the east shore of Guemes Island. My body is toast after rowing the length of Padilla Bay, making camp in Saddlebag Island State Park for the night. We are hummed to sleep by the flame-spouting industrial tangle of the Marches Point Oil Refinery across the water in Anacortes, filling the sky with an eerie light and offering a stark reminder of where the energy to drive our carbon economy is actually coming from.

It is a long slog against the wind in the morning down the final reach of Padilla Bay past the refinery and through the narrow,
seven-mile passageway of the Swinomish Channel, which separates Fidalgo Island from the mainland Skagit delta. I have now
circumnavigated the inner San Juans by making my home passage through this protected backdoor channel. We stop in La
Conner for breakfast after ten miles of vigorous rowing. This
feels like a homecoming of its own. La Conner is the only place
I have visited this year by all three modes of self-transport—by
boot, spoke, and paddle.

Robin and I catch the last of the ebb around the cliffs at Hawk
Point and out past Goat Island through the Skagit River delta.
The change of tide now carries us south through Skagit Bay toward Strawberry Point. I can feel the magnetic pull of familiar
home ground welcoming us near our journey's end. We drift with
the rising tide in brilliant sunshine up the long, gentle slope of
the Skagit Flats, searching for shallow channels to carry us
through sandbars loaded with waterfowl, and waiting for high
water to bring us all the way into Stanwood through the narrow
channel of West Pass. From here we cross into the marshy isolation of South Pass near the top of the flood, with powerful currents surging in from both north and south. We wait out the tide,
napping on the edge of the salt marsh channel until the ebb gives
us our ticket for passage into Port Susan.

I am retracing by water a route that I took on foot earlier in
the year, with a waterside vantage that helps fill out my picture
of the region's ecological sinews. We push down into Port Susan
past the chaotic outflow of the Stillaguamish River, which churns
the shallow bay into a cauldron of silty chop that spars with the
wind-driven waves. It is a long slog across the graveyard of snags
that have been carted by the river down from the mountains to

lodge here in the muddy shallows. The last miles are in heavy turbulence kicked up by the river's outflow, and we make a ragged landfall at Kayak Point in waves that nearly swamp the boat. It is almost dark, and after thirty miles of rowing, we trust our weary luck to find a camping spot in the crowded park. Our luck holds. A lone campsite reserved for paddle craft as part of the Cascadia Marine Trail system has been waiting, apparently, just for us.[1]

Our final morning takes us south around Camano Head and across Saratoga Passage for a ten-mile row to my hometown harbor in Langley. Jay is there to meet us and has brought my bicycle with him. Robin and I give each other a big hug and high-five in parting. We load our gear in the back of Jay's Jeep and hoist the *Barbara Goss* onto its rack, as I concede again to the surrogate use of his car to get my gear home. But as usual, there will be no car ride home for me. I jump on my bicycle to ride the five miles back home to the Maxwelton Valley.

Two weeks, and two hundred miles by paddle, have taken me to the wildest edges of the Salish Sea. It has taken me back in time through the lens of Native cultures striving to recover the mythic pathways that have bound them to this place for centuries. With each journey completed, I come home to a more complete sense of place. The valley sparkles in the August sunshine as I draw near to home, and my body feels unleashed to be back on my bicycle again. I turn past Woodland Hall to the house I built with my own hands on a forested hillside. I call through the door, but Sally isn't there, so I walk down through the commons to our community vegetable garden, where I know I will find her waiting for me.

CHAPTER 17

Closing the Circle

o   o   o

> What makes a place special is the way it buries itself inside the
> heart, not whether it's flat or rugged, rich or austere, wet or arid,
> gentle or harsh, warm or cold, wild or tame. Every place, like every
> person, is elevated by the love and respect shown toward it, and
> by the way in which its bounty is received.
>
> —RICHARD NELSON, *The Island Within*

Today marks the fall equinox, the final seasonal marker of my year, and the weather shows it. Rain spits at the cabin of the *Martina*, my familiar home-away-from-home tied to the dock in Cornet Bay, as we sit crammed around the galley table drinking beer and drying our clothes by the stove. Kristin and two friends, Emi and Noel—experienced kayakers all—joined me for this last kayaking adventure of the year, completing my circumnavigation of Whidbey Island and Puget Sound. We ended our trip at dusk tonight in the pouring rain as we paddled—hooting and hollering like kids—through the tidal rapids and whirlpools of Deception Pass. It was a dramatic finale, and we were all glad to arrive at our destination with kayaks all facing upright in the water. It's hard to say which I've enjoyed more, these glorious fall days in the open strait, or the company of friends to share in what has often been a solitary journey over these last nine months.

Here at the equinox, I can feel the steep slope of darkness moving back over the land, pulling with it an age-old blanket of rain and fog. It is a comforting feeling for one who has always loved this transition from summer into fall, a time for pulling back from the heavy work of summer, with the harvest mostly in, and only a few late runs of salmon still waiting to be caught. That is how I'm feeling tonight. Every fiber of my being is ready to slow down. Our final race through the pass got us to the shelter of protected water ahead of darkness by the barest of margins. It was a perfect entry into the fall season.

I've been pushing myself hard during these last months, as hard as I ever did on the fishing grounds. It is what the summer calls out of me. After tonight, I'm ready to ease back on the throttle, shifting my focus to a more inward harvest of writing and teaching. I still have three months until the winter solstice that will conclude my year in circumference, but already I've done most of what I set out to do, more than I thought possible to expect. I have never forgotten what launched me on this journey to begin with, that deep hunger for an alignment of action and conviction in the face of a great threat to humanity's future. I have not forgotten the urgency of the crises we face. But somewhere along the way, in the adventure of this homecoming pilgrimage, I left behind my fear about what lies ahead, a weight I've been carrying for too long. I am less encumbered by despair, even as I have fallen back in love with the place I call home and the gifts of local community.

Dinner tonight is a group effort, a simple vegetable stir-fry using fresh greens from Sally's garden back home. The beer is my favorite Northwest microbrew, and as the equinoctial storm adds its fury to the darkness outside, our stories pour out with the kind of gusto and pleasure that can only come on the heels of a real-life adventure like today's.

There is much to tell. After my return from Cowichan Bay, I continued south into the heart of Puget Sound on a solo trip, stitching by paddle stroke the places of my childhood into the present configuration of my life. I stayed with friends Holly and John in Indianola, where I spent so many days fishing from the pier as a kid, then paddled on through Agate Passage into Liberty Bay. At that poignant homecoming, I stayed with my cousin Jennifer at her cottage on the bay, where she has come home with her husband Joe to live after all these years. The bond we share in that place also worked its magic in dropping away the years that have come between us. I slept outside by the waters that lulled me to sleep through my childhood summers, held by a sense of renewed connection with family in a familiar and beloved landscape.

In a moment of rich serendipity, I stopped in Suquamish at the Port Madison Indian Reservation to meet with Marilyn, the woman in the canoe whose radiant presence so captured my heart in Cowichan Bay. A friend from Bainbridge Island had recognized her from a picture I posted in my blog and offered to arrange for this meeting. It felt just right to arrive at her tribal community having paddled all the way from home. The Suquamish Tribe will host next summer's coastwide canoe rendezvous, taking up where Cowichan Bay left off.

I arrived at the community dock in Agate Passage as the tribe was putting finishing touches on its new ceremonial longhouse in preparation for the event: an impressive "House of Awakened Culture," with carved cedar house posts and doors opening onto a spectacular view of Port Madison. This is the first longhouse that the Suquamish Tribe has built since the U.S. government burned Chief Seattle's Old Man House in 1870. Marilyn remembers stories from her father of the secret ceremonies held by the tribe when he was a child, at the burned-out site of the Old Man House. The traditions never died, they just went underground. She herself has been involved in the canoe revival since its beginning in 1989, and her first Tribal Journey was up the British Columbia coast to Bella Bella in 1993, a trip of several weeks by canoe that tested her to the core and changed her life.

As they set out on that trip, an elder told her that she must find her gift during the journey and bring it back to her community when she returned. She decided that her love of traditional weaving was a special gift, and she has taught weaving classes ever since. She has also been a canoe leader on each subsequent journey, traveling to every part of the Salish Sea. The canoe she skippered to Cowichan Bay this summer is called *Spirit of Raven,* and next summer she will stand as an elder herself at the huge tribal gathering that will take place there. To sit with Marilyn on her own home ground felt like a privilege, closing yet another circle in my own pilgrimage of homecoming.

My journey brought me back through the heart of the city, paddling all the way up to Hamm Creek in the Duwamish watershed, and along Seattle's humming waterfront, where sea lions still mingle with freighters, and fifty thousand revelers danced to rock music at the Hemp Fest in Myrtle Edwards Park. All of this is home. These searing contrasts are my life. There is no way to go but forward from here.

o o o

IN THE MORNING, my companions head back into the city to rejoin busy lives. I sit alone again at the galley table. As gusts of wind heel the boat over against its mooring lines, I feel glad that we chose to push on last night through those final ten miles of exposed shoreline despite our weariness. I am right where I want to be in this storm. The charts I have spread on the table are filled with detail and nuance that they didn't have nine months ago. They depict a broader landscape, more intricate channels, subtler islands and currents, more intriguing river towns and deltas, foothills and hidden valleys that pour out of the markings on the map and into my living memory. A hundred new adventures cast themselves upon my imagination as I pore over the charts. How could I ever be bored inside this circle again?

But most of these adventures can wait until next year. There is no need to be greedy. Each season has its assigned task. I look forward to this inward turn, this pull toward hibernation that I share with so many of my fellow mammals at the threshold of winter. For now, I set thoughts into my journal, enjoying my morning cup of tea, happy that I am here in this harbor and not still out in the strait with these blistering gusts of fall wind.

Later this morning, I will catch an Island County bus down the long length of the island, retracing the miles that took several days of paddling to cover on the water. Tomorrow, I will catch more buses into the city to resume my work at the VA Hospital. Traveling by bus and bicycle seems second nature to me now. I'm in no hurry for this year to be over, and I hardly think of my car anymore. I don't resent the inconvenience. It doesn't even feel like a sacrifice. It's more like a privilege. I know exactly why I'm doing this.

I roll up my charts and put them away. I wash last night's dishes, dry them, and place them in their racks on the galley wall. Each movement, each task, rolls out of me in an unhurried way, and there is honest pleasure in doing them. That is the way of my days more often now. It isn't that much of an effort. I step out on deck one last time to feel the cold gusts of wind on my face, the blasts of salt air. I gaze across the shallow bay to the channel between timbered islands, where the tide is surging by on its way to the pass. For the last two months, I've been fed by these waters. It is hard to know, anymore, where I end and they begin. I sling my pack over my shoulder and walk up the finger of the county dock, where a bus will take me back down the island, back to the center of my circle, back to the heart of home.

EPILOGUE

We shall not cease from exploration
And the end of all our exploring
Will be to arrive where we started
And know the place for the first time.

—T. S. Eliot, "Little Gidding"

The winter solstice has finally arrived. I've come all the way around to where I began this journey one year ago today. I'm throwing a big party to celebrate the occasion. This has been a community undertaking from the beginning, and I want to express my gratitude. I went public with this effort early on, and the island is a small place. All through the year, I've received gestures of support from friends and neighbors who have made their own action commitments in response to what I've been doing. Some have chosen to go car-free one day a week. Others pulled their bicycles out of storage and started riding again. Some have traded in their customary exotic winter vacations for a getaway closer to home. Others have committed to eating food that is more locally grown as their way of participating in the spirit of this cause. I would have made the journey anyway, with or without such support, but the experience has been a shared one, and I have rarely felt more cared-for by my community. Though I have gotten discouraged at times and have often felt solitary, I have rarely felt alone.

So for this winter solstice, I have rented my neighborhood community hall, hired a local marimba band, and am throwing a huge party and salmon bake. As my friend Rick likes to say, "If you want to change the world, throw a better party." To that I would add that if you want your friends to come, make it a salmon bake. It works every time. I've saved some Skagit River chum salmon that I caught this fall in Saratoga Passage, right along the shores of Whidbey Island. The Skagit chums are the best of their kind in the region, the biggest and most succulent of local chum runs, and I've selected the best of the best. This will be a salmon bake fitting for the occasion.

The only trouble is, we have a blizzard outside today. It looks like Siberia around here. Snow is a rare event in the lower elevations of Puget Sound, and this is the biggest snow we've had in two decades. The roads and highways are sheet ice, travel is at a standstill throughout the region, and the long hill down to Thomas Berry Hall is closed to cars for the last half-mile. Most of my friends from off-island have had to cancel. Everyone who does come will walk the last half-mile in the snow and the dark.

"This is perfect," I think. "People have to *walk* to my year-end celebration. Anyone who didn't get a chance to share in my adventures will get their chance tonight." Virtually every other event in the community has been canceled, but this show will go on, even if only a handful of people show up. I haven't figured out a way to reschedule the winter solstice. Even the marimba band members have refused to pull out and somehow managed to get their bulky instruments down to the hall during the heavy snows of the afternoon. There should be plenty of baked salmon to go around.

In the end, it comes together perfectly. Eighty hearty souls make the trek, and everyone is in the mood to celebrate. It's the solstice, after all, the most beautiful winter solstice anyone can remember. I show a homespun DVD with highlights and pictures from the year. I give a little speech to my captive audience of friends, many of whom then take their turn reflecting on what the year has meant to them. All the while, the snow keeps falling, its beauty enfolding us in the magic of the season. Then the band fills the hall with the most joyous music I've heard in a long time. It's not really an option to sit on the sidelines. We dance our hearts out, and when it's all over, Sally and I walk home on trails through the forest with Dan, Christian, and Abigail—the only brave souls who made it here tonight from across the water—to see what Siberia really looks like under moonlight at the midnight hour. We walk far down to the open fields and marshes of the valley, reveling in the snow. When we finally get home, I pull out my choicest bottle of Scottish single malt and the conversation continues in a quieter hue within our intimate circle of friendship. None of us want the night to end. It has been a remarkable year on every front, personally and globally, and it has come to a close with the most memorable winter solstice of my life.

o o o

NOTHING I HAVE DONE THIS YEAR would stand out in a chronicle of great achievements. But that wasn't the point. This year was not a stunt. I did not do this to join the *Guinness Book of World Records* or to impress my friends. I am not entering a contest or offering a ten-point plan. Yet if there is any integrity in what I have done, I will not stop here. This year was simply my own first step toward a more enduring practice of place.

Our climate is changing faster than any of us thought possible. Personal efforts to change our patterns of carbon consumption are only one leg in a tripod of shifts that must include bold new climate initiatives at all levels of government and a rapid transition to a clean-energy economy. But even the best legislative and green-technology initiatives will fall short without a broadly shared commitment to manifest these changes in our own lives. This is the critical third leg of the stool that has been missing. While 98 percent of federal funding for climate-change research is currently directed to the physical and natural sciences, only 2 percent is devoted to the "human dimensions" of the crisis—our role in creating it, the immense social impacts of the crisis, and what it will take to unleash our capacity to respond on a human level. Yet if climate change has been fundamentally caused by human behavior, then its solutions must ultimately lead us back to the behaviors that have carried us to the precipice in the first place.[1] That's why finding the will and the courage to embark on appropriate personal changes is so crucial now and constitutes one of the great adventures of our times.

The corresponding political and economic shifts will flow, as they always have before, from the ground up, through the ballot box of daily personal choices and through the quest for a greater authenticity in our lives—a sense of belonging that can never be reduced to material well-being alone. Especially in the near term, while the engines of government and commerce lurch rudderless between past and future visions of economic "prosperity," it is our moment to step up as leaders, in whatever ways we can, testing and proving these changes on the stage of our own lives. It is for those of us who have consumed and benefited the most from our current carbon binge to volunteer for the changes that can hold us over into a future worthy of our children and grandchildren.

What I have done this year was never intended as a blueprint for others to follow, but my hope is that it has offered evidence that a spirit of adventure is lurking in the choices that are available to each one of us, here and now, wherever we may find ourselves, and in whatever ways we can imagine. If the scope of this shift is to be realized, such changes must engage our hearts as well as our minds, our livelihoods as well as our leisure hours, our core understanding of what constitutes a life well lived.

Nor was this year meant as a permanent blueprint for my own future. I have not banished cars from my life, or travel to distant places. But the experience has fundamentally altered my relationship with transportation options. I will use my car much less often now, relying on the bus and my bicycle whenever that is a reasonable option, and my sense of what constitutes a reasonable option has expanded considerably from a year ago. When I do drive, I will make it the most fuel-efficient car currently available, and I will carpool much more often, combining errands with my wife or traveling to events with friends who are also going. It isn't that hard to do. It isn't as hard as I thought it would be. It is simply part of my practice now.

I can travel outside my circle again, but I have far less need to do so. When I do, I have rediscovered the pleasure of train travel as an alternative to jets, and I now arrive at my destination knowing that I've been on a journey. I will continue to claim my time in transit as *lived* time rather than *lost* time. Mostly, though, I will stay closer to home. The more I explore my home ground, the more it comes alive, and I have put to rest the illusion that I am limiting myself by doing so.

Everything we need to be happy really is near at hand. I keep meeting others who have found the same to be true as they've made similar shifts in lifestyle. It's almost never as hard as people expect, and the benefits always seem to outweigh the costs.

So what if it proves inconvenient at times? Surely we can bear a little inconvenience in order to deliver a livable planet to our children. The changes I have volunteered for this year had been staring me in the face for a long time. They are changes that will become involuntary soon if we give our tacit consent to a runaway climate by refusing these changes now. How convenient is a twenty-foot rise in sea level likely to be?

o   o   o

TIME IS NOW OF THE ESSENCE, and audacity's stock is rising fast. The odds against a business-as-usual future are getting longer by the day. Given the culture of denial about climate change that persists in the media, it is easy for ordinary citizens to miss not only the severity of our crisis, but also how quickly it is worsening. In the short time since I began my year in circumference, NASA laser images from space have revealed that the Greenland and Antarctic ice sheets are thinning three times faster than previously thought, a development that one University of California–Berkeley climatologist has called "ominous and distressing."[2] This astonishing news was buried deep in the *Seattle Times,* while "Our Top 5 Towns for Outdoor Fun" topped the headlines. I entered my year in circumference amid predictions that the Arctic Ocean may be ice-free in summer by the end of the twenty-first century, a situation that has not occurred in over fifty million years.[3] I leave the year contemplating a drastically reduced time frame for the disappearance of late-summer sea ice in the Arctic, perhaps no more than five years from now, by the latest projections. According to environmental writer George Monbiot, "the trajectory of current melting plummets through the graphs like a meteorite falling to earth."[4]

Meanwhile, in a year dominated by financial meltdown and corporate bailouts, even as Barack Obama was being sworn in as president of the United States, a Pew Research Center poll showed that climate change has slipped to last place in a list of twenty priority issues for Americans, far behind jobs and the economy, education, health care, "moral decline," military spending, and other perennial issues still judged more pressing by a majority of Americans.[5] My year comes to a close amid the same bewildering gap between public perception and scientific consensus that is fueling our rush into climate catastrophe.

Yet as Glenn Prickett of Conservation International has pointed out, "Mother Nature doesn't do bailouts."[6] We cannot mandate a rise in the freezing temperature of water by legislative decree or shore up collapsing ice fields with emergency loans from the federal government. When the history of our era is written many decades hence, Barack Obama, terrorism, and the financial meltdown may be footnotes to what Bill McKibben, scholar in residence at Middlebury College, has called "the meltdown meltdown."[7] Our time for dickering with the basic truth of climate change is over.

I chose 2008 as the year I would face my own complicity in the climate crisis, and it has turned out to be quite a year on the world stage as well. Barack Obama's election shifted the balance of power toward greater political engagement with climate initiatives. But it was also the year when, in Thomas Friedman's words, "both Mother Nature and Father Greed hit the wall at once."[8] Paul Gilding called it the year of "the Great Disruption": "When we look back, 2008 will be a momentous year in human history. Our children and grandchildren will ask us, 'What was it like? What were you doing when it started to fall apart? What did you think? What did you do?'"[9]

These were precisely the questions that launched me on my year in circumference twelve months ago. They remain my questions now as I look forward from here. Will I have a compelling answer for my grandchildren when they ask, *What did you do?*

How did you respond when our climate first started to come un-
raveled, when you knew at last how firmly you held our future in
your own hands?

The snow that falls outside my window tonight begs these
same questions. It is most remarkable for how rare it has become.
It falls not in the usual heavy sleet, but in light, wispy flakes born
of subfreezing temperatures that will keep it with us for days.
There isn't a whisper of wind or sound, and every branch is articulated with a thick mantle of white. It is as if the night forest
is being illuminated by a light inside the earth itself. This snow is
a final moment of grace in a year filled with gracious moments.

I grew up longing for the gift of snow in winter, for the way it
transformed the world before my eyes into a palace of white el-
egance, cleansed of rubble and noise. It never lingered as long as
I wished, giving way all too soon to the rain I knew so well. As I
watch these snowflakes falling outside my window tonight in
the quiet hours before dawn on this winter solstice, I am that
spellbound child again. I know that I am looking at a scene my
grandchildren may not share. The time when such snow is a rare
visitor even on the high peaks of the Cascades and Olympics may
not be far off, and my heart nearly breaks at the thought.

Everything changes. It has always been so. Our lives pass
swiftly away. To be human is to swim in a sea of intertwined
beauty and loss. Yet the losses we now contemplate are of a different order of magnitude, beyond the imagining of any former
generation of human beings. In the daily scramble of love and
work, it is easy to miss the scale of what we face. It is easy to
confuse our climate crisis with a litany of lesser ills we'd simply
rather ignore.

Yet it is not the human way to surrender what is most precious to us without rallying the full measure of our courage and

fortitude to the cause of its survival. This is the moment of truth into which all previous generations have delivered us, with the fate of all future generations now resting in our hands. Imagine! We have entered a perfect storm of our own making. The living earth on which we sail, the cradle of all homelands and all possible homecomings, is in grave danger of sinking. Every hand is needed on deck. What greater adventure could anyone ask for?

ACKNOWLEDGMENTS

At no point during the living of this year or the writing of this book have I felt alone on the journey.

Thanks first to my wife Sally Goodwin, who was there for me the whole way, and to my children Kristin and Alex Hoelting. Their encouragement, enthusiasm, and shared spirit of adventure have been a gift from start to finish.

This book might never have been written without the generous and astute counsel of my agent Lindsay Edgecombe of Levine Greenberg Literary Agency in New York, and the always-insightful guidance of my editor at Da Capo Press, Renée Sedliar. The book is immeasurably better because of them both, and the experience of writing it immeasurably richer. Gratitude also to Arielle Eckstut of Levine Greenberg, and to Drew Kampion; both did much to prepare the ground for this book.

My debt to Gary Snyder as a teacher is evident throughout this book, and it would be difficult to exaggerate his influence on my life and work. I am deeply indebted to Jon Kabat-Zinn, Shodo Harada Roshi, Daichi Storandt, and Zoketsu Norman Fischer for extraordinary guidance on the path leading home.

Special thanks to those who offered lodging and hospitality during my many explorations around Puget Sound by boot, spoke, and paddle, including Brad Furlong and Eileen Butler of Fir Island; Lauren Jaye and Billie Robinson of La Conner; Howard Shapiro of Mount Vernon; Cynthia and David Trowbridge of Greenbank; Eikei-san of Tahoma Zen Monastery; Jennifer and Joe Merrick of Poulsbo; Shinjo Jyl Brewer of Vashon Island; Christian Swenson and Abigail Halperin; David Kearney, Muriel Kelly, Joe Ryan and Lee Nelson, all of Seattle; Ron and Eva Sher of Bellevue; Leon Somme and Shawna Franklin of Body, Boat, Blade on Orcas Island; Jeff Iverson of Friday Harbor; Sandi and Richard Chamberlain of Victoria, B.C.; Holly Hughes and John Pierce of Chimacum and Indianola; Diane Bunting of Gig Harbor; Andy and Nancy Willner of Enumclaw; Saul and Shelley Weisberg of Bellingham; and Daya and Shanti of Penn Cove.

Among the many remarkable friends whose support lit the way during this project were Doug Kelly, Dan Kowalski, Rick Jackson, Dave Anderson, Ross Chapin, David Gunderson, Jim Shelver, Fritz Hull, Peter Evans, Rick Ingrasci and Peggy Taylor, Larry Daloz and Sharon Parks, Charles Terry and Betsy MacGregor, Carmen Cook and Michael Hansen, Stephanie Ryan and Craig Fleck, Dorit and Vito Zingarelli, Leslie Cotter and David Whyte, Jay Thomas, Steve Scoles, Larry Rohan, Ray Williams, Gordon Peerman, Christian Swenson, Lance Loder, Robin Clark, Bruce Tickell, Marilyn Wandrey, Emi Morgan, Rick Paine, Aaron Racicot, Jim Kramer and Carol MacIlroy. My brother Kim, sisters Leslie and Dana, and mother Patricia, island neighbors all, provided a welcome respite and a place at the table whenever I needed it.

And finally, I have never felt a greater sense of belonging in my local community. Expressions of support, friendship, conviviality, and shared purpose abounded during my year, giving me a thousand new reasons to stay closer to home.

NOTES

Notes to Introduction

1. To take an online carbon footprint survey, go to www.climatecrisis.net/takeaction/carboncalculator/. This link is to Al Gore's organization We Can Solve the Climate Crisis. There are many similar versions of carbon-footprint calculators available online. Seeing where we actually stand in our own patterns of carbon consumption can be a tremendously helpful motivator, as well as giving specific and valuable information about where we can make the biggest impact in lowering our personal carbon footprint.

2. Using this Carbon Neutral Company online calculator, www.carbonneutral.com/cncalculators/flightcalculate.asp, and assuming a round-trip flight from Seattle to Paris with a stopover in New York, I would be responsible for *about* five or six months of emissions from driving a 20-mpg car for 6,000 miles (that's roughly the average American car's fuel efficiency and roughly the average number of miles driven every six months). (This information is courtesy of Eric de Place, senior researcher at Sightline Institute in Seattle [www.sightline.org/].)

3. Mark Binelli, "Greenland Melting: The End of the End of the World," *Rolling Stone*, July 10–24, 2008.

4. In addition to ibid. and Elizabeth Kolbert, *Field Notes from a Catastrophe: Man, Nature, and Climate Change* (New York: Bloomsbury USA, 2006), 189, Al Gore's documentary *An Inconvenient Truth* (2006) remains a compelling and highly motivational summary of climate science, though recent scientific findings are even more alarming than what is represented in his documentary. Gore is successful in bringing dry scientific statistics into stunning visual focus and in telling moving stories that bring the numbers to life at a heart level. He also

succeeds in bringing a can-do and hopeful spirit to his conclusions, rather than leaving the viewer more despairing. See also Intergovernmental Panel on Climate Change, *Climate Change 2007: Synthesis Report* (Geneva, Switzerland: IPCC, 2007), www.ipcc.ch/publications_and_data/publications_ipcc_fourth_assessment_report_synthesis_report.htm. See also James Hansen, "Global Warming Twenty Years Later: Tipping Points Near," briefing to U.S. House Select Committee on Energy Independence and Global Warming, June 23, 2008, www.columbia.edu/~jeh1/2008/TwentyYearsLater_20080623.pdf.

5. Kolbert, *Field Notes from a Catastrophe*, 189.

Notes to Chapter 1

1. Gary Snyder, *The Practice of the Wild* (North Point Press, San Francisco, 1990), 18.

2. James Howard Kunstler, *The Geography of Nowhere: The Rise and Decline of America's Man-Made Landscape* (New York: Touchstone, 1993).

3. Alan Thein Durning, *The Car and the City* (Seattle: Northwest Environment Watch, 1996), 9.

4. Laura Esther Wolfson, "Proust at Rush Hour," *Sun Magazine*, March 2009, 13.

5. Northwest Environment Watch, *Cascadia Scorecard: Seven Key Trends Shaping the Northwest* (Seattle: Northwest Environment Watch [now called Sightline], 2004), 31, available at www.sightline.org/publications.

6. Kunstler, *The Geography of Nowhere*, 11.

7. Information through the Puget Sound Partnership, www.psp.wa.gov.

8. Timothy Egan, *The Good Rain: Across Time and Terrain in the Pacific Northwest* (New York: Knopf, 1990), 22.

9. John M. Findlay, "A Fishy Proposition: Regional Identity in the Pacific Northwest," in *Many Wests: Place, Culture, & Regional Identity*, ed. David M. Wrobel and Michael C. Steiner (Lawrence: University of Kansas Press, 1997).

10. Alan Weisman, *The World Without Us* (New York: Picador Press, 2007), 48–49.

11. Ibid., 24.

Notes to Chapter 2

1. Clarke Abbey and David Petersen, *Postcards from Ed: Dispatches and Salvos from an American Iconoclast* (Minneapolis: Milkweed Editions, 2006), quoted in *Sun Magazine*, October 2006, 17.

2. Rebecca Solnit, *Wanderlust: A History of Walking* (New York: Penguin Books, 2000), 28.

3. Ibid., 9.

4. Weisman, *The World Without Us,* 52–54.

5. See Solnit's summary of bipedalist theory in Solnit, *Wanderlust,* 30–44.

6. Mary Leakey, quoted in ibid., 41.

7. Bruce Chatwin, *In Patagonia* (New York: Penguin Books, 1977), xiv.

8. Edwin Bernbaum, *Sacred Mountains of the World* (San Francisco: Sierra Club Books, 1990), 44.

9. Gary Snyder, *The Practice of the Wild* (San Francisco: North Point Press, 1990), 98.

10. Carl Honoré, *In Praise of Slowness: Challenging the Cult of Speed* (New York: HarperCollins, 2005).

11. Jean-Jacques Rousseau, *Confessions,* quoted by Solnit, *Wanderlust,* 19.

12. Solnit's extensive investigation of the impacts of walking on these and other eminent philosophers is illuminating to this conversation (Solnit, *Wanderlust*).

Notes to Chapter 3

1. Lyanda Lynn Haupt, *Pilgrim on the Great Bird Continent: The Importance of Everything and Other Lessons from Darwin's Lost Notebooks* (New York: Little, Brown, 2006), 62.

2. See U.S. Geological Survey, "Surface-Water Data for Washington," at http://waterdata.usgs.gov/wa/nwis/sw.

3. I teach a program called Mindfulness-Based Stress Reduction (MBSR), which was developed by Dr. Jon Kabat-Zinn and run by the Center for Mindfulness in Medicine, Health Care, and Society. See Jon Kabat-Zinn, *Full Catastrophe Living: Using the Wisdom of Your Body and Mind to Face Stress, Pain, and Illness* (New York: Delacorte, 1990);

or learn more about MBSR at Center for Mindfulness in Medicine, Health Care, and Society, University of Massachusetts Medical School, "30 Years of International Distinction," www.umassmed.edu/cfm/home/index.aspx?linkidentifier=id&itemid=41252.

4. Vaclav Havel, *Disturbing the Peace: A Conversation with Karel Huizdala* (New York: Alfred A. Knopf, 1990). Havel made these remarks in 1986, three years before he became president of the Republic of Czechoslovakia.

Notes to Chapter 4

1. Statistics drawn from the North Cascades Institute, www.ncascades.org.

2. See, for example, Iain D. Couzin et al., "Effective Leadership and Decision Making in Animal Groups on the Move," *Nature,* February 2005.

3. David Livingston, quoted in Helen Whybrow, *Dead Reckoning: Great Adventure Writing from the Golden Age of Exploration* (New York: Outside Books, W.W. Norton, 2003), 18.

4. David Livingston, quoted in Phil Cousineau, *The Art of Pilgrimage: The Seeker's Guide to Making Travel Sacred* (Boston: Conari Press, 1998), 225.

Notes to Chapter 5

1. Gary Snyder, *The Practice of the Wild* (San Francisco: North Point Press, 1990), 43.

2. Ibid., 42.

3. Gary Snyder, quoted in Dana Goodyear, "Profiles: Zen Master," *The New Yorker*, October 20, 2008, 75.

4. Haupt, *Pilgrim on the Great Bird Continent*, 261–262.

5. Ibid., 262.

6. Snyder, *The Practice of the Wild*, 82.

7. David Abram, with Gary Snyder, Jim Dodge, and Nanao Sakaki, talk delivered at Ethics and Aesthetics at the Turn of the Fiftieth Millennium Symposium, Stanford University, Stanford, CA, May 16, 1998.

8. Henry David Thoreau, *Walden* (New York: Modern Library, 1965), 115.

9. Wendell Berry, "The Peace of Wild Things," in *The Selected Poems of Wendell Berry* (Berkeley, CA: Counterpoint, 1998).

Notes to Chapter 6

1. BikeWebSite, "Bicycle Trivia," www.bikewebsite.com/trivia.htm, drawn from S. S. Wilson, "Bicycle Technology," *Scientific American*, March 1973. See also A. C. Nuned and R. Vincent, "The Bicycle: An Historical Outline," talk presented to South County Museum, Narragansett, RI, July 16, 2000, and manuscript, Physics Department, University of Rhode Island, Kingston, available at www.phys.uri.edu/~tony/bicycle/bikehist.html.

2. The editorial was written after decades of failed attempts to invent a credible mechanical horse (quoted in David V. Herlihy, *Bicycle: The History* [New Haven, CT: Yale University Press, 2004], 55).

3. Avital Binshtock, "Trendsetter," *Sierra*, September–October 2009, 9.

4. See John H. Lienhard, "Leonardo's Bicycle," www.uh.edu/engines/epi888.htm. For a rebuttal of its authenticity, see "Leonardo da Vinci Bicycle Hoax," www.cyclepublishing.com/history/Leonardo%20vinci%20bicycle.html.

5. David Herlihy, *Bicycle: The History* (New Haven, CT: Yale University Press, 2006), 22.

6. Ibid., 75 and 78.

7. Ibid., 294.

8. Sightline Institute, "Why Bikes Are a Sustainable Wonder," www.sight-line.org/research/sust_toolkit/solutions/bicycle.

9. Della Watson, "Bikes!" *Sierra,* March–April 2009, 38.

Notes to Chapter 7

1. Gary Snyder, unpublished Maritime Pacific Northwest version of his poem "Long Hair," used by permission of Gary Snyder.

2. Mary Beth Faller, "Outdoor Play Has Lost Some of Its Appeal," *Seattle Times,* September 6, 2003, available at http://community.seattletimes.nwsource.com/archive/?date=20030906&slug=outdoorplay06.

3. Research and Innovative Technology Administration, Bureau of Transportation Statistics, "Highlights of the 2001 National Household Travel Survey," report BTS03-05, Washington, DC, 2003, www.bts.gov/publications/highlights_of_the_2001_national_household_travel_survey/.

4. Richard Louv, *Last Child in the Woods: Saving Our Children from Nature-Deficit Disorder* (Chapel Hill, NC: Algonquin Books, 2005), 2–3.

5. Katherine Millet, "People: Nurture & Nature," *Chicago Wilderness* magazine, summer 2007.

6. Louv, *Last Child in the Woods,* 10.

7. Gary Paul Nabhan, *Cultures of Habitat: On Nature, Culture, and Story* (Washington, DC: Counterpoint, 1997), 72.

8. A movement has grown up in response to Richard Louv's work; it is called "No Child Left Inside." For more on this movement, see Richard Louv's "Leave No Child Inside: The Growing Movement to Reconnect Children and Nature, and to Battle 'Nature Deficit Disorder,'" *Orion* magazine, November–December 2008.

Notes to Chapter 8

1. See Kathleen Dean Moore, "Silence Like a Scouring Sand," *Orion* Magazine, November–December 2008.

2. Ibid.

Notes to Chapter 9

1. Quoted in Mike Sato, *The Price of Taming a River: The Decline of Puget Sound's Duwamish/Green Waterway* (Seattle: The Mountaineers, 1997), 19.

2. Washington Department of Ecology, "Dirt Alert: Tacoma Smelter Plume," www.ecy.wa.gov/programs/tcp/sites/tacoma_smelter/ts_hp.htm.

3. Monica Shaw, "Simpson Tacoma Kraft Reaps Rewards from Recovery Boiler and Precipitator Upgrades," *Pulp & Paper,* July 2003, available at http://findarticles.com/p/articles/mi_qa3636/is_200307/ai_n9279362/.

4. Mike Sato, *The Price of Taming a River: The Decline of Puget Sound's Duwamish/Green Waterway* (Seattle: The Mountaineers, 1997), 22.

5. Beal won the Environmental Law Institute's National Wetlands Award in 2003.

6. Sato, *The Price of Taming a River,* 38.

7. Robert McClure, "City Will Repair Wetlands Harmed by New Complex: Standing His Ground Paid Off for Activist," *Seattle Post-Intelligencer,* December 1, 2005.

8. For more information on the Duwamish, see Duwamish River Cleanup Coalition, www.duwamishcleanup.org.

9. Mary Lou Slaughter, interview by John Iwasaki, "Ceremony Marks Opening of New Duwamish Longhouse," *Seattle Post-Intelligencer,* January 4, 2009.

10. King County, WA, Department of Natural Resources and Parks, "Ancients of the Green," June 2003, ww.govlink.org/watersheds/9/pdf/Ancients ofGreen_back.pdf.

Notes to Chapter 10

1. Edwin Bernbaum, *Sacred Mountains of the World,* (San Francisco: Sierra Club Books, 1990), chs. 2 and 4.

2. Gary Snyder, *Earth House Hold* (New York: New Directions Books, 1969), 100–101.

Notes to Chapter 11

1. Yang Wan-Li, "Night Rain at Kuang-K'ou," in *Heaven My Blanket, Earth My Pillow: Poems from Sung Dynasty China,* trans. Jonathan Chaves (Buffalo: White Pine Press, 2004). Yang Wan-Li (1127–1206) was a Sung Dynasty poet.

2. See, for example, WeatherBill.com, www.weatherbill.com/assets/LandingPageDocs/Top-10-Rainiest-Cities-Summary.pdf.

3. Kenneth Brower, *The Starship and the Canoe* (New York: Harper & Row, 1971), 46.

4. Yang Wan-Li, "Night Rain at Kuang-K'ou," in *Heaven My Blanket, Earth My Pillow: Poems from Sung Dynasty China,* trans. Jonathan Chaves (New York: Weatherhill Books, 1975), 107.

5. See, for example, Patty Glick, "Fish Out of Water: A Guide to Global Warming and Pacific Northwest Rivers," National Wildlife Federation, Novem-

ber 2006, www.nwf.org/news/story.cfm?pageId=B78FFA91-0385-8B0A-44A6 DFA8FC022F09.

Notes to Chapter 12

1. George Vancouver, quoted in U.S. National Park Service, North Cascades National Park Web site, 2002, www.north.cascades.national-park.com/.
2. Gary Snyder, *Practice of the Wild*, 101.
3. Ibid., 102.
4. David D. Alt and Donald W. Hyndman, *Roadside Geology of Washington*, (Missoula, MT: Mountain Press, 1984).
5. Mauri S. Pelto, "The Disequilibrium of North Cascade, Washington Glaciers, 1984–2007," North Cascade Glacier Climate Project, Nichols College, Dudley, MA, available at www.nichols.edu/DEPARTMENTS/Glacier/diseqilibrium.html.
6. See, for example, data from NASA's Earth Observatory at http://earth observatory.nasa.gov/Features/Paleoclimatology_IceCores/.

Notes to Chapter 14

1. Steven C. Brown, "Vessels of Life: Northwest Coast Dugouts," in *The Canoe: A Living Tradition*, ed. John Jennings (Toronto: Firefly Books, 2002), 75.
2. Brower, *The Starship and the Canoe*, 45.
3. John Jennings, *The Canoe: A Living Tradition* (Toronto: Firefly Books, 2002), 80.
4. Ibid., 85.
5. Ibid., 77.
6. Bill Reid, *Out of the Silence* (New York: Harper & Row, 1971), 27–38.
7. Jennings, *The Canoe*, 78 and 81.
8. Ibid., 94.
9. Eugene Arima, *Building Dugouts*, in *The Canoe: A Living Tradition*, ed. John Jennings (Toronto: Firefly Books, 2002), 97.
10. Brower, *The Starship and the Canoe*, 71.
11. Quoted in Kenneth R. Lister, "The Kayak and the Walrus," in *The Canoe: A Living Tradition*, ed. John Jennings (Toronto: Firefly Books, 2002), 123.

Notes to Chapter 15

1. Drew Kampion, *The Book of Waves*, 3rd ed. (Lanham, MD: Roberts Rinehart, 1997); used by permission of the author.

2. For more on GreenFaith, see GreenFaith, Interfaith Partners for the Environment, Web page, www.greenfaith.org/index.html.

3. Insights drawn from Al Gore, speech at Media Center of the Associated Press, October 5, 2005, New York.

4. Elizabeth Fenn, "The Great Smallpox Epidemic," *History Today* 53, no. 8 (August 2003). See also Elizabeth Fenn, *Pox Americana: The Great Smallpox Epidemic of 1775–82* (New York: Hill & Wang, 2001).

5. Gary Paul Nabhan, *Cultures of Habitat: On Nature, Culture, and Story* (Washington, DC: Counterpoint, 1997).

Notes to Chapter 16

1. For information about the Cascadia Marine Trail, see the Washington Water Trails Association Web site, www.wwta.org/index2.asp.

Notes to Epilogue

1. Jon Gertner, "Why Isn't the Brain Green?" *New York Times*, The Green Issue, April 19, 2009.

2. David Perlman, "Satellite Shows 'Ominous' Polar Melting," *Seattle Times*, September 24, 2009.

3. John Noble Wilford, "Ages-Old Icecap at North Pole Is Now Liquid," *New York Times*, August 19, 2000.

4. George Monbiot, "Forget the Polar Bears—The Climate Crisis Is About All of Us," *Guardian*, December 3, 2008.

5. Pew Research Center, "Why Americans Don't Act on Climate Change," September 8, 2006, available at www.livescience.com/environment/090806-environmental-psychology.html.

6. Glenn Pricket, quoted in Thomas Friedman, "The Inflection Is Near?" editorial, *New York Times*, March 7, 2009.

7. Bill McKibben, "President Obama's Big Climate Challenge," *Yale Environment 360*, November 8, 2008.

8. Friedman, "The Inflection Is Near?"

9. Paul Gilding, quoted in ibid.

PERMISSIONS